# Syntax: A Linguistic Introduction to Sentence Structure

E. K. Brown and J. E. Miller

Hutchinson
London  Melbourne  Sydney  Auckland  Johannesburg

Hutchinson & Co. (Publishers) Ltd
An imprint of the Hutchinson Publishing Group
17–21 Conway Street, London W1P 6JD

Hutchinson Group (Australia) Pty Ltd
30–32 Cremorne Street, Richmond South, Victoria 3121
PO Box 151, Broadway, New South Wales 2007

Hutchinson Group (NZ) Ltd
32–34 View Road, PO Box 40–086, Glenfield, Auckland 10

Hutchinson Group (SA) (Pty) Ltd
PO Box 337, Bergvlei 2012, South Africa

First published 1980
Reprinted 1983

Set in VIP Times Roman by Preface Ltd, Salisbury, Wilts.

Printed in Great Britain by The Anchor Press Ltd
and bound by Wm Brendon & Son Ltd,
both of Tiptree, Essex

**British Library Cataloguing in Publication Data**
Brown, E. K.
    A linguistic introduction to sentence structure.
    1. Grammar, Comparative and general – Syntax
    I. Title    II. Miller, J. E.
    415    P291

ISBN 0 09 138620 9 cased
        0 09 138621 7 paper

# Contents

6   *Contents*

# Preface

We would like to explain briefly why we have decided to write an introduction to syntax when there are many such books already on the market.

This volume arose from the teaching of syntax to first-year undergraduate students in the University of Edinburgh. Since the first-year course is designed to give students a general overview of linguistics, we thought that the syntax component should cover those basic concepts that have been and still are being used in the description of the syntactic structure of languages. This decision rules out those many textbooks that purport to be introductions to syntax or to grammar in general but are really introductions to transformational grammar. Of course, many basic concepts – constituent structure, embedding, recursion, inter-sentential relations, and so on – are integral parts of transformational grammar, but they are not exclusive to this particular approach to description. Other equally basic concepts – dependency (syntagmatic) relations, propositional processes and participants, the notions of theme and rheme, topic and comment, and so on – are not well handled in transformational models. Of the other textbooks available, none treats the range of concepts we want to consider in enough detail to form the single text round which a course could be built.

We recognize the commanding position that the transformational approach has assumed in the field of syntactic description over the past decade. It is still the dominant linguistic paradigm and has contributed more to our understanding of the nature of language than any other single model: indeed the companion volume to this is a fully formalized transformational grammar. But the concepts we wish to discuss are independent of and prior to any single model of grammar: it is precisely notions such as constituent structure, embedding, recursion, dependency relations and so on that any model seeks to account for, and linguists criticize one or another model precisely because it deals with one or another of these concepts inadequately. Our approach does not rule out formal grammar. A formal approach to language description is one of the corner stones of linguistics, and we hope to encourage students to look at the formal structure of language. It will be clear that much of the formalization we introduce in Parts one and two derives from a transformational approach, and we introduce some transformational rules. This book is not intended, however, to be an introduction to a fully formalized transformational grammar, and a formal approach is not exclusive to transformational grammar. The companion volume, however, Brown and Miller, 1982, discusses the problem of constructing a fully formalized transformational description of constituent structure, compares two transformational models and explores ways of formalizing other aspects of syntax.

There is another reason, external to linguistics, why we take this approach. At least half of the students who take a first-year course do not proceed any further with linguistics, though many do continue language study, and have occasion to use grammars. Most, if not all, detailed grammars of English or other languages are not set out as a formalized transformational grammar, but rather make informal use of such concepts as constituent structure, subject and object, complement and adjunct, agent and patient, government and concord, and so on. At least part of our purpose therefore is to train students to understand such concepts, so they can make the best use of the grammars they come across.

This book has been written with undergraduate students in mind, but it should be suitable for beginners at any level. We think it appropriate to have as few references as possible in the actual text, as our subject matter is those basic concepts that have become the common property of linguistics. The references at the end of the book give some idea of the sources from which we have drawn inspiration: they are not an exhaustive list of the writings on each topic, but an indication of books the student should find accessible.

# Introduction

It is indisputable that language is central to all communities of human beings. One of the first tasks of the young human being is to learn the language of the society into which he or she is born, and it takes many years to acquire the mastery of language expected of mature adults. Language is essential for the regulation of every community: the instruction of its young, the creation of laws, the development of its culture, the identification of its members. Consequently, language, as well as being a fascinating phenomenon in itself, is a necessary part of any investigation into human social organization and psychology.

This book is concerned with language for its own sake. To be more accurate, it is concerned with one part of language, namely syntax. But before we embark on the study of syntax, we should consider some general questions about the nature of language study. Let us begin by examining an instance of one person talking to another. If both speaker and hearer are mature speakers of the same language and neither suffers from any defects – such as deafness or laryngitis – that impede the production and the hearing of speech, we can say that the speaker produces a sequence of sounds, and that the listener hears the sounds and understands the message. This rudimentary account ignores many factors necessary in a detailed description of communication by language, but it will suffice for present purposes.

If both participants were literate, and perhaps not in close proximity, the speaker could have decided to convey his message in writing. The person receiving the message would then have been required to read a series of marks on paper, the marks being organized in sequences of different lengths separated by spaces. If the message was a long one, there might be several series of marks, each series being separated from the other by a space on the paper. Of course, the sequences are ordinarily called words and the series are ordinarily called sentences.

If we compare a written message with a tape-recording of a spoken message one obvious discrepancy is that nothing in the series of noises corresponds to the spaces between the words on paper, not even a pause or a slight cough. Furthermore, while there may be slight pauses corresponding to the gaps between the sentences, there need not be. The machine records a sequence of mere noises. If the language being spoken is one we know, we can interpret the noises, reconstructing the words, phrases, and sentences encoded in them. But if we know nothing of the language being spoken, we will make nothing at all of the transmission.

It is obvious – once it has been pointed out – that the same message can be conveyed either in speech or writing. This suggests that the notion of 'language' is rather more abstract than one might suppose. Language, we might say, does not intrinsically depend on either speech or writing (or indeed on any specific means of expression, like the system of manual signs employed by the deaf), but is a more abstract notion. We might say that a language is the system of relationships that a speaker has in his mind, and that the language can be expressed in speech or writing or by another medium. The linguist usually works with this more abstract notion of language. At the same time much can be said about written and spoken language in general or about a written and spoken language in particular, witness the success with which linguists write descriptions of other languages and assiduous students can acquire enough knowledge from these descriptions to communicate in them.

These remarks about a speaker and a listener have an important consequence for anyone who wishes to study language. To talk about language in any sensible fashion we have to draw a number of distinctions that are not normally drawn overtly in school grammars of languages.

In the first place, languages are organized on two levels: the *level of expression* – to put it crudely, the level of the noises in which the message is encoded – and the *level of content*. The word 'content' is unfortunate, since this level encompasses both the organization of words into sentences and the meanings that are associated with these words and sentences, but it is the standard term.

The linguist needs a sound knowledge of both levels of organization. Since language may be viewed as something abstract and messages can be encoded in sounds or writing, in principle the study of the level of expression will extend to both writing systems and sound systems. In practice, most attention has focused on the expression of language in sound, reflecting the general consensus among linguists that spoken language is more basic than written language. The study of the level of expression of sounds belongs to phonetics and phonology. Phonetics is concerned with the description of physical sounds, the functioning of the organs that are involved in their production and the range of sounds the speech organs can produce, and phonology is concerned with the ways different languages make systematic use of sounds for the transmission of messages. We shall not be directly concerned with either in this book.

We said in the previous paragraph that spoken language is more basic than written language, yet the written language enjoys greater prestige in all communities in possession of a writing system and a literature. Written language has a greater range of vocabulary, a more complex syntax and, except perhaps in hastily composed letters, none of the stops, starts and repetitions of spoken language. So great is the power of written language that in some formal situations, such as the delivering of judgment in court or the preaching of a sermon, it is felt appropriate to use the syntax and vocabulary of written language for proceedings conducted in speech.

Nevertheless, it is the spoken language which is fundamental. Every normal human being learns to speak before he or she learns to read and write. Even where literacy is universal most people conduct most of their communication in speech (including radios, television sets and telephones), and many books and newspapers are written in a style that approaches the style of spoken language.

The history of languages contributes two facts that put the primacy of spoken language beyond doubt. Firstly, no case is known of a community that had a written language before it had a spoken one. Speech always developed a long time before the emergence of a writing system. The second is that changes in language over time by and large originate in the spoken language and gradually find their way into the written language.

From the level of expression let us pass to the level of content, bearing in mind that the term 'content' is too narrow. Study of the content level has traditionally been split between syntax and semantics. Syntax is concerned with ways in which words combine to make sentences, and semantics deals with meaning. Traditionally a third component was also recognized – morphology, dealing with the structure of words. It is evident that if sentences can be split up to make words, words can be split up into smaller units. For example, *ineffectiveness* consists of four parts: *in*, *effect*, *ive* and *ness*. Morphology is the subject of Part two of this book. It is in many ways a sort of 'bridge' between the content and the expression level. It is related to syntax in a natural manner since the parts of words can be considered as participating in the structure of sentences along with the words themselves. Morphology is also relevant to the study of the expression level, because the structure of words is relevant to the functioning of systems of sounds. However, that aspect of morphology is not of major concern in this book.

The relationship between syntax and semantics is difficult and controversial. It has always been recognized that there is some distinction to be drawn between the meaning and the structure of sentences, but it is far from clear just where this boundary should be drawn. Language is a means of conveying meanings of various kinds, and it would be surprising indeed if considerations of meaning and of structure were totally separate. This book takes the view, however, that syntactic and morphological structure should be studied in their own terms as far as possible, the results furnishing a basis for investigations into semantics. Syntax and morphology are gateways to meaning, and it is important to have secure syntactic and morphological criteria against which intuitions about meaning can be measured. But, as we shall see, discussions of syntax cannot, and should not, totally exclude considerations of meaning.

In the course of our discussion we will need to redefine and refine a number of concepts and terms commonly used in language description. One we can usefully tackle immediately is the 'sentence'. In ordinary usage this term refers sometimes to the actual sequences of sounds produced by a speaker, sometimes to an orthographic unit, and sometimes to something much more abstract. In this book we use the term 'utterance' to refer to actual sequences of sounds, and restrict the term 'sentence' to the more abstract use. We consider the sentence to be a unit described in the syntax at the abstract level of content.

In order to understand why we make this distinction, consider the relationship between a sentence and its corresponding utterances. More than one utterance corresponds to a given sentence, in fact, a multitude of utterances. Take the sentence which we may represent orthographically as *What did you think of the programme on Comecon?* Even in the speech of one and the same speaker this sentence may be expressed (or realized) by a large number of different utterances. If speech is slow there may be a sound in the utterance corresponding to the last letter in *what* and a separate sound to each of the letters in *did*, to the first letter in *you* and to the last two letters in *you*. (To talk of 'separate sounds' in this way is to skate over some very formidable problems in the analysis of speech.) But if the speaker speaks at even ordinary conversational speed there may be only one separate sound corresponding to the last letter in *what* and the first letter in *you*. This part of the utterance might be represented as *whadja*, with *dj* representing one sound.

The discrepancy between the number of 'letters' and the number of separate sounds in our sentence may be considerable. Moreover, other factors increase the number of possible utterances corresponding to our sentence – all within the speech of our one speaker. For example, the speaker's attention may be distracted, causing him or her to repeat a word, or perhaps to miss out a word entirely. The speaker may inhale a crumb of toast and finish the utterance in gasps and coughs. The speaker may suffer from laryngitis that has all but paralysed some of the organs of speech, so the utterance is deformed.

Furthermore different speakers can produce a range of utterances that are interpreted as realizations of our original sentence. The quality of voice, for instance, is clearly different between men and women; and no two men or women have exactly the same quality of voice. Similarly, speakers of the different accents of English may not aim at the 'same' sounds. If all these factors are put together the utterances which can realize our sentence vary enormously.

Yet all of these different utterances are related by the hearer to the same, abstract, sentence. Native speakers clearly practise such an abstraction in everyday conversation. Normally we simply do not notice if a word is repeated or a couple of sounds are slurred (unless the interference is so great that the intended sentence cannot be reconstructed). Indeed we are often able to guess at the complete sentence after hearing only part of the utterance. It is this abstract notion of the sentence that the linguist usually works with.

Let us accept then that the sentence is an abstract unit. Linguists set up such a unit to explain how we relate a range of utterances to the same abstract sentence, and to explain patterns within the sentence. For the moment we can suppose that these patterns are built up of words: it turns out that the only satisfactory way to make sense of the arrangements of words is to consider the patterns they form within sentences.

Words are dependent on each other in many different ways. For example, they may have to occur in a certain order. In English, words like *the* and *a* precede the nouns they go with, but in some other languages what corresponds to *the* in English is placed after the noun. Again, one word may not be able to occur unless another word is present. In the sentence *Foreign books are expensive*, foreign cannot occur unless there is a word like *books*. The forms of words may also differ according to what other words are present in the sentence. In Latin, for instance, the adjective corresponding to *good* is *bon-*, the dash indicating that various items can be added. If the adjective goes with a noun like *puer* it ends as *bonus* but if it goes with a noun like *puella* it ends *bona*. These relationships or dependencies between words can be sensibly described only if we establish the sentence as a unit in our description. We define the sentence then as an abstract unit postulated in order to account for the dependencies between units of syntactic structure.

When the abstractness of language was first mentioned, along with the distinction between the levels of content and expression, there was a short discussion of the relationship between written and spoken language. Linguists, it was argued, have good reason to assign priority to spoken language. Closely related to the linguists' attitude to spoken and written language is a very important point concerning the task of describing the syntax of a language.

To a great extent we treat the topics that used to be gathered together under the heading of 'grammar', a word that for many people has a strong association with the idea of 'good grammar'.

The popular understanding seems to be that the grammar of a language, whether your native language or a foreign language, contains information that enables its user to write and speak the language correctly. This understanding has some foundation, but the notion of correctness is far from simple.

The complexities of the notion can be illustrated by the situation in Britain. A child learning English in Exeter, Manchester or Edinburgh produces utterances that satisfy the expectations of the people he or she comes in contact with: relatives, the children he or she plays with, the local shopkeepers. (This is the simplest of cases. For many children the learning of the appropriate English is not so straightforward, for instance the child of Bengali-speaking parents in an area inhabited by English speakers.) The child cannot string any sort of noises together in any order. He or she must produce approximately the noises that the people roundabout produce, and the noises must be combined into sequences as they are by those other people.

Every community has rules of language that have to be observed by its members. The person who does not observe them is not understood and, more seriously, is open to ridicule. Conversely, the child who produces appropriate utterances speaks correctly from the point of view of the local community.

When the child goes to school, he may speak incorrectly from the point of view of his or her new community. At some stage in his or her education the child is encouraged to adapt to a new standard of correctness, usually that of the literary language. Different children adapt to different degrees. The question whether adaptation is necessary or desirable is highly emotive and divisive, and one we do not tackle here. From a linguistic viewpoint, the literary language is only one dialect of English, even though many may consider it the 'correct' form. All dialects of English, literary and non-literary, have their own rules, and these rules are capable of description. The grammar itself makes no evaluative judgements – it is users of the language that make such judgements, for reasons (like, for instance, social prestige) external to grammatical considerations.

What is considered to be 'correct' usage can change over time. Let us illustrate this. Twenty years ago the linguistic observer in Britain would have recorded utterances that could be related to sentences like *This book is different from that book* and *This book is different to that book*. A manual of 'faults' to be avoided by the public speaker would have listed the *different to* construction as one to be avoided. The linguist, however, would have observed and recorded utterances corresponding to sentences with the *different to* construction. He would also have brought them into his description. He might also have sought to account for the rise of this construction by noting the similarity in meaning between *X* being 'different from' *Y* and *X* being 'opposed to' *Y*, or by observing the occurrence of *to* with adjectives like *opposite* and *opposed*. Change has not stopped there. In the late 1970s the linguist might record utterances related to sentences like *This book is different than that book*. He might bring this too into his description, accounting for the construction by noting the connection between saying that *X* and *Y* are 'different' and that *X* and *Y* are 'to be compared'. The comparative construction makes use of *than*, as in *X is smaller than Y*, and we note constructions like *other than* and *rather than*.

The *different than* construction is probably even less acceptable to the authors of public-speaking manuals than the *different to* one. Yet many speakers of English use both constructions, and in the course of time both may become acceptable even to the purist. If the linguist declined to record such constructions he would not only be falsifying the facts of the language, but he would also be throwing away data that affords an insight into how a language functions as a system, and how such systems change.

We do not assert that linguists never come across 'incorrect' data – our previous discussion of slips of the tongue, the omission of words and so on illustrated that they do. We maintain, however, that 'correctness' is a notion relative to particular uses of language and to particular dialects or subdialects. The description of a language may concentrate on the literary dialect of the language or on some other dialect, but it is inappropriate to assert that the former deals with 'good' and the latter with 'bad' grammar.

Finally let us say that the study of language can be different and exciting. No complete grammar of any language, be it a literary language or a dialect, has yet been written. Even the enormous amount of work done recently on the syntax of English, far from solving all the problems of English, has only served to increase the number of complexities that require investigation.

Anybody with a little training in syntax (and in other branches of linguistics) will find much to occupy his attention. Let us recall that people have to be taught to observe; whether it be the doctor learning to observe and 'read' the human body; the artist learning to observe and 'read' great paintings; or the geologist and geomorphologist learning to observe and 'read' the landscape. At the very least, a knowledge of syntax should enable the student to observe and 'read' the utterances he hears, opening his ears to a multitude of curiosities.

Part one

# Constituent structure

# 1 Constituent structure

The analysis of the structure of sentences was traditionally known as 'parsing'. Part of the *Oxford English Dictionary*'s definition of PARSE is: 'to resolve (a sentence etc.) into its component parts of speech and describe them grammatically'. The two operations suggested by this definition suffice for our present purposes:

(i)  the analysis of the sentence into its relevant parts;
(ii) the grammatical description of these parts.

These two operations are clearly closely related, and in linguistic work have commonly been referred to as constituent structure analysis. A constituent is some proper subpart of a sentence relevant to its analysis. Part of a constituent structure description of a language, therefore, tells us how to break sentences down into their constituent parts, and which strings of words are, and which are not, considered to be constituents. Or, seen the other way round, the description tells us how the smallest constituents can combine to form other, larger, constituents, and how these, in their turn, can form yet larger constituents until we have constructed a sentence. This suggests that there are different types of constituents, and we need to know the degree of likeness and difference between different types, which constituents can combine with which other constituents to make sentences, what order constituents can, or must, occur in, and so on: this involves the naming of different types of constituent so that we can identify them.

Let us, as an example, consider how to describe the structure of the sentence:

1  The dog frightened the child

We have to make three initial assumptions, all of them justified in due course. Firstly, although we are considering only a single sentence, it is not the only sentence in the language, and we can, indeed must, assume that we can use our knowledge of other potential sentences to guide our analysis. The description we give to this sentence must be compatible with the analysis we would like to make of other sentences we might have chosen: our ultimate aim is the description not of a single sentence but of the language as a whole.

Secondly we assume that the smallest constituents with which we are concerned are the five words represented in **1**. This assumption begs a number of questions. For one thing, it is clearly not quite true, since a word like *frightened* is analysable into the smaller constituents *frighten* and *-ed*, on the analogy of other forms of FRIGHTEN like *frighten-ing*, *frighten-s* or indeed *frighten* in sentences like:

> **2a**   Dogs frighten children
> **2b**   The dog is frightening the child
> **2c**   The dog frightens the child

and so on.[1] We also know that constituents like *-ed*, *-ing* and *-s* occur with other verbs like KILL: *kill-ed*, *kill-ing*, *kill-s*. We consider the analysis of words in due course; for the present we need merely to acknowledge that the word is a traditionally recognized unit, and that a unit of this sort indeed seems a relevant constituent in English.

Our third assumption concerns the sentence. Suppose we use the neutral term 'string' to refer to any sequence of constituents: we can then refer to the words *the dog* or *frightened the child* or indeed the whole of **1** as strings without a commitment as to their status as constituents or any identification of the type of constituents we believe them to be. What entitles us to refer to the string **1** as a sentence, when the other strings mentioned do not seem to be sentences? Unfortunately, as with the word, there are considerable problems about the identification of sentences: to call a string a sentence implies that it has a certain sort of unity, but it is far from easy to describe exactly what sort of unity a string needs to have for it to be referred to as a

1 We use small capitals to refer to the dictionary or lexical entry of particular items. Thus FRIGHTEN is the lexical entry which relates the actually occurring forms of FRIGHTEN, like *frightens*, *frightening*, *frightened* etc. The form we use is the one typically chosen in English dictionaries. For further discussion see page 166.

sentence. We might regard the study of syntax as an attempt to answer just this question. For the time being we merely accept that **1** is a sentence; again our provisional justification is that it is supposed that we would all agree that **1** is indeed a sentence.

**1** The dog frightened the child

With these three assumptions in mind we can turn to the analysis of **1**. What relevant units can we discern? At an intuitive level *the dog*, *frightened* and *the child* appear relevant constituents in a way that strings like *frightened the* or *dog frightened* do not. Furthermore, again at an intuitive level, the strings *the dog* and *the child* seem to be constituents of the same type. We can back these intuitions by formal criteria if we consider the relationships between our sentence and other sentences in the language. Basically two types of criteria are used: one has to do with features of a constituent related to its internal structure, the other with aspects of the external distribution of the constituent. Both of these criteria show that a particular constituent has the unity that justifies its being treated as a unit.

Consider first the strings *the dog* and *the child*. In their internal structure, we note that both strings contain the word *the*, that this word does not co-occur with *frightened*:

**3** *The dog the frightened the child[2]

and that it must be the initial word in its constituent:

**4** *Dog the frightened child the

Furthermore, these strings can be substituted by a single word, and the sentence as a whole remains grammatical:

**5a** Fido frightened the child
**5b** The dog frightened Johnny
**5c** It frightened him

Similarly, these constituents can be substituted by other, longer, strings, which we consider to be 'expansions' of the strings in question, and the sentence remains grammatical:

2 Here and throughout the book an asterisk (*) indicates an ungrammatical sentence.

**6**   The big dog frightened the child next door
  The big dog that lives next door frightened the child

Similar substitutions and expansions are not possible for strings like *frightened the*. If we now turn to the word *frightened*, we can make comparable observations. Since it is a single word, and we are treating words as the smallest constituents, we can say nothing about its internal structure, but it can certainly be substituted by various expansions:

**7a**   The dog has frightened the child
**7b**   The dog may have frightened the child

We may note that the expansions appropriate here (*has*, *may have*) are impossible with constituents like *the child*:

**8a**   *The may have child frightened the dog
**8b**   *May have the child frightened the dog

just as the expansions appropriate to constituents like *the child* are impossible with constituents like *frightened*:

**9a**   *The dog big frightened the child
**9b**   *The dog frightened that lives next door the child

So much for the internal structure of constituents: particular types of constituent may have characteristic structural properties (*the child*, but not **child the*), complex constituents may be substitutable by single words (*the dog*, *Fido*, *it*) and constituents may be appropriately expanded (*the dog*, *the big dog*; *frightened*, *has frightened*).

The second criterion has to do with the external distribution of a particular constituent: in what range of environments can the constituent be found? Does it retain its integrity as a constituent in other structural positions within sentences? Consider once more the strings *the dog* and *the child*. To begin with they are mutually substitutable:

**10a**   The dog frightened the child
**10b**   The child frightened the dog

but neither of them is substitutable for *frightened*. Next note that these strings retain their unity in sentences like those in **11**, all of which, you would probably agree, are systematically related to our original sentence **1**:

**11a**   *The child* was frightened by *the dog*
**11b**   It was *the dog* that frightened *the child*
**11c**   What *the dog* did was frighten *the child*
**11d**   What happened to *the child* was that *the dog* frightened it

We may also note the relevant question and answer sequence:

**12a**   What frightened *the child*? *The dog*
**12b**   What did *the dog* frighten? *The child*

The constituents we are interested in have a unity difficult, or perhaps impossible, to dissolve. We also note that the substitutions and expansions discussed above show exactly the same unity, since substitution of *Fido* or *the big dog that lives next door* for *the dog* in any of the sentences in **11** or **12** still yields grammatical sentences. There is no way in which strings like *frightened the* show a comparable unity.

The discussion shows, then, that there is some justification for regarding the constituents of our sentence as:

The dog – frightened – the child

The discussion also shows that constituents like *the dog* and *the child* are constituents of the same type, whereas *frightened* is a constituent of a different type. Following traditional usage we call constituents like *the dog* Noun Phrases, abbreviated as NP, and constituents like *frightened* a Verb, abbreviated as V.

Our first analysis, then, suggests that the sentence has three constituents, which we can represent by the string:

**13**   NP + V + NP

(Note that we use string to refer both to strings of words, and to strings of constituent names.)

We should now consider the constituents of these constituents since the NP clearly has internal structure: it consists of the word *the* followed by either *child* or *dog*. *Child* and *dog* appear to be the same sort of constituent since they are mutually substitutable for each other, and different from either *frightened* or *the* since neither is substitutable for either of these words: we will refer to them, again following the traditional terminology, as Nouns abbreviated as N. We have already noted that *the* is a different type of constituent from either of the Ns we have identified or the V: we have noted that it does not co-occur with a V, and that it may co-occur with an N, but that if it does it must precede the N in the NP: there are no strings *dog the* or *child the*. Again following traditional terminology, we call *the* an Article, abbreviated as Art.

Since we have agreed to stop with the word, no further analysis is possible. Let us see how it meets the two requirements set out at the beginning of the chapter (page 21).

We have analysed the sentence into a tripartite structure:

**14** NP + V + NP

we have analysed each of the NPs into a structure

**15** Art + N

and we have identified each of the words as belonging to one of three types of constituents:

**16** *frightened* is a V
*dog* and *child* are Ns
*the* is an Art

We have also given a partial grammatical description of these items. *The* is an Article, an item which can only occur in an NP, and must precede the other constituent of the NP, the N. Ns only occur in NPs and they must follow the Art. The V *frightened* occurs between two NPs: there are no sentences:

**17** *Frightened the child the dog
*The dog the child frightened

There are two common ways of representing this information about constituent structure. One is to indicate constituent structure by bracketing:

**18** (((The)(dog))(frightened)((the)(child)))

There are brackets round each word, since each word is a constituent. Since the strings *the dog* and *the child* are also constituents, these are also bracketed. Since the sentence as a whole is a unit, there are brackets round the whole string. (There are always as many right-facing brackets as left-facing.) Bracketing shows the constituent structure but omits information about the type of constituent. This can be included by labelling each bracket with a suitable subscript:

**19**  $_S(_{NP}(_{Art}(the)_{Art}\ _N(dog)_N)_{NP}\ _V(frightened)_V$

$_{NP}(_{Art}(the)_{Art}\ _N(child)_N)_{NP})_S$

The subscript identifying the type of constituent is to the left of the bracket at the beginning of the constituent, and to the right of the bracket at the end of the constituent. Alternatively we can put subscripts only on the opening bracket:

**20**  $_S(_{NP}(_{Art}(the)_N(dog))_V(frightened)$

$_{NP}(_{Art}(the)_N(child)))$

Representations of this kind are called labelled and bracketed strings.

Sometimes, however, such representations are not easy to read, especially if there is a good deal of structure to represent; an alternative method, often preferred, is the tree diagram, illustrated in Figure 1.

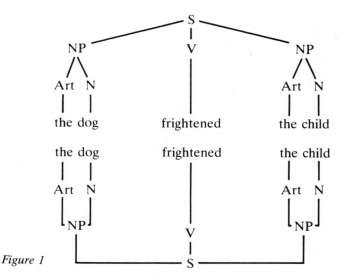

*Figure 1*

Whichever way up the tree is, it conveys the same information as the labelled and bracketed string. It is more usual nowadays to find tree diagrams as in the top half of Figure 1, with the constituents depending from the S node. In tree diagrams, those places where there are labels are called nodes: thus we can refer to the NP node, the V node, and so on. Where two or more lines lead from a single node this is called branching: thus the S and NP nodes branch. The other nodes do not branch – all nodes do not have to branch.

At this point it is convenient to introduce further technical vocabulary. First, the notion of domination: a node is said to dominate all the constituents that are traceable back to it. Thus in Figure 1, the first NP dominates the string *the dog*, but it does not dominate, say, *frightened*. A more particular notion is that of immediate domination: a node A is said to immediately dominate another node B if B is traceable back to A with no other node intervening. Thus S dominates everything in the sentence – indeed it has to do so – but it only immediately dominates NP, V and NP. S does not immediately dominate Art + N.

A different way of talking about the same relationships uses the term constituent: corresponding to the notion of domination is the notion of constituents. Thus, *the* and *dog* are constituents of the first NP. Similarly, corresponding to the notion of immediate domination is the notion of immediate constituents: Art and N are the immediate constituents of the first NP. Concomitant with constituent is the notion of a construction: two or more constituents are in construction with each other if they are dominated by the same node. Thus Art and N are in construction in the first NP. Finally 'family tree' terminology is often used to describe the relationships between items; thus in Figure 1, NP, V and NP are daughters of S, the leftmost NP being the left daughter, and the rightmost NP being the right daughter. Analogously, the leftmost NP is the left sister of V (both are daughters of the same mother), and the rightmost NP is the right sister of V, for the same reason.

A final observation about the analysis of Figure 1 is to note its hierarchical structure: the sentence is analysed into its immediate constituents, each of these constituents into its immediate constituents, and so on. The hierarchical nature of the analysis illustrates what appears to be a universal principle of the organization of human languages, that they have hierarchical syntactic structures. It is not immediately obvious why this should be so, nor why this analysis is preferable to an analysis in terms of a single string (a 'string constituent analysis') as illustrated, for sentence **1**, in Figure 2.

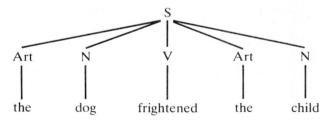

*Figure 2*

Let us compare Figures 1 and 2. Firstly, Figure 2 does not indicate that the NP is a relevant sentence constituent, yet our previous discussion suggests it is an important constituent, in that a number of generalizations about syntactic structure can be more clearly formulated using such a constituent. Secondly, a hierarchical analysis shows that the relationship between any pair of constituents must be considered in terms of relationships established within the tree as a whole; mere contiguity for instance is not necessarily a particularly interesting relationship. Thus, in Figure 1, there is a close relationship between the contiguous items *the* and *dog*, they are constituents of NP, but there is no immediate relationship between *dog* and *frightened*, even though they are contiguous. Rather the V *frightened* has a relationship to the NP *the dog*, since both are constituents of S. This can be seen more clearly if we compare the relationships between the strings *the child* and *frightened* in the two sentences analysed in Figures 3 and 4. (We do not justify the analysis of Figure 4 further here – it can be established in just the way we have established our analysis of **1**.) The string *the rumour that the dog chased the child* is an NP which has the sentence *the dog chased the child* embedded in it (such structures are further discussed on pages 134ff.). In Figure 3 both *the child* and *frightened* are daughters of S: in traditional terms *the child* is called the 'subject' of the verb *frightened*; this sentence would be used when the child in question 'did' the 'frightening'. In Figure 4 *the child* is a daughter of the embedded S, and in traditional terms the 'object' of the verb *chased* (it is 'the child'

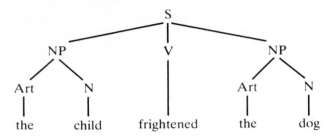

*Figure 3*

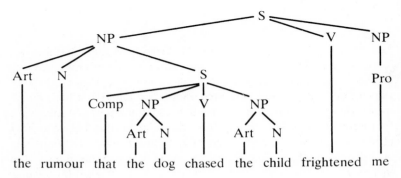

*Figure 4*

that is 'chased'), and *frightened* is a daughter of the
superordinate S. Whereas in Figure 3 *the child* is the subject of
*frightened*, in Figure 4 the subject of *frightened* is the NP *the
rumour that the dog chased the child*. The relationship between
the contiguous items *the child* and *frightened* is close in Figure 3,
but remote in Figure 4.

Finally, if we adopt a hierarchical analysis we discover that
'the same' constituents keep appearing at different places within
constituent structures. We have already observed this in the case
of the NP: we may now observe in Figure 4, that this is also
true of sentence structures, since one sentence of the structural
form NP + V + NP is embedded inside another sentence of
precisely the same form. This 'nesting' property of constituents
is an important characteristic of language, and one to which we
shall return.

**Technical terms**

bracketing
branching
constituent
constituent structure
construction
daughter of
domination
hierarchical structure
immediate constituent

immediate domination
in construction with
labelled and bracketed string
labelling node
sister of
string
substitution
tree diagram

# 2 Form classes

The previous chapter discussed the sentence:

**1** The dog frightened the child

and assigned to it the constituent structure of Figure 5.

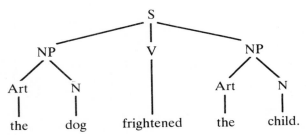

*Figure 5*

Many hundreds of sentences in English can be analysed in an analogous fashion, for example:

**2a** The dog chased the child
**2b** The cat killed the bird
**2c** The child hit the dog
**2d** The dog caught the cat

etc. In these sentences the words fall into groups that are mutually substitutable within the sentence structure shown in Figure 5, as summarized in Figure 6.

Selecting one word from each column yields an acceptable sentence with the analysis of Figure 5. Tables like these, which may be familiar from foreign-language teaching manuals, are called substitution tables, since they use the principle of simple substitution. They are also very simple grammars.

| the | dog<br>child<br>cat<br>bird | frightened<br>chased<br>killed<br>hit<br>caught | the | dog<br>child<br>cat<br>bird |
|-----|-----|-----|-----|-----|

*Figure 6*

A set of words like {*dog, child, cat, bird*} where the individual words are mutually substitutable is known as a word class. Our analysis has established three classes; the class containing the one member {*the*}; the class containing {*dog, child, cat, bird*}; and the class containing {*frightened, chased, killed, caught, hit*}. We have named them, following traditional usage, respectively, Art(icle) N(oun) and V(erb).

Word classes are not the only classes of item needed in a grammar, as is clear from the discussion in the preceding chapter, where we saw that strings of words like *the dog* and *the child* also need to be accounted for: we identified these as Noun Phrases (NP). For this reason linguists have usually preferred the more general term form class, since form may be applied indifferently to words, parts of words, strings of words, etc. Our substitution table can accommodate information about form classes other than word classes by labelling and bracketing within the table, as shown in Figure 7.

| | | S | | |
|---|---|---|---|---|
| NP | | V | NP | |
| Art | N | | Art | N |
| the | dog<br>child<br>cat<br>bird | frightened<br>chased<br>killed | the | bird<br>dog<br>cat |

*Figure 7*

Two important and closely related points about form classes are, first, the membership or the internal structure of the class in question, and second, its distribution.

As far as word classes are concerned we can only list their membership, since we are not considering here the internal structure of words. Thus, the class of Articles consists of the word {*the*} (so far the only article we have met); and so on. In the case of other form classes it would be absurd and cumbersome to state their membership in terms of strings of words: the class NP consists of the strings {*the dog, the cat, the bird* . . .}; etc. Instead we describe their internal structure in terms of other form classes: the class NP consists of strings of the form Art + N, leaving to our description of the membership of Art and N a specification of what these classes contain.

We now turn to the question of distribution. By the distribution of an item, we mean the set of environments in which it occurs. In sentence 1 the distribution of *frightened* is:

3   The dog __ the child

the sign __ indicating the place within the sentence, the environment, in which this item occurs. Similarly we can say that the distribution of *the* is the two environments:

4a   __ dog frightened the child
4b   The dog frightened __ child

But to state environments in this way is highly redundant; we can make a more economical statement of distribution by using notions of class membership, since this makes the most economical statement of the relevant environment. In this case *frightened* is a V, and the distribution of V is:

5   NP __ NP

Similarly the distribution of *the* is the most economically stated by stating its membership of the class Art and that the distribution of Art is:

6   NP (__ N)

i.e. articles precede nouns in NPs.

For each of the classes discussed so far a description can be made in terms of both criteria: the membership, or the internal structure of the class in question; and the distribution of the class. In this way we can begin to make a grammatical description of various classes. What is an Article? An Article is a class of words, including *the*, which occurs in Noun Phrases preceding a Noun.

Form classes may contain as members not only single words, but also strings of words and indeed other form classes. Consider the membership of the class NP. Let us first widen our data base to include sentences like:

**7a**   The boy chased Fido
**7b**   Fido chased the child
**7c**   Fido chased John

This data introduces a new form class, with the membership {*Fido, John*}.

We call this class Proper Names (PN). The distribution of PN is different from that of N in that members of this class may not be preceded by an Art (**The Fido*). We have already assigned strings Art + N to a class labelled NP. We must now consider whether the class PN is itself a member of the class NP, or whether PN and NP are quite separate classes. If PN and NP are considered quite separate classes, the analysis is as shown in Figures 8 and 9.

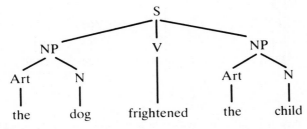

*Figure 8*

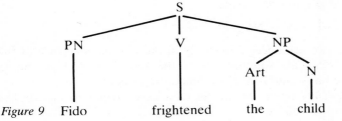

*Figure 9*

In this analysis the two sentences concerned appear rather different, since at no level do they have the same structure: the immediate constituents of the two sentences are:

**8**  NP + V + NP (Figure 8)
PN + V + NP (Figure 9)

If, on the other hand, PN is considered a subclass of NP, the analysis is as shown in Figures 10 and 11.

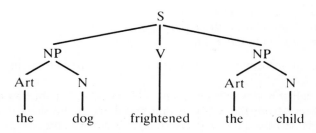

*Figure 10*

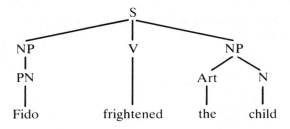

*Figure 11*

Under this analysis the two sentences have the same structure at the most 'fundamental' level since the constituents of the sentence are, in both cases:

**9**  NP + V + NP

and the two sentences differ only in the internal structure of the initial NP. This solution seems the more satisfactory on an intuitive basis, and formal evidence supports it.

First of all, let us widen the data base further to include the following sentences:

**10a** The boy yawned
**10b** The dog slept
**10c** Fido yawned
**10d** John slept

As before, we consider strings like *the dog* and *the boy* as strings with the structure Art + N, and members of the class NP. *Fido* and *John* are once more members of the class PN. *Yawned* and *slept* also form a substitution class, traditionally called Intransitive Verbs, which we abbreviate as VI. Members of this class cannot be put into the same class as words like *frightened*, *chased*, etc., since these items are not mutually substitutable – there are no sentences:

**11**  *The dog yawned the boy
*Fido frightened

etc. We therefore re-label the class containing *frightened*, *chased*, etc., as the class Transitive Verb, abbreviated as VT. This raises the question of why we refer to VT and VI as different sub-classes of *verbs*, a question to which we return later.

Using these two new verb classes, VT and VI, if we analyse NP and PN as distinct classes, we end up with six distinct sentence types:

| | | |
|---|---|---|
| **12a** | NP + VI | (*sentences* **10a,b**) |
| **12b** | PN + VI | (*sentences* **10c,d**) |
| **12c** | NP + VT + NP | (*sentence* **2**) |
| **12d** | NP + VT + PN | (*sentence* **7a**) |
| **12e** | PN + VT + NP | (*sentence* **7b**) |
| **12f** | PN + VT + PN | (*sentence* **7c**) |

whereas if we take PN as a subclass of NP we need account for only two types of sentence:

**13**  NP + VI
NP + VT + NP

The distinction between Art + N and PN is now a matter of the NP. This leads to a more economical description, particularly if we seek to extend our data base still further, as we will. This solution also makes possible a more economical statement of the distribution of our two verb classes. If NP and

PN are distinct classes, then we must describe the distribution of our verbs in such terms as:

**14**   VI occurs in the environments: NP __ #; PN __ #[1]
VT occurs in the environments: NP __ NP; NP __ PN
PN __ NP; PN __ NP

If we consider PN a subclass of NP, a more economical statement results:

**15**   VI occurs in the environment NP __ #
VT occurs in the environment NP __ NP

The evidence we have considered has been entirely based on the substitutability of PN for strings Art + N. Also, the external distribution of PN is the same as that of strings Art + N, as can be determined by the appropriate substitutions in sentences like **11–12** discussed in the previous chapter. All this strongly suggests that PN and Art + N form a single class, NP.

Let us now turn back to the statements of 15. Might not VI and VT + NP themselves constitute a form class, sometimes labelled Verb Phrase (VP)? An argument in favour of this analysis is the fact that these strings are clearly substitutable for each other following the initial NP:

**16**   $NP + \begin{Bmatrix} VI \\ VT + NP \end{Bmatrix}$

Furthermore, using the sort of argument adopted earlier (cf. discussion of Figures 8 and 9), an analysis of this sort shows that at the most fundamental level all our sentences have the same structure, as shown in Figures 12 and 13.

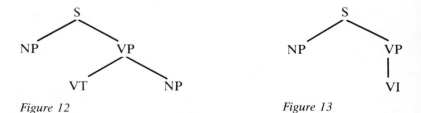

*Figure 12*                    *Figure 13*

1 The symbol # indicates a 'constituent boundary': in this case the end of the sentence. We use this symbol to indicate that VI does not occur with a following NP, as distinct from VT.

(Structure below the NP level is not shown since it is irrelevant to the argument.) All the sentences are now analysed as having the single structure:

**17** NP + VP

rather than as being of two distinct structures. This analysis is fine, but is only partially supported by other kinds of evidence. For instance, the NP has a unity in external distribution, but comparable evidence for the unity of the VP is not so strong. For instance, although we do find sentences like:

**18** John kissed Mary and Harry did so too
(i.e. Harry – kissed Mary)

where *did so* might be thought of as a substitution for the VP; we also find sentences like:

**19a** John kissed Mary and Charlie Agnes
(i.e. Charlie – kissed – Agnes)
**19b** John kissed and Harry fondled Mary
(i.e. John kissed – Mary)

where constituents other than the VP are involved; so evidence in favour of identifying a constituent of the VP type is less conclusive than that leading us to recognize the NP. It can, however, prove a useful constituent to have recognized, as will be seen later, and it has the advantage that all our sentences are analysed as having the same structure at the 'deepest' level: i.e. NP + VP.

**Technical terms**

distribution         substitution table
environment         word class
form class

# 3 Constituent structure grammar

In chapter 1 we said that two of the tasks of a grammar are to provide a systematic account of the constituent structure of sentences and to account for the distribution of forms into classes. In this chapter we produce a formal and explicit grammar for the data discussed so far. To begin with it is convenient to summarize our description.

**A:** Constituent structures. The constituent structures discussed in the previous chapters can be summarized as:

1   A Sentence (S) has the constituents: $NP + VP$

    A Verb Phrase (VP) has the constituents: $\begin{Bmatrix} VT + NP \\ VI \end{Bmatrix}$

    A Noun Phrase (NP) has the constituents: $\begin{Bmatrix} Art + N \\ PN \end{Bmatrix}$

**B:** Word class membership. There are a number of ways the description can be arranged. We can organize our description so that it answers the question, 'What is the membership of the classes VT, VI, . . . , etc.?' or so that it answers the question, 'To what class (VT, VI, . . . , etc.) does a particular word belong?' The first question would be appropriately answered by a description which enumerates the membership of each class:

2   Art: *{the}*
     N:   *{dog, child, boy, cat}*
     PN: *{Fido, John}*
     VT: *{frightened, chased}*
     VI: *{yawned, slept}*

The second question can be answered by providing a 'lexicon' or word list in which the class membership of each individual word is specified. For convenience, and to follow traditional dictionaries, this list can be arranged alphabetically, though a list arranged by some other principle, or even an unordered list serves our purpose equally well. A lexicon looks like this:

**3**  boy: N       dog: N       slept: VI
    cat: N       Fido: PN       the: Art
    child: N       frightened: VT       yawned: VI
    chased: VT       John: PN

The description above is itself a grammar in that it constitutes, as required, a systematic account of the language. We shall, however, further formalize our grammar, by using the following sysmbols:

| *symbol* | *interpreted as:* |
|---|---|
| $\rightarrow$ | 'consists of', 'has the constituents', 'is to be expanded as' |
| + | 'followed by' |
| {X,Y} | 'either X or Y, but not both' |
| $\left\{ \begin{array}{c} X \\ Y \end{array} \right\}$ | 'either X or Y, but not both' |

The first symbol is used in rules like:

**4**  S $\rightarrow$ NP + VP

In ordinary language we can interpret this as meaning, 'The sentence consists of the constituent NP followed by the constituent VP.' Rules of this sort are known as 'rewrite rules'. In rewrite rules there must be only a single symbol on the left-hand side of the arrow: the right-hand side of the arrow may have one or more symbols. If the left-hand side of the arrow is not restricted to a single symbol it is unclear exactly what is a constituent of what; for instance:

**5**  A + B $\rightarrow$ X + Y + Z

This rule could mean X + Y is an expansion of A and Z an expansion of B:

**6**

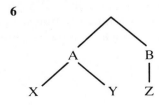

or the rule could mean X is an expansion of A, and Y + Z is an expansion of B:

**7**

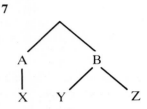

To specify the first analysis the rules are:'

**8**   A → X + Y
  B → Z

To specify the second analysis the rules are:

**9**   A → X
  B → Y + Z

Our rules must lead to an explicit and unambiguous account of constituent structure: for this reason we must only ever expand one symbol at a time, and hence only one symbol may be on the left-hand side of the arrow.

The second symbol, +, indicates an ordering relationship between constituents. Thus the rule:

**10**   A → X + Y

means that A is to be expanded into two constituents, X followed by Y. If the constituents may be in either order, the rule states this explicitly:

**11**   $A \rightarrow \begin{Bmatrix} X + Y \\ Y + X \end{Bmatrix}$

This leads us to our two rule types involving 'curly' brackets. Curly brackets indicate choices and mean that the symbol on the left of the arrow may be expanded into one and only one member of the set of items enclosed within curly brackets. The alternatives are on different lines, when writing constituent structure rules:

**12**   $A \rightarrow \begin{Bmatrix} X + Y \\ P + Q \end{Bmatrix}$

The alternatives are on the same line and separated by commas, when writing rules for the insertion of lexical items:

**13**   $A \rightarrow \{X, Y, Z\}$

Using this formulation we can write our grammar like this:

**14 A**   *Constituent structure rules:*

$$1 \ S \quad \rightarrow NP + VP$$

$$2 \ VP \rightarrow \begin{Bmatrix} VT + NP \\ VI \end{Bmatrix}$$

$$3 \ NP \rightarrow \begin{Bmatrix} Art + N \\ PN \end{Bmatrix}$$

**B**   *Lexical rules:*

4 Art → {*the*}
5 N   → {*dog, child, boy, cat*}
6 PN → {*Fido, John*}
7 VT → {*frightened, chased*}
8 VI  → {*yawned, slept*}

Rules **1–3** are called constituent structure rules since they introduce and develop constituent structures. We call the first symbol, S, the initial symbol, since it is this symbol that is expanded first and the derivation of the whole sentence starts with this symbol. In this grammar the symbols Art, N, PN, VT and VI are terminal symbols since the constituent structure rules cannot develop them further. VP and NP can be further developed by the rules and are called non-terminal symbols. This grammar uses the first of our two suggested approaches to lexical insertion – the lexical rules enumerate the class membership of each terminal symbol. The second approach to lexical insertion, the one using a lexicon, involves scrapping the lexical rules above and replacing them by a lexicon as in **3** above and a general lexical insertion rule:

**15**   *Lexical insertion rule:*

For any terminal symbol of the constituent
structure rules, select from the lexicon a
word that is described as being a member of
the class named by the terminal symbol in
question and attach this word as a daughter
of the relevant symbol.

The output of both grammars (constituent structure rules and lexical rules, *or* constituent structure rules, lexical insertion rule and lexicon) is exactly the same. There are certain advantages in using the approach involving the lexical insertion rule and a lexicon, and this is the approach we shall use. However, the lexical insertion rule is, formally speaking, a different type of rule from the constituent structure rules – it is not a rewrite rule as the constituent rules are:[1]

This proposed grammar can be used for an explicit analysis of the sentences in our data. We start with the first rule, that sentences have a structure NP + VP. This can be represented by the partial tree in Figure 14:

*Figure 14*

Note the convention in drawing trees from the grammar that a rule like S → NP + VP is interpreted as 'write the symbol S, and draw from it as many branches as there are constituents on the right-hand side of the rule, and label the node at the end of each branch by the appropriate symbol'; and similarly for the other rules. Tree diagrams can be drawn on the basis of the rules of the grammar. A grammar will contain information about the possible structural configurations in the data it seeks to account for. A tree diagram shows the structural configuration of some one particular sentence. The second rule in our grammar develops the VP as either VT + NP or as VI. We chose the first alternative, Figure 15:

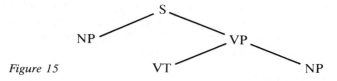

*Figure 15*

1 The rules presented above as 'constituent structure rules' are an informal presentation of what are known in Transformational Grammars as 'Phrase Structure Rules'. The Lexical Insertion Rule is an informal presentation of a type of 'Transformational Rule'. Transformational Rules are discussed at more length on pages 102ff. For a fully formal account of the properties of Phrase Structure Rules and Transformational Rules the reader is referred to any of the books specifically about transformational grammar listed on pages 386–7.

The third rule says that NP is to be developed as either Art + N or as PN. There are two NPs; let us choose one of each, Figure 16:

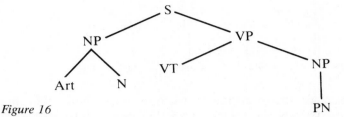

*Figure 16*

We now come to the choice of lexical items. By the lexical insertion rule we may insert from our lexicon words with the appropriate class membership. This gives the sentence shown in Figure 17:

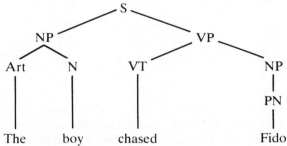

*Figure 17*

The same result is obtained by using the lexical rules instead of the lexical insertion rule. We have produced a labelled and bracketed analysis of a sentence; providing we have operated the grammar correctly – and providing that the grammar itself is correct – we should have a grammatical sentence, as indeed we do. The grammar also produces a definition of what is meant by a grammatical sentence: a sentence that our grammar generates is, by definition, a grammatical sentence. Other strings are not. Our particular grammar can generate only a tiny number of sentences in English, but the principle is clear: the grammar defines grammatical sentences.

We can also use our grammar to analyse sentences. However, the particular way we have chosen to write the grammar entails a somewhat cumbersome procedure. Consider the sentence:

**16**   The boy chased the cat

Our lexicon assigns these words to classes as shown in Figure 18:

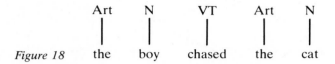

*Figure 18*

Inspection of the constituent structure rules shows that the sequence Art + N constitutes an NP, but that no other sequence of forms is a possible constituent. Incorporating this information, we get Figure 19:

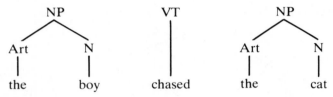

*Figure 19*

Inspecting the constituent structure rules again, we see that VT + NP constitutes a VP; and finally we note that NP + VP constitutes an S. Incorporating this information in a tree diagram (Figure 20), we once more have a labelled and bracketed analysis of a sentence:

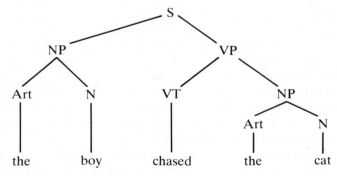

*Figure 20*

In principle a grammar tells you how to construct a sentence, or how to analyse a sentence into its relevant parts, and in both cases assigns a labelled and bracketed description to the sentence. It also accounts for sentences other than those on which it was immediately constructed – in other words it predicts which sentences of the language are grammatical and assigns descriptions to them. Grammars that can do this are generative grammars. Our grammar can do all of these things, though in the form we have here only for a very limited part of English. Later chapters expand the description.

**Technical terms**

category
constituent structure rules
expansion
generative grammar
grammatical
initial symbol

lexical insertion
lexical rule
non-terminal symbol
rewrite rule
terminal symbol

**Exercises**

1  *Some verb classes in English*

This is an exercise in verb subclassification.

1  The man seemed angry
2  The man laughed
3  The man terrified the children
4  The children cried
5  The woman telephoned the policeman
6  The policeman looked strong

There are three different sentence structures and hence three different subclasses of verb. The relevant environments for the subclassification of the verbs are shown below. Say which verbs occur in which environments:

The verbs      . . .      occur in the environment __ Adj
The verbs      . . .      occur in the environment __ NP
The verbs      . . .      occur in the environments __ #
(The environment __ # means the verb occurs with no following constituent.)

Draw a tree diagram for each sentence type. Use the class labels VCop (Copulative verb); VT (Transitive verb); and VI (Intransitive verb) for the three classes of verb identified above.

Now consider the following additional data:

**7** The man ran away
**8** The man hid under the hedge
**9** The policeman looked down
**10** The policeman saw the man
**11** The policeman caught the man
**12** The woman was happy
**13** The policeman stood near the playground

This data introduces two new sentence types and hence two new verb subclasses (and also includes further examples of structures we have already analysed). What are the environments for these two new verb classes? Use the additional constituent labels PP (Prepositional phrase) and Part(icle), and use the labels VbPP and VbPart for the two new classes of verb. A Prepositional phrase has the constituents Prep(osition) + NP. The class Prep includes items like {*under*, *near*, *in*, *on* ...}. The NP can be any NP as described earlier.

Example 14 in this chapter presented a grammar for a restricted set of English sentences. Extend this grammar to include the data from this exercise. The extended grammar should generate all the sentences in the data and others of a similar pattern and assign to each a constituent structure tree.

## 2   The structure of the NP in English

There are restrictions on the possible order of constituents in English. We find NPs like *all their old cotton dresses*, *a lovely pale blue silk shirt*, *five worn-out jumpers*, but not NPs like *\*their all old cotton dresses*, *\*a pale lovely silk blue shirt*. Construct twenty NPs each of not more than six words using as 'head noun' one of the following: *dress*, *shirt*, *jumper*, *sock*, *petticoat*, *apron*, *blouse*, and as 'premodifiers' of the head noun appropriate items from the following list:

the, big, new, her, five, all, lovely, worn-out, woollen, blue, spectacular, small, my, two, few, splendid, quite, silk, pale, your, a, old, some, red, cotton, very

(The notions 'head noun' and 'premodifiers' are discussed further on pages 254–5: in NPs of the sort you are asked to consider the head noun is always the final, and obligatory, constituent, which may be preceded by a number of optional premodifiers.)

(a) Assign each word above to one of the form classes:

Quant(ifier) *all, several* . . .  Num(eral) *five, two* . . .
Art(icle) *a, the* . . .  Adj(ective) *blue, red* . . .
Poss(essive) *my, your* . . .  Int(ensifier) *very, pale* . . .

(b) There are ordering restrictions on the adjectives – thus *old blue dress* but not *\*blue old dress*. Assign adjectives to 'order classes' labelled Adj$_1$, Adj$_2$, etc. (Can you make any semantic generalizations about these order classes?)

(c) There are also co-occurrence restrictions on the Quantifiers, thus *all their socks*, but not *\*several their socks*. Assign Quantifiers to one of the two subclasses Quant$_1$ and Quant$_2$.

(d) Write formulae to show possible orders of elements in the NP (and to exclude impossible orders): e.g. *all blue dresses* (Quant Adj N); *all dresses* (Quant N). Try and collapse the formulae into a single general statement using brackets for 'optional' constituents: e.g. (Quant)(Adj) N – which will cover the examples above: the N is an obligatory constituent and so is unbracketed. You will need to add a note about the difference between singular and plural head nouns – to account for the fact that we find *a* with singular NPs (*a red sock \*a red socks*) and *all* with plural NPs (*all red socks, \*all red sock*), etc.

# 4 Some verb classes in English

Implicit in the preceding chapter is the notion that decisions about constituent structure have implications for the description of class membership, and vice versa, and that these decisions have implications for the type of grammar we write. Some of these problems can be illustrated by considering a classification of some verbs in English. The criterion used is the number and type of constituents that follow a verb, a very traditional criterion. It is what follows the verb that is criterial: what precedes the verb is non-criterial since all verbs must be preceded by a 'subject' NP. Some traditionally recognized verb classes include the following:

### 'Copular' or 'linking' verbs

These occur in the environment:

1 $- \begin{Bmatrix} NP \\ Adj \end{Bmatrix}$

**2a** John is a soldier
**2b** John is strong

These verbs, of which the 'copula' $BE^1$ is the prime exemplar, may be followed by either an adjective, as in **2b**, or an NP, as in **2a**; if they are followed by an NP the NP must agree in number with the subject NP of the sentence:

**3**  He is a soldier
**4**  They are soldiers
**5** *They are a soldier. *He is soldiers

---

1 It will be recalled that we introduced the convention of referring to the dictionary or lexical entry of a particular item by the use of small capitals (see note 1, page 22). Thus BE is the lexical entry relating the various forms of BE – *am, is, are, were*, and so on.

(There are some exceptions to this generalization, for example if the NP to the right of BE contains a 'collective' noun; *They are a crowd of lazy idlers*; *They are the best regiment in the army*.)

Only copular verbs can be followed by either an NP or an Adjective so we can treat NP and Adj here as members of a single form class, defined by the environment $V_{Cop}$—. We call this form class, again following traditional terminology, Predicate (Pred). This means we must change the statement at the head of this section to read, These occur in the environment:

**6** __ Pred

We then need a rule in our grammar to the effect:

**7** $\text{Pred} \rightarrow \begin{Bmatrix} \text{NP} \\ \text{Adj} \end{Bmatrix}$

The introduction of the labelled node, Pred, has two advantages: it offers a unique environment for the classification of copular verbs, and it enables us to identify which NPs are 'predicate NPs'. We need to know this to ensure that predicate NPs agree in number with the subject of the sentence. Other copular verbs include SEEM, BECOME, LOOK.

### 'Intransitive' verbs

These occur in the environment:

**8** __ #
**9a** The women wept
**9b** The children cried

Such verbs can occur as the final constituent of a sentence, as is implied by the statement in **8** that they occur in the environment of #, a symbol indicating a constituent boundary. The relevant constituent boundary in this case is the right hand end of the VP, for reasons which will become apparent. Intransitive verbs include DIE, TALK, WORK.

### 'Transitive' verbs

These occur in the environment:

> **10**　＿ NP
> **11a**　The dog bit the man
> **11b**　The child thrashed the dog

Verbs like BITE and THRASH were traditionally called transitive verbs because 'the action of the verb' was considered to 'pass over' from the subject to the object.[2] Transitive verbs cannot typically occur without a following NP:

> **12a**　*The dog bit
> **12b**　*The child thrashed

With all true transitive verbs, for any sentence of the form:

> **13a**　NP + V + NP
> **13b**　The dog bit the man

there are corresponding sentences of the form:

> **14a**　The man was bitten by the dog
> **14b**　What the dog did to the man was bite him
> **14c**　What happened to the man was that the dog bit him

Such sentences are impossible with copular verbs:

> **15a**　He became a soldier
> **15b**　*A soldier was become by him
> **15c**　*What happened to the soldier was that the man became him

Other transitive verbs include KILL, COOK, FIND.

2 The grammar discussed in the preceding chapter, and elaborated at the end of this chapter, can be used to give a formal definition to the terms 'subject' and 'object'. The subject NP is that NP which is immediately dominated by S; the object is that NP immediately dominated by VP. In these terms the NP dominated by Pred which occurs after the copula verb BE discussed in 1–7 is not an object NP – in traditional terms it is referred to as a 'complement'. Notions such as subject, object, complement, etc. are discussed in more detail on pages 330ff.

**'Di-transitive' verbs**

These occur in the environment:

**16** __ NP + NP
**17** John gave Mary the book

These verbs are called 'ditransitive' since they are typically followed by two NPs, and most verbs in this class must be followed by two NPs.[3] Characteristically, sentences of the form illustrated in **17** have corresponding sentences where the two NPs are reversed in order and a preposition, typically *to*, is introduced:

**18a** John gave Mary the book
**18b** John gave the book to Mary

Like sentences containing transitive verbs, sentences like those in **18a,b** correspond to sentences like:

**19a** Mary was given the book by John
**19b** The book was given to Mary by John

Either object NP can become the subject of the corresponding 'passive' sentence. Other di-transitive verbs include PRESENT, TELL, TAKE.

**'Intransitive locative' verbs**

These occur in the environment:

**20** __ PP
**21a** The lamp stood on the table
**21b** The gun leant against the wall

Most verbs of this class require to be followed by a PP:

**22a** *The lamp stood
**22b** *The gun leant

3 In terms of our previous definition of object, such verbs may be said to have two objects – hence the description 'di-transitive'. The two objects are usually distinguished as the 'indirect object', the first of the two NPs in the structure shown, and the 'direct object', the second of the two NPs. (For further discussion see chapter 19.) In sentences with only one object, like **11**, this is called the direct object.

The P P typically indicates a location, hence the name for this class of verbs. Other intransitive locative verbs are HANG, SIT, SLUMP.

### 'Transitive locative' verbs

These occur in the environment:

23   __ NP + PP
24   John stood the lamp on the table
25   Mary leant the gun against the wall

Frequently, as in the examples given, these verbs correspond to the verbs found as intransitive locative verbs, except for the object N P immediately following the verb. These verbs resemble transitive verbs in that there are corresponding sentences like:

26   The gun was leant against the wall by Mary
27   What happened to the gun was that Mary leant it
     against the wall

and so on, in a manner analogous to transitive verbs (as 17). They differ from simple transitive verbs in that, typically, they require to be followed by a PP as well as an NP. We find no sentences:

28   *John stood the lamp

etc. These verbs differ from di-transitive verbs in that they cannot be followed by two N Ps:

29   John stood the lamp on the table
30   *John stood the table the lamp.

Other transitive locative verbs are PUT, LAY, HANG.

We have looked at six different verb classes. Each can be distinguished in terms of the environments in which the members of the class can occur, and in terms of the sentences that can be related to a sentence containing a verb from a particular class. Some of these have been illustrated; others the reader is left to discover for himself.

How might we account for these different verb classes in a formal grammar? One way is to label each of the verb classes, producing a constituent structure grammar of the following sort:

**31**     $S \rightarrow NP + VP$

$$VP \rightarrow \begin{cases} V_{cop} + Pred \\ V_i \\ V_t + NP \\ V_{dt} + NP + NP \\ V_{il} + PP \\ V_{tl} + NP + PP \end{cases}$$

($V_{cop}$ = verb copulative; $V_i$ = verb intransitive, and so on)

$$Pred \rightarrow \begin{Bmatrix} Adj \\ NP \end{Bmatrix}$$

together with a set of lexical rules of the form:

**32**  $V_{cop} \rightarrow \{\text{SEEM, TURN, APPEAR}, \ldots\},$

  $V_i \rightarrow \{\text{DIE, TALK, WORK, SMILE}, \ldots\}.$

and so on.

An approach of this sort poses difficulties. It leads to the establishment of a large number of verb classes: we already have six, and with little difficulty can establish more. This makes the second rule in our grammar cumbersome. Furthermore, we find that a considerable amount of 'cross-classification' is involved: i.e. many verbs occur in more than one class – examples we have seen are the verbs STAND and LEAN. An alternative approach is to have a lexicon listing the class membership of each verb, and a lexical insertion rule as discussed in the preceding chapter. This approach leads to the listing in the lexicon of the different class memberships of each verb, in the form:

**33**  STAND $V_{il}$, $V_{tl}$

and so on, but does not solve the clumsiness of the constituent structure rules.

A different approach lists in the lexicon the environments in which a particular verb can occur, without actually seeking to name each individual verb class. Thus we list STAND as:

**34**  STAND V; __ (NP) PP

In this representation V indicates that STAND is a verb. We call such characterizations (and others like N, Adj, Prep, etc.) 'inherent subcategorization' since they describe the form class to which a particular item belongs, which seems to be an inherent property of the item itself. The representation __ (N P) P P indicates that STAND must occur with a following P P, and may, optionally, occur with an immediately following N P. This is equivalent to saying that STAND is either an intransitive locative, or a transitive locative verb, since these two environments define these verb classes. We call such characterizations 'strict subcategorization': this always refers only to the syntactic environment relevant to the sub-categorization of the item in question which means other constituents of the V P. This approach simplifies our grammar: instead of listing individually all the different expansions of V P we can present the rules as follows:

**35**   $S \rightarrow NP + VP$

$$VP \rightarrow V\left(+\left\{\begin{matrix} \\ (NP) \end{matrix}\begin{matrix} Pred \\ \left(+\left\{\begin{matrix} PP \\ NP \end{matrix}\right\}\right)\end{matrix}\right\}\right)$$

$$Pred \rightarrow \left\{\begin{matrix} Adj \\ NP \end{matrix}\right\}$$

Recall that, by our conventions, items curly-bracketed together are alternatives; items in ordinary parentheses are optional. The V P rule here allows us to produce the strings: V + Pred; V; V + N P, V + P P, V + N P + N P; V + N P + P P – this is just the set of environments described above. The strict sub-categorization frames for a given verb include just those categories that are introduced as sisters of V in the N P. Note that only the sisters of V are necessary for strict subcategorization.

We shall also have to amend the lexical insertion rule given on page 43. Our rule will now be:

**36**   *Lexical insertion rule*

For any terminal symbol of the constituent structure rules, select from the lexicon a word that is described as being a member of the class named by the terminal symbol in question and attach this word as a daughter of the relevant symbol. If the item selected is characterized by a strict subcategorization frame, then the environment into which the item is inserted must not conflict with the strict subcategorization frame.

## Technical terms

| | |
|---|---|
| copula | linking verb |
| complement | object |
| copular verb | predicate |
| di-transitive verb | strict subcategorization |
| inherent subcategorization | strict subcategorization frame |
| intransitive verb | subject |
| indirect object | transitive verb |
| intransitive locative verb | transitive locative verb |
| locative verb | |

## Exercises

### 1

The text of this chapter distinguished six verb classes. To which of these classes do the following verbs belong? Note that some belong to more than one class. For each verb draw up a lexical entry like that shown in the text for STAND:

| | | | | |
|---|---|---|---|---|
| SEEM | LIE | LIVE | ANTAGONIZE | HANG |
| SPREAD | SING | LOCK | FIND | CRY |
| APPEAR | SHOOT | EAT | GROW | DIE |
| SMELL | GROWL | WRITE | GIVE | PASS |
| PUZZLE | REMAIN | ARRIVE | BECOME | SEND |

### 2

We noted in the text that sentences like *Moggy is a cat* and *Kate bought a cat* are, at one level of structure, apparently similar – NP V NP – but that we need to distinguish between copular verbs (like BE) and transitive verbs (like BUY). Summarize the reasons for making this distinction.

Now consider the following sentences:

**1**   The girls made John happy (NP V NP Adj)
**2**   The committee elected John Chairman (NP V NP NP)
**3**   The committee gave John a cheque (NP V NP NP)

Using the same sorts of criteria that you used to distinguish between copular and transitive verbs, distinguish between the three apparently similar sentence types (in particular think of syntactically related sentences – *The committee elected John as Chairman*, etc.). To which of the verb classes you establish do the following belong:

| | | | | |
|---|---|---|---|---|
| GIVE | PRESENT | VOTE | CONSIDER | OFFER |
| THINK | MAKE | SHOW | CHOOSE | IMAGINE |

*3*

Many of the verbs that we have looked at so far can take NP objects, where the NP is expanded to dominate a noun (like *The hunters shot* THE LIONS). Many verbs can also have sentences as objects:

I believe *that the world is flat*
I think *that Edinburgh is a lovely city*

Suppose that such sentences, which we will examine in more detail later, have a structure like this:

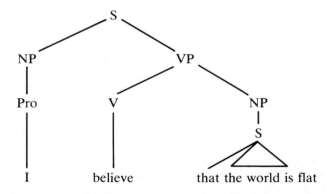

Note that in the analysis proposed the sentential object of the verb is treated as an NP which has been expanded as *that + S*.

(This analysis will be defended in more detail later on.) For our present purposes we describe the relevant environment as:

— S

and we can add this environment to the other environments discussed above. We note one further similar environment, illustrated by:

I told Mary that I loved her (NP V NP S)

Given these two new environments, write lexical entries for the following verbs. For example:

TELL    V, __ NP NP (I told Mary a bedtime story)
           V, __ NP S    (I told Mary that I loved her)

| ASSUME | PERSUADE | ARGUE | FORETELL | PREDICT |
| SAY | TELL | EXPECT | SUPPOSE | ASSURE |
| DENY | HEAR | AGREE | PROMISE | SUPPOSE |

# 5   Formal grammars

Grammars of the sort discussed so far are referred to as 'formal' grammars. Formal here can be taken in two senses.

In one sense the grammar is formal in that it is concerned with the distribution of forms, but not with the sense of individual forms, nor with the meaning of whole sentences nor whether any appropriate context of use can be found for the sentence. It is concerned only with the distribution of forms. Form classes are established in terms of their distribution – items with the same distribution are placed in the same form class. In this sense 'formal' may be opposed to 'notional'. A notional description would include in the same class items held to have a common element of meaning, but not necessarily with the same distribution.

The distinction between a formal and a notional approach can be illustrated by considering the following data from the African language Akan, from central and southern Ghana:

| 1a | Kofi ware | *Kofi is tall* |
| 1b | Kofi reware | *Kofi is getting tall* |
| 1c | Kofi aware | *Kofi has grown tall* |
| | | |
| 2a | Kookoo no bere | *the cocoa is ripe/red* |
| 2b | Kookoo no rebere | *the cocoa is ripening* |
| 2c | Kookoo no abere | *the cocoa has got ripe* |
| | | |
| 3a | Kofi kasa | *Kofi speaks* |
| 3b | Kofi rekasa | *Kofi is speaking* |
| 3c | Kofi akasa | *Kofi has spoken* |
| | | |
| 4a | Kofi yɛ kɛseɛ | *Kofi is big* |
| 4b | Kofi reyɛ kɛseɛ | *Kofi is getting big* |
| 4c | Kofi ayɛ kɛseɛ | *Kofi has become big* |

Sentence sets **1** to **3** contain the verbs WARE 'to be or become tall'; BERE 'to be or become ripe or red'; KASA 'to speak'. Set

**4** has a verb Yɛ 'to be or become' followed by an adjective KɛSEɛ 'big'. We can identify the verbs in formal terms as those forms that can be inflicted by various verbal affixes: the **a** sentences contain the simple verb stem; the **b** sentences the prefix *re-*; the **c** sentences the prefix *a-*.[1] By contrast adjectives, like KɛSEɛ, are invariant, so there are no sentences like:

    **5**  *Kofi kɛseɛ
        *Kofi rekɛseɛ
        *Kofi akɛseɛ

Furthermore adjectives must, as in English, be preceded by a copular verb, in this case the verb Yɛ 'to be or become'. Verbs do not co-occur with the copula, so we do not find:

    **6**  *Kofi yɛ ware
        *Kookoo no yɛ bere

In formal terms items like WARE 'to be tall' or BERE 'to be red' are clearly verbs, just as KASA 'to speak' is a verb. Grouping WARE 'to be tall' and KɛSEɛ 'big' into the same class falsifies the facts of the language. Both are 'descriptive' words, but their grammatical behaviour is different, and the grammar should be based on grammatical considerations (like the ability to bear verbal affixes) rather than notional considerations (like the fact that they are descriptive words).

We can make the same point by considering the following English sentences:

    **7**  John talks; John is talking
    **8**  The fruit ripens; The fruit is ripening
    **9**  The fruit is ripe; The fruit is getting ripe

TALK and RIPEN in **7** and **8** are clearly verbs (they occur in the verbal forms *ripen*S and IS *ripen*ING, etc.); equally clearly RIPE in **9** is an adjective (it occurs with the copula, BE, and in constructions with the verb GET). We cannot use the verb RIPEN with the syntax of an adjective, nor the adjective RIPE with the syntax of a verb, as can be seen by comparing **8** and **9** with the ungrammatical:

    **10**  *The fruit ripes; *The fruit is riping
    **11**  *The fruit is ripen; *The fruit is getting ripen

---

1 This is not the whole story since tonal distinctions are also involved, and these are not marked. However this account is adequate for our purposes.

The fact that RIPE and RIPEN are lexically related, though true, is irrelevant: RIPE is an adjective and RIPEN a verb. In attempting to describe the grammar of a language, formal criteria are to be preferred to notional criteria.

Members of a formally established form class may have a common notional element; indeed this is often the case and is no surprise if we hold that language is a system for communicating meanings. On the other hand the principles behind the establishment of formal and notional classes are quite different, and formal criteria are in general preferable.

The second sense of formal implies that the grammar should be formalized, that is, presented in terms of a set of formal rules, like those of the previous chapter, explicitly and economically. It must be clear just what data is accounted for and how it is being accounted for, just what assumptions are made about the nature of the language, and just what claims about the structure of the language are presented. In this sense formal is opposed to informal.

Formal in the first sense does not necessarily exclude considerations of meaning: this would be impossible and undesirable. Ostentatious attempts to expel considerations of meaning have usually allowed meaning to creep surreptitiously back under some other guise. We can see how meaning is smuggled in if we consider the sort of problem sometimes presented for analysis to beginning linguistics students. Such problems often present data from a little-known language which can sometimes be analysed without knowing the meaning of the sentences, rather like a puzzle from a Sunday newspaper. Here is an example from Scots Gaelic (we have omitted glosses to demonstrate a formal analysis):

12　Bha an cù dubh
13　Bha an cat bàn
14　Bha Calum mór
15　Bha an cù sgìth
16　Bha Calum sgìth
17　Bha Màiri beag
18　Bha an gille mór
19　Bha an cù beag
20　Bha Màiri bàn
21　Bha an gille beag
22　Bha an cat mór
23　Bha Màiri beag

We are provided with the additional information that these strings are all sentences, and that no other word order is possible for these sentences – the following, for example, are impossible:

24  *An cat dubh bha
25  *Bha cat an dubh
26  *Bha dubh an cat

etc. We are also told that strings like:

27  *Bha an Calum sgìth
28  *Bha cat dubh

are not found.

It is possible to write a grammar for this data without knowing what the sentences mean, using only the techniques of expansion and substitution. Thus, we allocate *dubh*, *sgìth*, and *beag* to the same form class since they are all mutually substitutable following *bha an cù* (**12**, **15**, **19**). *mór* and *beag* are mutually substitutable in **18** and **21**, and *beag* and *bàn* are substitutable in **17** and **20**. Since these classes have overlapping membership we assume that all these items are members of the same form class, which we give the arbitrary label A. We could test this supposition, if a Gaelic speaker were handy, by enquiring whether a string such as:

29  Bha an cù mór

which we do not find in our data, but which this analysis predicts, is well formed. (It is.)

Next we note that our data includes a class of words (*cù*, *gille*, *cat*) that only occur after *an*, and we see from the ungrammaticality of **28** that at least one member of this class cannot appear without a preceding *an*: we assume this is typical of the class, which we give the arbitrary label B.

There is a class of words in our data never preceded by *an*: *Calum* and *Màiri*, and **27** shows that *Calum* at least may not be preceded by *an*. We give this class the arbitrary label C. This leaves only *bha* and *an* unaccounted for; the evidence suggests these must be considered separate one-member classes, D and E. So much for simple substitution. We can summarize our findings in substitution tables, one for each string type (Figures 21 and 22):

| D | E | B | A |
|---|---|---|---|
| bha | an | cu<br>cat<br>gille | dubh<br>bàn<br>sgìth<br>beag<br>mór |

*Figure 21*

| D | C | A |
|---|---|---|
| bha | Calum<br>Màiri | dubh<br>bàn<br>sgìth<br>beag<br>mór |

*Figure 22*

At this point we note that strings of the form E + B appear substitutable for members of the class C. This suggests a new form class, F, which can be expanded as either E + B or C. This too we can represent in the substitution table (Figure 23):

| S | | | |
|---|---|---|---|
| D | F | | A |
| | E | B | |
| bha | an | cù<br>cat<br>gille | dubh<br>bàn<br>mór<br>beag<br>sgìth |
| | C | | |
| | Calum<br>Màiri | | |

*Figure 23*

Or we can write a little grammar for our data:

**30** $S \rightarrow D + F + A$

$$F \rightarrow \begin{Bmatrix} E + B \\ C \end{Bmatrix}$$

*Lexical rules*:

$D \rightarrow \{bha\}$
$E \rightarrow \{an\}$
etc.

At this point we must give up our pretence. If we had glossed the sentences – glosses for a few of the sentences are shown below, and reference to the lexicon below will yield glosses for the others – the reader would quickly have identified the class arbitrarily labelled A as a class of Adjectives, B as a class of Nouns, C as a class of Proper Nouns, D as a copular verb and E as an article. Using these more familiar class names we could write the grammar:

**31**  *Constituent structure rules*

$S \rightarrow VCop + NP + Adj$      Copular verb/
Noun Phrase/
Adjective

$$NP \rightarrow \begin{Bmatrix} Art + N \\ PN \end{Bmatrix}$$      Article/Noun
Proper Noun

*Lexicon*:

*an* Art 'the'
*bha* VCop 'was'
*cat* N 'cat'
*bàn* Adj 'white; fair haired (of people)'
etc., etc.

Exercises like this with or without glosses are useful. They encourage a formal (rather than a notional) approach to description; they illustrate the principles of distributional analysis; and they can be used to practise writing formal grammars. They also draw the student's attention to the ways in which languages can differ with respect to such features as constituent order within the sentence or class membership: note the difference in constituent order between English (subject + verb + complement) and Gaelic (verb + subject + complement). In the Akan data at the beginning of the chapter the class Verb in Akan includes items that translate as Adjectives in English. The exercises also illustrate, albeit in an oversimplified way, an approach to language analysis: sentences with similar structure are gathered together so that they may be compared directly and the likenesses and differences between them clearly observed.

Such exercises are, however, artificial. The data has been carefully selected and arranged: and it is here that meaning has crept surreptitiously in. A random sample of data from a native speaker of a language speaking naturally would not look anything like the data we have examined; it would be impossible to make a formal grammar on the basis of a dozen or so utterances collected at random.

*Lexicon for the Gaelic data:*

| | |
|---|---|
| *an*  Art 'the' | *cù*  N 'dog' |
| *bàn*  Adj 'white' | *dubh*  Adj 'black' |
| *beag*  Adj 'small' | *gille*  N 'boy' |
| *bha*  Vcop 'was' | *Màiri*  PN 'Maire' |
| *Calum*  PN 'Calum' | *mór*  Adj 'big' |
| *cat*  N 'cat' | *sgìth*  Adj 'tired' |

The sentences **12–23** translate as

The dog was black **(12)**
The cat was white **(13)**
Calum was big **(14)**
*etc.*

## Technical terms

formal (of forms) vs. notional
formal (formalized) vs. informal

## Exercises

The data in this and the following exercise are from Scottish Gaelic.

*1*

(a)   Group the words into classes: use the class names Art(icle); N(oun); PN (Proper Noun); VT (Transitive verb); VI (Intransitive verb); Pro(noun).

(b)   Find an appropriate translation meaning for each word.

(c)   Write a grammar for these data and incorporate it into the grammar given in the text.

| | | |
|---|---|---|
| 1 | Chunnaic mi an cù | I saw the dog |
| 2 | Bhuail e an gille | He struck the boy |
| 3 | Ghlac Calum breac | Calum caught a trout |
| 4 | Reic Calum an cù | Calum sold the dog |
| 5 | Sgrìobh mi litir | I wrote a letter |
| 6 | Ghlac Calum an cù | Calum caught the dog |
| 7 | Bhuail Tearlach an gille | Charlie struck the boy |
| 8 | Chunnaic an cù Calum | The dog saw Calum |
| 9 | Bhàsaich Tearlach | Charlie died |
| 10 | Fhuair Tearlach cù | Charlie got a dog |
| 11 | Sheinn mi | I sang |
| 12 | Bhàsaich an cù | The dog died |
| 13 | Chunnaic Calum cù | Calum saw a dog |

*2*

In the sentences below, there is an additional constituent not present in the corresponding sentences in the previous exercise. Let us refer to this as a Prepositional Phrase (PP). What are the constituents of the PP? Use the class name Prep(osition) in addition to the class names already available to you.

Enlarge the grammar you wrote for the previous exercise to accommodate this new data.

| | | |
|---|---|---|
| 1 | Bhuail Tearlach an gille le bata | Charlie struck the boy with a stick |
| 2 | Ghlac Calum breac anns an linne seo | Calum caught a trout in this pool |
| 3 | Chunnaic mi an cù aig an dorus | I saw a dog at the door |
| 4 | Sgrìobh mi litir gu Calum | I wrote a letter to Calum |
| 5 | Bhàsaich Tearlach anns an Eadailt | Charlie died in Italy |

*3*

The following data are from Kwahu, an Akan language from Ghana:

| | | |
|---|---|---|
| 1 | ɔkyerɛkyerɛfoɔ no rekasa | The teacher is speaking |
| 2 | abɔfora no regoro | The child is playing |
| 3 | Amma regoro | Amma is playing |
| 4 | Kofi rehwɛ ɔkyerɛkyerɛfoɔ no | Kofi is looking at the teacher |
| 5 | ɔkyerɛkyerɛfoɔ no reboa Amma | The teacher is helping Amma |
| 6 | ɔkyerɛkyerɛfoɔ no reboro abɔfora no | The teacher is beating the child |
| 7 | abɔfora no resu | The child is crying |
| 8 | Amma reboa abɔfora no | Amma is helping the child |

(a)   Group the words into classes: use the class names – Article (Art), Noun (N), Proper Noun (PN), Verb Transitive (VT), Verb Intransitive (VI).

(b)   Find an appropriate translation meaning for each word based on the English gloss. Since we are assuming that words are the smallest constituents of interest to us, you will have to identify a word like *regoro* as a member of the class VI and give it a gloss like 'is playing'.

(c)   There are two types of Noun Phrase (NP) shown in the data. What are the constituents of these NPs?

(d)   Write a grammar for this data.

(e)   Using your grammar, draw tree diagrams to represent the grammatical structure of sentences **1** and **6**.

# 6 Optional and obligatory constituents

We have noted that the subject NP is non-distinctive for purposes of verb sub-classification (page 50). Since all sentences require a subject NP, only what follows the verb can be distinctive. Let us now consider some other constituents that are non-distinctive for the purpose of verb subclassification. Consider these sentences:

1 The women wept in the bathroom
2 The dog bit the man in the bathroom
3 John gave Mary the book in the bathroom
4 John stood on the table in the bathroom
5 John stood the gun against the wall in the bathroom

We can analyse each of these sentences as having a constituent *in the bathroom* in construction with one of our example sentences from Chapter 4.[1] Traditionally these constituents are

---

1 Some of these sentences are ambiguous. For example, 2 could be analysed as:

    **i** The dog – bit – the man – in the bathroom
or as: **ii** The dog – bit – the man in the bathroom

In sentence **i** the constituent *in the bathroom* indicates where the man was bitten, and can be related to sentences like:

    **iii** It was in the bathroom that the dog bit the man
          Where the dog bit the man was in the bathroom
          Where did the dog bite the man? In the bathroom

In sentence **ii** the constituent *the man in the bathroom* is an NP. This sentence is related to other sentences like:

    **iv** It was the man in the bathroom that the dog bit
          Who did the dog bite? The man in the bathroom

We are immediately concerned with the first of these analyses, **i**. (We return to the other analysis later.) We also observe that constituents like *in the bathroom* do not typically occur in sentences with copular verbs:

    **v** *John is tall in the bathroom

This is why such sentences are not included in **1–5**.

called 'adverbs', and specifically 'adverbs of place', since they indicate where the action took place. There are a number of things we should observe about these constituents in deciding the constituent structure of **1–5**. Firstly, in each case *in the bathroom* is an optional constituent: without it, an acceptable sentence remains. By contrast we cannot leave out the constituent immediately following the verb. We can have:

>   **6**   The dog bit the man

but not

>   **7**   *The dog bit in the bathroom

Secondly the constituent *in the bathroom* is not criterial for verb subclassification: it can occur with all the verb classes illustrated, so cannot be criterial. Finally, constituents like *in the bathroom* can occur in a distinct sentence, for example:

>   **8**   The women wept. This happened in the bathroom
>   **9**   John stood the gun against the wall. This happened in
>   the bathroom

**8, 9** roughly paraphrase the sentences **1, 5**. Note that we cannot find sentences resembling **8, 9** which correspond to any of the other constituents in **1–5**:

>   **10**   *The dog bit. This happened to the man

This last characteristic of constituents like *in the bathroom* is particularly valuable when we contrast them with superficially similar constituents like *against the wall* and *on the table* in sentences **4** and **5**. The following are acceptable:

>   **11**   John stood on the table. This happened in the
>   bathroom
>   **12**   John stood the gun against the wall. This happened in
>   the bathroom

but the following are nonsense:

>   **13**   *John stood. This happened on the table
>   **14**   *John stood the gun. This happened against the wall

In Chapter 4 we observed that the constituents criterial for strict subclassification are those constituents that are sisters of V, and daughters of VP with V. This suggests that we should consider our adverbial constituents as constituents of some node other than VP. We will treat them as sisters of VP, and daughters, along with VP, of S, as shown in Figure 24.

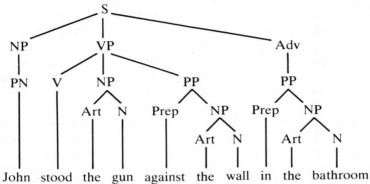

*Figure 24*

This analysis is captured in the following grammar:

**15**    $S \rightarrow NP + VP \;\; (+ Adv)$
$VP \rightarrow V(NP) \left( \begin{Bmatrix} PP \\ NP \end{Bmatrix} \right)$
$Adv \rightarrow PP \;\; \cdot$
$PP \rightarrow Prep + NP$
$NP \rightarrow \begin{Bmatrix} Art + N \\ PN \end{Bmatrix}$

This grammar clearly distinguishes those PP that are within the VP – and are hence constituents criterial for strict subclassification, as with STAND – from those PP not in the VP. These latter are adverbs and not criterial for subclassification.

Traditionally items like adverbs are called 'modifiers'; traditional grammars indeed often refer to 'modifying adverbs'. (We discuss modification in more detail on pages 254–9.) In informal notional terms, a modifier is a constituent that restricts the possible range of reference of some other constituent. In the sentence *the woman wept in the bathroom*, the adverbial constituent *in the bathroom* modifies the 'nuclear' sentence *the woman wept* by specifying the particular place in which the action described by the nucleus took place. We use the term 'scope' to refer to the constituents which the modifier modifies: thus the scope of the modifier *in the bathroom* is the nuclear sentence *the woman wept*. Syntactically, modifiers are optional constituents, and this is shown in the first rule in **15** by enclosing the adverb constituent in brackets. The scope of the modifier can, to some degree, be shown by the rule that introduces it. In the case of **15** the adverb is introduced as an optional constituent of the sentence, so its scope is the other constituents of the sentence, i.e. the nuclear sentence. Adverbial expressions like *in the bathroom* are thus 'sentence adverbs' or 'sentence modifiers'.

The previous paragraph referred to the constituent *the woman wept* as 'nuclear'. We can draw a useful distinction between 'nuclear' and 'non-nuclear' constituents. Nuclear constituents of the sentence are NP + VP and all that is immediately dominated by VP. Other sentence constituents, like Adv, are non-nuclear. Nuclear constituents are either obligatory for the sentence to be accepted as grammatical, or criterial for verb subclassification. Non-nuclear constituents are optional, and, typically, modifiers. Frequently, non-nuclear constituents can be placed in a separate sentence, as illustrated by **8** and **9**. In these terms PPs deriving from an expansion of VP are nuclear, PPs deriving from Adv are non-nuclear. Nuclear sentences are the most 'basic', simplest, sentence types in the language. Defining nuclear sentences is not, however, entirely straightforward.

The distinction between nuclear and non-nuclear constituents is not a simple matter of optionality. We saw, for instance, in the previous chapter that the NP that immediately follows a verb like STAND is not obligatory: both *He stood the lamp on the table* and *The lamp stood on the table* are grammatical. It is, however, nuclear, as it is part of the necessary strict subcategorization frame. Other verb classes with optional but nuclear constituents include 'verbs of motion' like RUN, WALK:

    **16**   John is running
    **17**   John is running to school

where the *to school* constituent is nuclear but not obligatory: **17** cannot be paraphrased by

    **18**   *John is running. This happened to school.

Another similar case involves verbs like READ and WRITE which take an optional object N P:

**19** John is reading
**20** John is reading a book

The constituent *a book* can hardly occur in a distinct sentence on the model of **8** or **9**. Furthermore it makes no sense to say that *a book* 'modifies' *John is reading* in a comparable fashion to the way *in the bathroom* modifies *the woman wept* in the sentence *The woman wept in the bathroom*.

Let us now look further at the expansion of the Adv node shown in the third rule of the grammar in **15**. The constituents we have been concerned with are traditionally called 'adverbs of place': are there other types of constituent that may be called adverbs of place? Are there other types of adverb in addition to adverbs of place? The answer to both questions is yes.

First, consider another type of adverb of place:

**21** The dog bit the man upstairs

(**21**, like **2**, is ambiguous as between the bracketing *The dog – bit – the man – upstairs* and *The dog – bit – the man upstairs*. We are concerned with the former analysis.) In **21** *upstairs* has the same distribution as the P P *in the bathroom*. This suggests they belong to the same form class, which we call $\text{Adv}_{\text{place}}$.

This leads to the constituent structure rule:

$$\textbf{22} \quad \text{Adv}_{\text{place}} \rightarrow \begin{Bmatrix} \text{PP} \\ \text{Place adverb} \end{Bmatrix}$$

where P P expands into a prepositional phrase, and Place adverb dominates such items as *upstairs*, *downstairs*, *here*, *there*, etc.

Sentences with $\text{Adv}_{\text{place}}$ constituents correspond to interrogative sentences of the form:

**23a** Where did the dog bite the man?
**23b** Upstairs/In the bathroom, etc.

Consider two other types of adverb, adverbs of time and adverbs of manner. Adverbs of time, as the name suggests, locate events, etc. in time:

**24a** The dog bit the man yesterday
**24b** John lived in London for twenty years

Once again there are prepositional phrases (*for twenty years*) and simple time adverbs (*yesterday*). Sentences with adverbs of time correspond to interrogative sentences with *when*:

**25**   When did the dog bite the man?

In independent sentences, adverbs of time most naturally follow rather than precede adverbs of place (though both orders may occur):

**26a**   The dog bit the man upstairs yesterday
**26b**   The dog bit the man yesterday upstairs

Whereas adverbs of time occur freely in sentence-initial position, adverbs of place there are often clumsier:

**27a**   Yesterday the dog bit the man
**27b**   Upstairs the dog bit the man

Adverbs of manner, as their name suggests, indicate the manner in which the event described by the verb is carried out:

**28**   The dog bit the man viciously

Once again there are manner adverbs (*viciously*) and prepositional phrases:

**29**   The man beat the dog with apparent enjoyment

Many manner adverbs are formed by the suffixation of *-ly* to the corresponding adjective form (*happy* : *happily*; *vicious* : *viciously*), and there is then a typical paraphrase *in an* [*Adj*] *manner*:

**30a**   The man beat the dog viciously
**30b**   The man beat the dog in a vicious manner

Manner adverbs typically follow the VP immediately and precede other adverbs:

**31a**   The man beat the dog viciously in the garden
yesterday
**31b**   ?The man beat the dog yesterday in the garden
viciously

Manner adverbs, unlike other adverbs, may also occur within the verb constituent, but occur less readily in sentence initial position.

**32a** The man viciously beat the dog
**32b** The man is viciously beating the dog
**32c** *The man in the garden beats the dog
**32d** Viciously the man beat the dog

Finally manner adverbs correspond to *how* in interrogative sentences:

**33a** How did the man beat the dog?
**33b** Viciously/With apparent enjoyment, etc.

Given this new data, we amend the first rule of **15** to:

**34** $S \rightarrow NP + VP \quad (+Adv_{manner}) \quad (+Adv_{place})$
$(+Adv_{time})$

together with appropriate rules, on the analogy of **22**, to accommodate the expansion of the adverb nodes. This leaves us with the problem of describing the 'alternative' placements of adverbs of manner and time (either within the verbal constituent or the sentence initially), which we return to in a later chapter.

Let us now turn to some optional constituents of the NP. The footnote on page 69 observed that the constituent *in the bathroom* could be understood as an adverb of place, which we have discussed, or as a constituent of the NP. If we understand it as an NP constituent, the analysis is that of Figure 25.

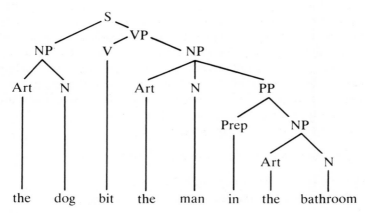

*Figure 25*

Under this analysis we consider the constituent *the man in the bathroom* to be an NP since it has the same distribution as an NP:

**35a** The man in the bathroom was bitten by the dog
**35b** Who did the dog bite? The man in the bathroom

etc. It corresponds to sentences of the form:

**36** The dog bit the man who was in the bathroom

where the constituent *the man who was in the bathroom* is also an NP. We defer consideration of such NPs, involving what are traditionally called 'relative clauses', to pages 137–44.

We can account for the structure of NPs like *the man in the bathroom* by proposing the constituent structure rules:

**37a** NP → Art + N (+PP)
**37b** PP → Prep + NP

Note that in **37a** PP is an optional constituent. We can, in the terms of our previous discussion, refer to it as modifying the constituents Art + N, and we see that the scope of the modification is defined by the rule. Such PPs are 'NP modifiers'. Just as adverb modifiers could be 'separated out' into a separate sentence, so too NP modifiers can be related to structures that have a relation to separate sentences – in this case the relative clause.

In using the rules **37a**, **37b** to derive a sentence, we need to 'cycle' through them: we apply **37a** to introduce a PP constituent, and then, having used rule **37b** to expand the PP, return to rule **37a** to expand the NP introduced by **37b**. This second application of **37a** may produce another PP, which in turn can produce another **NP**, etc. This property of 'cycling' through rules over and over again is called recursion (it is discussed in more detail on pages 134ff.). Recursive rules are necessary for structures like that in Figure 26.

Now consider the NPs in sentences like:

**38** The foolish boy stood on the burning deck

which we can analyse as in Figure 27.

Adjectives can be introduced into NPs by a rule like:

**39** NP → Art (+Adj) + N

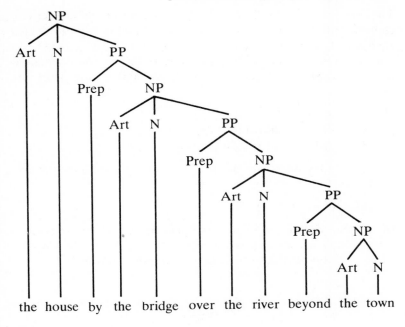

*Figure 26*

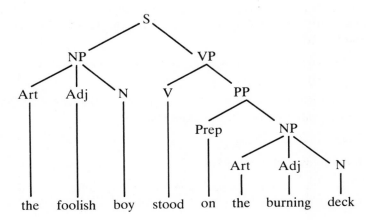

*Figure 27*

The rule correctly indicates the optional nature of adjectives, captures the fact that adjectives 'modify' nouns (reflected in a traditional characterization as 'modifying adjectives') and shows that the scope of the modification is the NP. But as it stands it does not allow us to account for NPs containing more than one adjective:

**40a**   A big red car
**40b**   A large old comfortable settee
**40c**   A large red ripe juicy plum

and so on. We therefore modify the rule by introducing a new notation:

**41**   NP → Art (+Adj)* + N

where the symbol * after a constituent means we can choose as many of this constituent as we wish – one in **38**, two in **40a**, and so on. The rule will lead to structures like that in Figure 28.

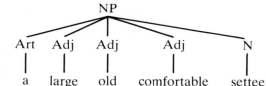

*Figure 28*

The implication of such structures is that all the adjectives modify the noun equally, and we see that an NP like **40b** can be paraphrased by

**42**   A settee which is large and [which is] old and [which is] comfortable

This rule is satisfactory for many similar adjective constructions, but obviously not for all. For example,

**43**   A dark red car

can hardly be paraphrased as

**44**   *A car which is dark and [which is] red (*compare* **42**)

but rather by

**45**   A car which is dark red

Similarly

**46** A red sports car

can be paraphrased by neither of

**47a** *A car which is red and [which is] sports (*compare* **42**)
**47b** *A car which is sports red (*compare* **46**)

In **43** *dark* modifies *red*, and *dark red* as a whole modifies *car*; in **46** *sports* modifies *car*, and *red* modifies *sports car*. This suggests the analyses in Figures 29 and 30 for **43** and **46** respectively.

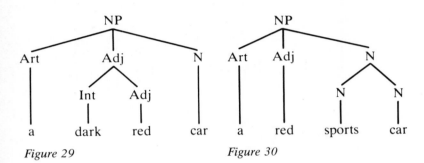

*Figure 29*            *Figure 30*

In Figure 29 *dark* has been categorized as an intensifier (Int). This class includes other items like *light, bright, brilliant, deep, very*, and so on, all of which may modify colour adjectives. In Figure 29 we have categorized *sports* as a noun, and the string *sports car* also as a noun. We do this because *sports* used as a separate item is a noun (*What sports do you play?*, *The sports have been rained off*, etc.) and because *sports car* is a 'compound noun' like *detective story, water mill, billiard ball*, etc., all of which typically have separate dictionary entries. (We discuss compound nouns further on pages 226–7.)

To accommodate structures like those in Figures 29 and 30 we need rules like:

**48a** NP → Art (+ Adj)* + N
**48b** (OP) Adj → Int + Adj
**48c** (OP) N  → N + N

Another notational convention is introduced: the symbol (OP) before a rule indicates that it is optional. In Figure 29 we use the rule **48b**, but not **48c**; in Figure 30 we use **48c** but not **48b**.

Rules like these generate large numbers of NPs, and go some way towards capturing the necessary relationships, of optionality, of modification and of the scope of modification, that we would want our grammar to account for. Without much ingenuity the reader will be able to think of other patterns of modification within NPs that are not shown by the rules, and he is invited to try and write rules to accommodate them.

Let us now summarize the rules of grammar we have so far considered: they are set out in Figure 31:

$$S \rightarrow NP + VP(+Adv_{manner})(+Adv_{place})(+Adv_{time})$$

$$VP \rightarrow V + \left( \left\{ \begin{array}{c} Pred \\ (NP) \end{array} \left( \left\{ \begin{array}{c} PP \\ NP \end{array} \right\} \right) \right\} \right)$$

$$Pred \rightarrow \left\{ \begin{array}{c} Adj \\ NP \end{array} \right\}$$

$$Adv_{manner} \rightarrow \left\{ \begin{array}{c} Manner\ adverb \\ PP \end{array} \right\}$$

$$Adv_{place} \rightarrow \left\{ \begin{array}{c} Place\ adverb \\ PP \end{array} \right\}$$

$$Adv_{time} \rightarrow \left\{ \begin{array}{c} Time\ adverb \\ PP \end{array} \right\}$$

$$PP \rightarrow Prep + NP$$

$$NP \rightarrow Art(+Adj)^* + N(+PP)$$

$$(OP)Adj \rightarrow Int + Adj$$

*Figure 31*  $(OP)N \rightarrow N + N$

We conclude the chapter with a brief discussion of syntactic ambiguity, since this matter has arisen several times in our discussion, and seems a natural consequence of the organizational principles of language. We have already noted that a sentence like:

**49**  The dog bit the man in the bathroom

is ambiguous as between two interpretations (Figures 32 and 33):

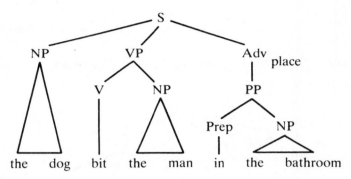

*Figure 32*

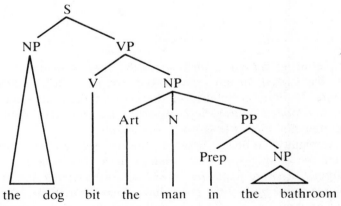

*Figure 33*

(Internal constituent structure is omitted where irrelevant to the argument.) Ambiguities of this sort may be called ambiguities of bracketing, since the ambiguity rests on whether *in the bathroom* is a constituent of NP (Figure 33) or is an adverb of place (Figure 32). Another type of ambiguity involves ambiguities arising from a particular item belonging to more than one form class, often called ambiguities of labelling: an example is shown in Figures 34 and 35.

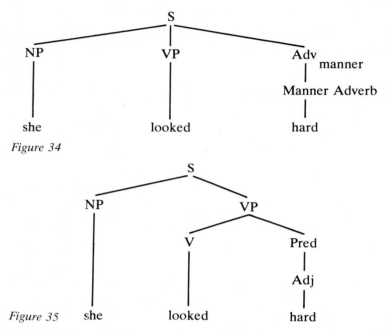

Figure 34

Figure 35

In Figure 34, *hard* is a member of the class of manner adverbs (cf. *she looked intently, she looked carefully*, etc.) whereas in Figure 35, it is a member of the class of predicate adjectives (cf. *she looked pretty, she looked careful*, etc.). The dual class membership of *hard* leads to the ambiguity.

Ambiguity has always exerted a special fascination: it can vary from the simple sort that children at a certain age revel in (*Wanted: a grand piano by an old lady with carved legs*) to the complex ambiguity that poets have found particularly fruitful. The grammarian's interest in ambiguity lies in the descriptive challenge it offers: if one particular string has two clear and distinct meanings, the grammar should ascribe to it two different analyses, compatible with its two meanings. The grammar we have been dealing with is capable of doing this. This is not to claim that our grammar can deal with all kinds of ambiguity – it can only cope with those that arise from labelling or bracketing or both. Ambiguities such as those in:

**50** The shooting of the hunters was disgraceful
I find it hard to sympathize with revolting students
Call me a taxi. OK, you're a taxi

fall outside our present scope. We shall try to deal with such ambiguities by machinery introduced in later chapters.

**Technical terms**

adverb (of place, time, manner)
ambiguity (of labelling and
  of bracketing)
basic sentence
cycle
modifier

non-nuclear constituent
nuclear constituent
obligatory constituent
optional constituent
recursion
scope

**Exercises**

*1  Ambiguity*

The ambiguity in the phrase *young men and women* can be shown by bracketing: *young (men and women)* – they are all young – as against *(young men) and women* – only the men are young. The difference can also be shown in tree diagrams:

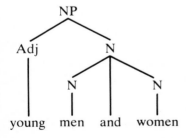 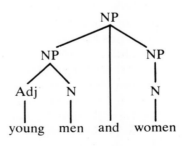

The following sentences are all ambiguous in one way or another: show their ambiguity by drawing appropriate tree diagrams.

1 My brother teaches history in a school for young boys and girls of wealthy parents
2 The bride and groom left early last night
3 He greeted the girl with a smile
4 We would like to attract more intelligent students
5 I bought an old French dictionary
6 They decided on the boat

Can you think of paraphrases that resolve the ambiguities one way or the other? How commonly do you think that strings like those illustrated are in fact ambiguous in the everyday use of language?

## 2 Optional and obligatory constituents

The text suggests that obligatory constituents are always nuclear, but that nuclear constituents are not always obligatory. It is further suggested that nuclear constituents are important for the strict subcategorization of verbs. In the sentences below the relevant constituents have been separated by strokes. Which of them would you consider to be obligatory and which non-obligatory, and which nuclear and which non-nuclear? You should give reasons to support your decisions: these may be based on the unacceptability of some sentence if a constituent is omitted, considerations that arise from strict subcategorization, considerations relating to possible transformations of the sentences in question and so on.

1 I/agree/with John
2 I/went/to the cinema/with John/yesterday
3 The fifteenth Music Festival/will be held/in the Assembly Rooms/in May 1979
4 John/went/to Bristol/in 1972
5 Harriet/always/plays/with a rubber duck/in the bath
6 Mary/will write/a letter/to mother/for you
7 Harriet/is/in the bath
8 They/elected/Charlie/president
9 We/sent/a parcel/to Mary/for Christmas
10 We/pierced/the membrane/with a needle
11 They/thought/Charlie/foolish

# 7 Selection restrictions

In our normal use of language we do not expect all linguistic forms freely to co-occur with all other linguistic forms. For example, intransitive verbs do not co-occur with a following NP; transitive verbs must co-occur with a following NP. The specification of such co-occurrence restrictions we have called 'strict subcategorization' and have proposed that this information should be included in the lexicon (pages 55–6). We have also seen that items can be characterized as Nouns, Verbs, Articles and so on, and have seen that this characterization too can be used to restrict co-occurrence. Articles co-occur with Nouns within the NP (*the man*, etc.), but not with Verbs (*\*the frightens*). We have proposed that this information should be included in the lexicon by marking individual items as N, V, Art and so on. We have called these descriptions 'inherent subcategorization' (pages 55–7).

This chapter examines another type of co-occurence restriction, 'selection restrictions', and considers whether these too should be included in our description. The notion of selection can be illustrated in the following:

1a The man admired the picture
1b *The picture admired the man
2a The picture frightened the man
2b *The man frightened the picture

Typically ADMIRE requires an animate subject expression, but will tolerate any object expression: in notional terms only animates can 'admire' things, but they can admire other animates, inanimates, abstract objects, and so on. This accounts for the acceptability of **1a**, and the oddness of **1b**. Conversely, FRIGHTEN takes any subject expression, but must have an animate object expression: in notional terms, one cannot 'frighten' things! We say that ADMIRE 'selects' an animate subject expression, and that FRIGHTEN 'selects' an animate object expression. Statements such as these are statements of selection restrictions.

Such statements rely on an intuition of what is the 'normal' or 'literal' use of language, and they beg an important question: are sentences like:

**3**   Sincerity admires the young poet

'unacceptable', since ADMIRE here has an abstract subject expression? Or are such sentences quite acceptable, but involve a 'figurative' or 'metaphorical' use of language? We exclude the possibility that *Sincerity* is a girl's name (in which case the sentence is perfectly well formed in terms of the selection restriction stated above, and is non-figurative). We might find such a sentence in some allegorical tale: in this case we would speak of 'personification'. Traditional grammars of Indo-European and other languages sometimes recognize this problem by giving a passing mention to various kinds of figurative language. In doing so they usually assume that the reader knows the difference between the literal and figurative use of language and makes allowances accordingly: implying that we can distinguish 'normal' states of affairs and a literal use of language from 'abnormal' states of affairs and figurative language. It is not at all clear just how this might be done, nor even, if it can be done, whether it is to be considered a specifically linguistic ability (like knowing that in English adjectives precede the noun they modify) or whether it rests on our knowledge of the world, or the way in which we choose to conceptualize the world. A thorough account of such matters is beyond our scope: the essential thing for the reader is to recognize that deep questions lie behind any attempt to include any information about selection restrictions in a grammar.

How might we take some account of such information in the grammar? Suppose we can somehow identify a 'literal' use of language and that we will restrict our description to this sort of language. In the case of FRIGHTEN and ADMIRE the necessary information is that the subject of ADMIRE and the object of FRIGHTEN should be animate. We can capture this generalization by subcategorizing nouns into classes of 'animate' and 'inanimate' nouns. We express this in terms of 'features' attached to the nouns. Thus MAN (and other similar nouns like

BOY, GIRL, CAT, DOG, etc.) has the feature [+animate] and
PICTURE (and other nouns like TABLE, CHAIR,
TYPEWRITER, etc.) has the feature [−animate]. We can now
use this categorization to specify a selection restriction for
FRIGHTEN and ADMIRE in much the same way as we
specified their strict subcategorization. ADMIRE can be inserted
into a structure of the form:

**4** $_{NP}(N[+animate])\_ NP$

We call such a structure a 'selection frame', and take it to mean
that ADMIRE requires an animate subject expression, but can
have any object expression. **4**, as stated, is obviously schematic
since it takes no account of other constituents that may be
relevant, such as other constituents of the subject NP, but it will
serve our purposes. Similarly a selection frame for FRIGHTEN
is:

**5** $NP \_ _{NP}(N[+animate])$

We add this specification to other specifications in the lexicon.
The lexical entries for ADMIRE and FRIGHTEN are now:

**6** ADMIRE   $V; \_ NP; _{NP}(N[+animate])\_NP$

FRIGHTEN   $V; \_ NP; NP - _{NP}(N[+animate])$

We have met the first two types of categorization: V indicates
that the items are verbs and __ NP indicates that they are
transitive verbs. The third specification is the selection
restriction. Whereas strict subcategorization only includes other
constituents from the VP, selection restrictions must also
include information about the subject, and indeed may have to
include still other constituents of the sentence as a whole not
relevant to strict subcategorization. Specifying verbs as in **6**
means we must also specify nouns with their appropriate
features. So our lexicon will include entries for nouns like:

**7** MAN      N; [+animate]
PICTURE   N; [−animate].

The specifications in **6** and **7** can now be used to account for the
acceptability of **1a** and **2a** and the unacceptability of **1b** and **2b**.
We will see exactly how this might be done in due course.

Before we do so, let us consider some other noun features that will be useful for a specification of selection restrictions. We will examine the features [±human], [±male], [±concrete], [±count] and [±common].

[±human] distinguishes between 'human' and 'non-human' animates. PRAY and MARRY, for example, co-occur with human nouns, since animals do not 'pray' or 'marry' (in a literal use of language). [±male] distinguishes between 'male' and 'female' animates: PREGNANT, for example, co-occurs with female animates and not with males. [±concrete] distinguishes between 'concrete' and 'abstract' nouns: FALL, for example, requires a concrete subject noun, since abstracts cannot 'fall'. [±count] distinguishes between 'count' and 'mass' nouns: count nouns are typically those nouns that are used to refer to discrete objects that can, in a literal sense, be counted (*one chair*, *two chairs*, etc.); mass nouns are typically those nouns that are used to refer to non-discrete objects, like OIL, BUTTER, CHEESE, that cannot be counted (*\*one butter*, *\*two butters*, etc.).[1] A verb like FLOW typically co-occurs with a mass rather than a count subject noun: we find *The oil flowed over the floor* but not *\*The chair flowed over the floor*. [±common] distinguishes between 'proper' nouns, like JOHN, FIDO and 'common' nouns like MAN, DOG.

Some of these features 'cross classify'. Thus, JOHN and FIDO are both [−common], and MAN and DOG are both [+common]; JOHN and MAN are both [+human] and FIDO and DOG are both [−human]. Similarly BEAUTY is [−concrete],[−count], TRUTH is [−concrete],[+count], CROWD is [+concrete],[−count] and MAN is [+concrete],[+count]. Others of them are 'hierarchical' – the distinction [±male] is contingent on the prior choice of [+animate], since sex is only distinguished in animates.

We can use the features to specify various nouns:[2]

---

1  BUTTER, and other mass nouns, can sometimes occur in sentences like *Our grocer stocks two butters, French and Danish*. But note that in such sentences *butters* has the sense 'kind(s) of butter'. We discuss cases like this in more detail on pages 242–4. For the present we assume that BUTTER is a mass noun.

2  For any lexeme we have given only one specification. In some cases the items in question have more than one possible use. Thus MAN in the sense specified indicates 'individual human male'; there is another sense of MAN as 'mankind': this use is [−count] and is not accounted for here. In the entry for

**8** MAN N; [+concrete],[+count],[+animate],
     [+human],[+male],[+common]

 WOMAN N; [+concrete],[+count],[+animate],
     [+human],[−male],[+common]

 JOHN N; [+concrete],[+count],[+animate],
     [+human],[+male],[−common]

 BEAUTY N; [−concrete],[−count],[+common],
     [−animate]

 OIL N; [+concrete],[−count],[+common],
     [−animate]

 DOG N; [+concrete],[+count],[+animate],
     [−human],[±male]

We can now use these features to specify selection restrictions for some of the verbs etc. discussed in the text:[3]

**9** FLOW $V; \_\_ PP; {}_{NP}(N[-count])\_\_$
     $_{PP}(Prep{}_{NP}(N[+concrete]))$

 PREGNANT $Adj; Cop \_\_ ; {}_{NP}(N[+female]) \_\_$

 FALL $V; \_\_ \#; {}_{NP}(N[+concrete]) \_\_$

 PRAY $V; \_\_ \#; {}_{NP}(N[+human]) \_\_$

 MARRY $V; \_\_ NP; {}_{NP}(N[+human]) \_\_$
     $_{NP}(N[+human])$

DOG we have specified [±male] to indicate the sense where DOG is used to refer to a canine irrespective of sex. Another sense of DOG would need to be specified as [+male] in contrast to BITCH [−male].

3 As with the nouns, the specifications are illustrative rather than exhaustive. A full specification of the entries would require to account for all possible uses. Even the examples as they stand need modification in some cases. For example the entry for MARRY should indicate that if the subject N is [+male] the object noun should be [−male] and vice versa. We could use the specification [α feature], meaning 'either + or −' and the specification [−α feature] to indicate the opposite polarity. So if [α male] has the value [+male], then [−α male] has the value [−male].

Together these descriptions account for the acceptability or otherwise of the following:

**10a**   The man/oil/dog fell
**10b**   *Beauty fell (*non-concrete subject*)
**10c**   The woman/dog is pregnant
**10d**   *The man/John is pregnant (*non-female subject*)
**10e**   *The dog prayed (*non-human subject*)
**10f**   *The woman flowed over the beauty (*count subject, non-concrete N in PP*)

The examples show the sort of judgements that formally stated selection restrictions force on us, and bring us back to a question mentioned at the beginning of the chapter – is 'figurative language' to be considered in some way 'deviant'? Perhaps what we recognize as 'metaphorical language' is language that 'breaks' a selection restriction. But since so much of our 'ordinary' use of language is 'metaphorical' we might question the validity of such an account – it is far from clear where, or how, to draw the boundary.

The discussion so far has assigned features to nouns on a semantic basis, in terms of some characteristic of the object, etc. that the noun in question is typically used to refer to. So, for example, we have assigned to WOMAN the features [+animate],[+human],[−male], etc. since this lexeme is indeed used to refer to 'animate human females'. We may now observe that all the features we have discussed have relevance for grammatical processes of one sort or another. For example, the pronoun typically used for [−human] nouns is *it*; the pronoun for [+human] nouns is *he* or *she* depending on whether the noun in question is [+male] or [−male]. Similarly we note that [−common] nouns do not usually co-occur with an article: *Fido* but not *the Fido*, *a Fido*, etc. There is a complex web of co-occurrence restrictions between articles, and nouns characterized as [±count]. Some of these are illustrated in **11** for NPs with no article, and with the articles *a*, *the* and *some*, when pronounced /sm/.

| **11** | | [+count] | [−count] |
|---|---|---|---|
| | singular | the chair | the butter |
| | | a chair | *a butter |
| | | *sm chair | sm butter |
| | | *chair | butter |

|        | [+count]   | [–count]    |
|--------|------------|-------------|
| plural | the chairs | *the butters |
|        | *a chairs  | *a butters  |
|        | sm chairs  | *sm butters |
|        | chairs     | *butters    |

The reader is invited to insert the NPs into a sentence frame like:

**12**   I am going out to buy __

Grammatical sentences are only possible with the unstarred forms: the starred forms produce ungrammatical sentences, as *I am going out to buy butter* but not *\*I am going out to buy chair*, etc. (we agreed, note 1, page 88, to disregard the reading 'kind of butter' 'packets of butter' for the examples involving *butter*). The other features can be shown to control similar grammatical restrictions. For these reasons, features like those we have discussed are known as 'syntactic features'.

We can use syntactic features for two rather different purposes: to specify certain grammatical restrictions (like those illustrated in **11**) and to control selection (as in **8**). We defer for the moment the question of whether it is sensible to use the same set of features for two rather different purposes (which may on occasion conflict).

Having demonstrated the relevance of syntactic features to what seem to be grammatical operations, we might account for them in the grammar itself rather than, as we have supposed hitherto, in the lexicon. We now consider the consequences of trying to incorporate subclassification into the grammar. At first glance this seems quite straightforward. We could use rules like:

**13**

$$ N \; \rightarrow \; \begin{Bmatrix} N_{animate} \\ N_{inanimate} \\ N_{human} \\ N_{non\text{-}human} \end{Bmatrix} $$

etc.; but this will not do since nouns are typically not just animate or human, but both animate and human etc. Perhaps rules like **14** might be appropriate:

**14**

$$N \rightarrow \begin{Bmatrix} N_{anim} \\ N_{inan} \end{Bmatrix}$$

$$N_{anim} \rightarrow \begin{Bmatrix} N_{anim,hum} \\ N_{anim,non\text{-}hum} \end{Bmatrix}$$

$$N_{anim,hum} \rightarrow \begin{Bmatrix} N_{anim,hum,common} \\ N_{anim,hum,non\text{-}common} \end{Bmatrix}$$

etc. Or perhaps rules like:

**15**

$$N \rightarrow \begin{Bmatrix} N_{hum} \\ N_{non\text{-}hum} \end{Bmatrix}$$

$$N_{hum} \rightarrow \begin{Bmatrix} N_{hum,anim} \\ N_{hum,non\text{-}anim} \end{Bmatrix}$$

$$N_{hum,anim} \rightarrow \begin{Bmatrix} N_{hum,anim,common} \\ N_{hum,anim,non\text{-}common} \end{Bmatrix}$$

etc. Or indeed any other ordering of these categories. **14** and **15** are clearly absurd: there is no obvious reason to prefer one type of subcategorization to another, and the number of rules must be immense to accommodate all possible combinations. The difficulty is that characterizations like animate : non-animate; common : non-common cross-classify (as we have seen). Rewrite rules cannot handle cross-classification in any satisfactory way. Furthermore rules like these lead to trees like that shown in Figure 36, which is ridiculous. From a syntactic point of view an NP contains only one N, not a series of constituents $N$, $N_{anim}$, $N_{anim,hum}$ etc.

A further problem arises if we use rules like this for purposes of selection as well: the 'direction' in which such restrictions apply. For example, in discussing FRIGHTEN and ADMIRE we said (page 85) that ADMIRE selects an animate subject, and FRIGHTEN selects an animate object. The direction of the selection is from verb to noun. This seems more natural than

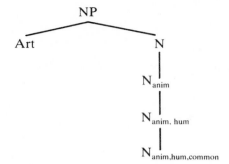

*Figure 36*

to say that an animate object selects FRIGHTEN as its verb. Unfortunately, if the subcategorization of nouns is to be handled in the grammar, then selection is most easily handled in terms of nouns selecting Verbs – the direction we would rather avoid. To see that this is so consider the grammar and lexicon in **16**:

**16**
$$S \rightarrow NP + VP$$
$$VP \rightarrow V + NP$$
$$NP \rightarrow Art + N$$
$$N \rightarrow \left\{ \begin{matrix} N_{anim} \\ N_{inan} \end{matrix} \right\}$$

MAN       $N_{anim}$

PICTURE   $N_{inan}$

FRIGHTEN   V; __ NP; N __ $N_{anim}$

ADMIRE     V; __ NP; $N_{anim}$ __ N

This grammar produces trees like that shown in Figure 37. The subject noun is categorized as $N_{inan}$. We cannot therefore lexicalize this tree with ADMIRE, since ADMIRE requires an animate subject. In other words, if the subcategorization of nouns is handled in the grammar, the direction of selection is from noun to verb; this seems inappropriate.

For reasons such as these it seems wrong to handle subcategorization in the grammar. We therefore return to our

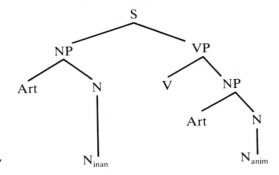

*Figure 37*

original proposal: the subcategorization of nouns should be a
matter for lexical specification. Given this decision, let us see
how lexical insertion is to be handled. We suppose that our
grammar has rules like:

17      S → NP + VP
        VP → V(+NP)
        NP → (Art+)N

and our lexicon has entries like those illustrated in **8** and **9**. We
need a lexical insertion rule along the following lines:

**18**   *Lexical insertion rule:*

        For any terminal symbol of the constituent
        structure rules:
        (i)     Select from the lexicon an item
                characterized as a member of the class
                named by the terminal symbol in
                question.
        (ii)    Attach this item as a daughter of the
                relevant symbol.
        (iii)   The subcategorization frame for the
                relevant item must not conflict with
                the environment in which the item is
                to be inserted.
        (iv)    The selection frame for the relevant
                item must not conflict with the
                environment in which the item is to be
                inserted.
        (v)     The V node is to be lexicalized first.

Let us see how the rules will work. The constituent structure rules of **17** can generate the tree of Figure 38:

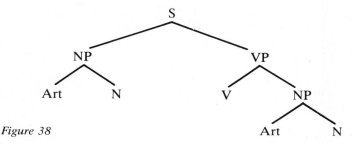

*Figure 38*

Lexical insertion must now take place. By condition (v) the V node is to be lexicalized first. Suppose we chose FRIGHTEN. It is a V, thus satisfying condition (i). Its strict subcategorization frame is __NP, which does not conflict with the environment into which we wish to insert it, thus satisfying condition (iii). Condition (iv) cannot apply since no selection environment is yet available. We may therefore attach this item to the relevant node, yielding Figure 39:

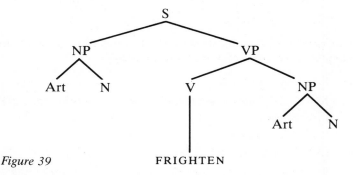

*Figure 39*          FRIGHTEN

We now come to the lexicalization of the N nodes. Condition (v) is satisfied – all the V nodes are lexicalized. Condition (iii) is vacuous since we have not specified subcategorization frames for the nouns in our lexicon. Condition (iv) must be satisfied since FRIGHTEN carries a selection frame. In terms of the frame we must select an animate object noun, but can select any subject noun. Thus we might lexicalize to produce Figure 40:

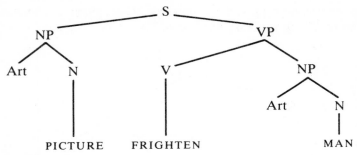

*Figure 40*

which will yield a sentence like:

**19**   The picture frightened the man

given the appropriate choice of articles, tense, etc.

We can extend the principle illustrated above to account for the co-occurrence restrictions we noted in **9–11** that exist between articles and mass nouns. Suppose we amplify the rules for the NP as follows:[4]

**20**   NP → (Art) N + Num          (Num = Number)
Num → $\begin{Bmatrix} \text{sing} \\ \text{pl} \end{Bmatrix}$          (sing = singular)
         (pl = plural)
Art → {*a, the, sm*}

Suppose also that the following general convention attaches to the lexicalization of the N node within an NP:

**21**   *Lexicalization of NP*

N[−count] may be inserted to N within the NP providing

(i)    Art is not *a*
(ii)   Num is not pl

N[+count] may be inserted to N within NP providing

(i)    If Num is sing; Art is present, but not *sm*
(ii)   If Num is pl; Art is not *a*

---

4 The first rule in **20** introduces a feature that we discuss in more detail on pages 187ff. We suppose that a plural NP like *the boys* is derived from a string Det + N + pl (*the + boy + −s*). Analogously, a singular NP like *the boy* derives from a string Det + N + sing (*the + boy*): in this case the item *sing* has no overt realization.

The rules of **20** generate trees like those of Figures 41(*a*) and 41(*b*):

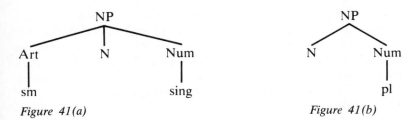

*Figure 41(a)*                                    *Figure 41(b)*

In terms of our rules for the lexicalization of NP, a [+count] noun, like BOY, can be inserted into the tree in Figure 41(*b*), since it does not offend the restrictions for [+count] nouns (yielding *boys*. (A [−count] noun could not be inserted into this tree since it offends rule (ii) for [−count] nouns.) By contrast, a [−count] noun can be inserted into Figure 41(*a*), since it does not offend the relevant rules; a [+count] noun could not. The lexicalization rules will allow for all of the possible NPs shown in **11**, and none of the impossible ones.

An approach of the sort illustrated blurs the boundary between what we might call 'grammatical' categorization, and what we think of as 'lexical' categorization. This is clearly true. However, the decision as to what is counted as 'lexical' and what 'grammatical' is not in any sense 'given': it is something the analyst needs to work out for the particular language that he is describing. We have in any case already seen advantages in treating such notions as 'transitive' and 'intransitive' for verbs as matters of strict subcategorization in the lexicon − in principle the case illustrated above is no different. There are other reasons why this approach is preferred. One is the sheer complication of writing constituent structure rules to account for the sort of distribution noted in **11**; this illustrates only a part of the whole complex web of co-occurrence restrictions between articles and nouns. A second reason has to do with the relation between categories like [±count] and various types of semantic characterization − a subject we will explore (pages 242–4).

We now return to the question raised on page 91: is it appropriate to use syntactic features both to control grammatical occurrence, illustrated in **11**, and selectional co-occurrence, illustrated in **10**? It does not seem appropriate for two main reasons, both to do with the fact that selection restrictions appear more a matter of semantic compatibility between lexical items than of the grammaticality of sentences as such.

A semantic and a syntactic characterization of some item need not be congruent. In setting up a set of syntactic features, we would be wisest to pay attention to syntactic facts. This can be illustrated with the category [±count] in English. Our initial characterization of the distinction was semantic – as between 'discrete' and 'non-discrete' objects. This characterization holds rather generally but not universally. Some nouns, like GRAPE, PLUM, PEAR are normally [+count]; others, like GRAPEFRUIT, APPLE, may be either [+count] or [−count], as can be verified by checking the nouns in NPs on the lines of **11**. I could enquire of a guest

**22**   Would you like some (sm) grapefruit?

but hardly

**23**   *Would you like some (sm) plum?

even though what was being offered was similar – in the one case a plate of segmented grapefruit and in the other a plate of stewed plums. The categorization of nouns as [±count] is not only to some degree idiosyncratic within a language; it is also idiosyncratic between languages.

This point, the mismatch between a syntactic and a semantic characterization, can be made even more clearly by reference to a language that has a grammatical category of 'gender'. In French, for example, all nouns are categorized as being in one of two classes (with a few exceptions which may be in both classes) which are usually given the names 'masculine' and 'feminine'. The grammar needs to know the gender of a noun in order that appropriate grammatical rules can be applied: for example the rules of 'concord' that ensure that a masculine noun co-occurs with the masculine form of the article, *le*, *un*, etc., and a feminine noun co-occurs with a feminine form of the article, *la*, *une*, etc. Gender distinctions in French are not typically a semantic matter, since all nouns are assigned to one gender class or the other (c.f. *le stylo* 'the pen', but *la table* 'the table') even when the notion of sex is irrelevant. We could handle this by a syntactic feature [±masculine], but that feature would hardly be appropriate for stating selection restrictions. For the correct selection restriction of an adjective like ENCEINTE 'pregnant', for example, we need to know the sex of the referent, not the grammatical gender of the noun. This is particularly clear in the case of those nouns that are masculine in gender but may be used to refer to individuals of either sex, like *le docteur* 'doctor'. This question also has marginal relevance in English: some kinds of object, like a 'ship' and a 'car', are often pronominalized with *she*, rather than *it* (one may perhaps speculate that this is because they are used to refer to objects men find attractive!), and conversely a 'baby' is often referred to as *it*.

The second reason is that a complete specification of the selection restrictions of some item clearly cannot be handled by syntactic features alone. Consider the verb EAT. In its literal sense this means 'consume as food'. The object NP might be specified as [+concrete] since we normally eat 'things'. But clearly not all 'things' are 'edible'. We might then suppose that we should add a feature [+edible]. If we do, this is clearly not a syntactic feature in the sense discussed, since it has no relevance at all for any grammatical process, syntactic co-occurrence restriction, etc. And even a feature like [+edible] does not solve all our semantic problems: what is to be classed as [+edible] depends on what is 'doing the eating'. Humans do not normally eat wood, coal, carrion or clothes – but termites, fires, crows and clothes-moth caterpillars do! Even a man might on occasion be said to *eat his hat* – though this might be considered 'figurative' language.

Our conclusion then is this: nouns are marked in the lexicon with a set of syntactic features (inherent subcategorization) which may be used to account for various grammatical features (like co-occurrence with articles). In a similar way verbs are marked with a strict subcategorization frame.[5] While it is possible to include a specification for selection restrictions using the syntactic features which characterize nouns, it is not desirable to do so: selection restrictions are primarily a matter

---

5 We have not considered any cases of nouns with strict subcategorization frames, but this is appropriate in some cases (see page 136). Similarly we have not considered inherent subcategorization for verbs, other than the marking V, though this too will be appropriate in some cases (see discussion on page 238).

for a semantic description. This suggests that we should not include within the grammar or the lexicon (insofar as it impinges on the grammar) the selection frames so laboriously established at the beginning of this chapter. This is exactly what we propose to do, but not because questions of selection are unimportant, or not a matter of interest for the linguist. They clearly are of considerable interest. Our proposal simply implies that we should not consider the specification of selection restrictions as a part of the grammatical description of a language. So the sentences marked in **10** as deviant are considered only as semantically and not as grammatically deviant. This seems a more suitable conclusion: so, for instance, with respect to **10b**, while the sentence might well be considered as 'unusual', it is not uninterpretable – but the onus of interpretation falls on the semantic component of a complete description, not on the grammatical component. This frees a semantic description of such matters from an unnecessarily intimate link with a particular grammatical description, which may in some cases unduly restrict its freedom. It also frees the grammatical description from a semantic description where the two are not congruent. Both consequences seem desirable.

The decision does not however mean that we wish to discard the lexical subcategorization of nouns in terms of syntactic features. We have seen that these can be useful to specify grammatical co-occurrence, etc., and we wish to retain them.

Nor does the decision imply that we wish to sever the bonds between the syntactic and the semantic description of a language. The discussion has made clear that there is some degree of congruence between semantic features, of the sort we might use for selection, and syntactic features, of the sort we might use to control grammatical co-occurrence, etc. This is why we were able to use syntactic features at the beginning of the chapter to make some quite useful remarks about selection. This should not surprise us – language is after all, a means of conveying meanings. The congruence between a semantic and a syntactic characterization should cause no surprise – it would be more surprising if there were a complete mismatch! Syntactic features, however, can only be used to account for the grossest facts about selection, and only insofar as they do not conflict with semantic characterizations. Our conclusion therefore is that selection restrictions are not part of a grammatical description.

**Technical terms**

cross-classification
feature
inherent subcategorization
lexicalization

selection restriction
selection frame
strict subcategorization

syntactic features used for subcategorization of nouns:
[±animate];      [±human];      [±male];      [±concrete]
(concrete : abstract);   [±count]   (count : mass);   [±common]
(common : proper)

**Exercise**

You are probably familiar with playground jingles like:

One fine day in the middle of the night
Two dead men got up to fight,
One blind man to see fair play,
Two dumb men to shout, 'Hurray.'
Back to back they faced each other,
Drew their swords and shot each other.

Would you wish to consider such jingles as 'ungrammatical'? If not, how could you handle a linguistic description of the obviously anomalous nature of such jingles?

# 8   Relations between sentences

Pairs of sentences like:

1   The cat has eaten the mouse
2   The mouse has been eaten by the cat

are related to each other both semantically and syntactically. The semantic relationship lies primarily in the fact that both sentences share the same 'agent' (*the cat*), responsible for the action described by the verb, and the same 'patient' (*the mouse*), affected by the action described by the verb. (Notions like 'agent' and 'patient' are discussed more fully on pages 288ff.) One could say that 1 describes the situation from the cat's point of view, and 2 describes the same situation from the point of view of the mouse (we shall discuss these questions on pages 357ff.); for our present purposes the relevant semantic relationship is that in both sentences the cat is the eater and the mouse is the eaten. This is reflected in the traditional description of sentences like 1 as 'active' (agent subject) and 2 as 'passive' (patient subject).

The structural relationship between these sentences can be diagrammed as in Figure 42.

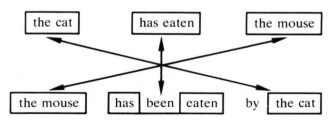

*Figure 42*

There are three syntactic differences between 1 and 2:

i   The NP (*the mouse*) that is the object of the verb in **1** 'becomes' the subject of the verb in **2**.

ii  Correspondingly, the NP (*the cat*) that is the subject in **1** has the preposition *by* adjoined to it to form the Prepositional Phrase (PP) *by the cat*, and this now follows the verb.

iii  In **1** the verbal constituent *has eaten* consists of the auxiliary verb *has* followed by the main verb *eaten*. In the passive sentence the verb constituent is changed by the addition of *been*, a form of the verb BE, which is added immediately after (and as a right sister to) the auxiliary verb. We call this form of the verb BE the 'passive auxiliary'. We discuss auxiliary verbs and the rules for the formation of verb forms later (pages 105ff.).

The active–passive relationship can be generalized to any sentence containing a transitive verb:

**3a**   The dog will bite the cat
**3b**   The cat will be bitten by the dog

**4a**   The man is beating the boy
**4b**   The boy is being beaten by the man

etc. As before, the objects of the **a** sentences 'become' the subjects of the corresponding **b** sentences; the subjects of the **a** sentences 'become' PPs with *by* and follow the verb, and a passive auxiliary, a form of BE, is introduced after the auxiliary (*will* BE *bitten*, *is* BEING *beaten*).

This suggests that we can generalize the syntactic statement of this relationship by abstracting away from particular lexical items in particular sentences, and state the relationship in terms of general syntactic structure, as in Figure 43.

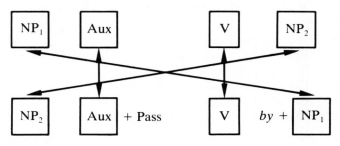

*Figure 43*

We can alternatively state the relationship in formulaic terms as:

$$\textbf{5} \quad NP_1 - Aux - V - NP_2$$
$$\Leftrightarrow NP_2 - Aux + Pass - V - by + NP_1$$

The formula is interpreted as follows. For any sentence that has a constituent structure analysis as shown on the left-hand side of the formula ($NP_1 - Aux - V - NP_2$), there is a corresponding sentence which has the analysis shown on the right-hand side of the formula ($NP_2 - Aux + Pass - V - by + NP_1$). The symbol '$-$' separates those constituents that are of relevance to the statement of the rule: we are not for example concerned with the internal structure of the NPs in question, since this is not relevant to the formulation of the relationship: both of the following are good active–passive pairs of sentences:

**6a**   The little old lady who lives upstairs has fed our cat
**6b**   Our cat has been fed by the little old lady who lives upstairs

**7a**   John painted that remarkable picture hanging on the wall over there
**7b**   That remarkable picture hanging on the wall over there was painted by John

We have used the symbol '$+$' to indicate that some particular pair of constituents form a construction: we want to indicate that the string $by + NP$ in the passive sentence is a constituent. The symbol 'Pass' indicates an appropriate form of the passive auxiliary BE. We have used the symbol '$\Leftrightarrow$' to indicate that the two structures are related.

Before considering the active : passive relationship further, we must turn our attention to auxiliary verbs. Consider the sentences:

**8a**   The dog bit the cat
**8b**   The dog has bitten the cat
**8c**   The dog is biting the cat
**8d**   The dog has been biting the cat
**8e**   The dog will bite the cat
**8f**   The dog may have bitten the cat

All the sentences have the same subject NP (*the dog*) and the same object NP (*the cat*). They differ in the internal structure of what we call the Verb Group. Each Verb Group consists minimally of a form of the verb BITE, which we call the main or lexical verb. It is always the last constituent. The main verb may be preceded by one or more other verbs – in our examples we have forms of the verbs BE, HAVE, WILL and MAY. We call these auxiliary verbs.

We will consider first those sentences like **8b–8f** which contain auxiliaries, and return later to consider sentences like **8a**, which has only a main verb. An appropriate constituent structure analysis for sentences **8b–8f** is, schematically, Figure 44:

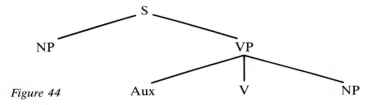

*Figure 44*

The node Aux dominates one or more auxiliary verbs, and V dominates the main verb.

The principle function of the main verb is to introduce the appropriate lexical content – all the sentences have to do with 'biting'. The principal function of the auxiliaries on the other hand is to relate the sentence to 'temporal' and 'aspectual' distinctions:[1]

**9a**  The dog *is* biting the cat (*now*)
**9b**  The dog *was* biting the cat (*yesterday afternoon*)
**9c**  The dog *will* bite the cat (*tomorrow, I expect*)

1 Temporal distinctions are often related to a grammatical category of 'Tense' – temporal distinctions (though not always tense distinctions, see pages 246–8) refer to the location of an event, etc. in time – before, after or concurrent with the moment of utterance.

'Aspectual' distinctions are often related to a grammatical category of 'Aspect'. Aspectual distinctions commonly refer to the distribution of an event over time. The main aspectual distinctions usually identified in English are 'progressive' (indicating that an action is, or was, etc. in progress: *the cat is/was biting the dog*), and 'perfective', indicating that an action has been completed (*the dog has bitten the cat*). Other aspectual distinctions often referred to in English include 'habitual' (*I drive to work*) and 'stative' (*I am clever*). The relationship between distinctions of tense and aspect and particular verb forms is complex and is discussed on pages 247–8.

or to estimations of the probability, likelihood, etc. of the event described in the sentence having taken place, being likely to take place etc.:

**10a**   The dog *may* have bitten the cat (but that's unlikely)
**10b**   The dog *could* have bitten the cat (but I hope it didn't)

One obvious difficulty about the analysis of auxiliary verbs in English is that each auxiliary requires that the verb, auxiliary or main, that immediately follows it, should take a particular form. So, if we have one of the auxiliaries MAY, WILL or CAN the following verb will be in its 'base' form:

**11a**   The dog will *bite* the cat
**11b**   The dog may *be* biting the cat
**11c**   The dog can't *have* bitten the cat

Such auxiliaries, and others like SHALL and MUST, are usually known as 'modal' auxiliaries (because one of their principle semantic functions is to mark the 'modal' distinctions of probability, etc. noted above). They constitute a form class insofar as they are mutually substitutable in a particular verb group, but no verb group can contain more than one of them:

**12a**   The dog may/will/must/could have bitten the cat
**12b**   *The dog may will have bitten the cat

If the auxiliary is a form of HAVE (usually called the 'perfective' auxiliary) then the following verb, main or auxiliary, is in the 'past participle' form. Exactly what shape the past participle takes depends on the particular verb involved, but it is frequently a form which ends in the suffix *-ed* or *-en*:

**13**   The dog *has* frighten*ed* the cat
        The dogs *have* bitt*en* the cat
        The dog *has* be*en* biting the cat

though not always:

**14**   The man has *hit* the dog
        John has *swum* the channel

To remind us of the formation rules for the perfective auxiliary we represent it as HAVE + pp, where HAVE reminds us that the auxiliary involved is a form of HAVE and pp indicates that the following verb is in the past participle form.

If the auxiliary is a form of the non-passive BE (usually called the 'progressive' auxiliary, since one of its main functions is to indicate that the action, etc. described by the verb is in progress) the following verb is in the *-ing* form:

**15**  The dog *is* bit*ing* the cat
The dog may *be* bit*ing* the cat

As before, to remind us of the formation rules for the progressive auxiliary, we describe this as BE + *-ing*: BE indicating a form of the verb BE (which one depends on what other verb this follows) and *-ing* to indicate that the following form is an *-ing* form.

If the auxiliary is the passive BE (which we call the 'passive' auxiliary since it is involved in the formation of passive verb groups), then the following verb once again is in the 'past participle' form:

**16**  The cat has *be*en frighten*ed* by the dog
The cat has *be*en bit*ten* by the dogs
The cat is *be*ing bit*ten* by the dog

We describe this as BE + pp, on the same principles as before. The last of the examples in **16** has both the progressive BE (BE + *ing*: IS *be*ING) and the passive BE (BE + pp: BE*ing* *bitt*EN). Both involve forms of BE, but are distinguished by the form of the following verb.

The above account shows a number of peculiar features about the structure of verb groups in English: in particular, the choice of a particular auxiliary has consequences for the verb that immediately follows it. This fact makes it extremely cumbersome to describe the English verb group using constituent structure rules, so we resort to the more 'abstract' type of representations of the auxiliaries as HAVE + pp, BE + *-ing* and BE + pp, noting that the representations pp and *-ing* relate to what happens to the following item. We can now say that the verb group consists of, minimally, a main verb, and the main verb may, optionally, be preceded by one or more auxiliaries. These must be in the order shown schematically in Figure 45.

In the example sentence the first auxiliary MAY is followed by the base form of the perfective auxiliary HAVE, *have*. This is

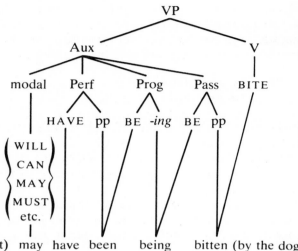

*Figure 45*

followed by the past participle form of BE, *been*. This BE is the progressive BE and is in turn followed by the *-ing* form, *being*. This BE is the passive BE, which is itself followed by the past participle form of the main verb, *bitten*.

In the example sentence in Figure 45 all the auxiliaries have been chosen. Obviously this is not obligatory: any combination of auxiliaries is possible, providing the order shown in Figure 45 is maintained. Note that if verb groups are formed with the auxiliaries in another order they are ungrammatical:

> **17** *Modal   Prog   Perf
> *The dog will be having bitten the cat
>
> **18** *Modal   Pass   Prog
> *The cat will be been biting by the dog
>
> **19** *Prog   Modal
> *The dog is canning bite the cat

We must now look at verb groups with no auxiliary:

> **20a**  The dog bites the cat (every day)
> **20b**  The dog bit the cat (yesterday)

The distinction shown between the forms *bites* and *bit* is generally described as one of 'tense', the form in **20b** being the 'past tense' form, and that in **20a** the 'non-past' form. The typical function of the 'past' form is to refer to events located in 'past' time, i.e. times previous to the moment of utterance of the sentence involved. The other form is usually contrasted as the 'non-past' form, not the 'present' form, since it is not typically used to refer to events taking place at the moment of utterance of the relevant sentence. The form often used in this sense is the present progressive (*the dog is biting the cat (at this moment)*), and this verb group involves the progressive auxiliary. A typical use of the non-past form is to refer to habits (as in **20a**), general truths (*dogs bite cats*), etc. In the orthographic form of the language the past form of verbs is generally formed by the addition of the suffix *-ed* to the stem of the main verb (*kill-ed*; *frighten-ed*; *want-ed*, etc.), but this is not the case for all verbs, as, for example, *bit* in **8a**, rather than *\*bited* (and similarly *run : ran*, *think : thought*, etc.). For now we follow the traditional account and simply refer to all such forms as 'the past form of KILL', 'the past form of BITE', etc. (for a fuller discussion see pages 168–9).

The past : non-past alternation shown in **20a,b** is also characteristic of verb groups that contain auxiliaries:

**21a**   The dog has bitten the cat
**21b**   The dog had bitten the cat

**22a**   The dog is biting the cat
**22b**   The dog was biting the cat

**23a**   The dog can bite the cat
**23b**   The dog could bite the cat

**24a**   The dog bites the cat
**24b**   The cat is bitten by the dog

**25a**   The dog bit the cat
**25b**   The cat was bitten by the dog

In all cases the first verb in the verb group shows the alternation in tense, however many items there are in the group. Only this first position in the verb group is open to this alternation, since the form of verbs other than the first is determined by what precedes them. This is most clearly shown in the last two pairs of examples. In **24a** and **25a** the first verb in the verb group is the main verb itself, and this consequently shows the tense alternation. In the corresponding passive sentences **24b** and **25b** the passive auxiliary is introduced before the main verb: the passive auxiliary is now the first verb in the verb group, and consequently shows the tense alternation: the main verb itself must be in the past participle form, since this form, as we have seen, is the form that follows the passive auxiliary.

How are we to treat these facts? The description we adopt (discussed further on pages 207–10) treats tense as a sort of auxiliary, and, furthermore, as the first auxiliary in the verb group. This entails saying that this tense auxiliary is not realized itself as a discrete item, but that its presence is felt as a marker on the first item to follow it within the verb group. This gives it a status much like *-ing* and pp in our description of the progressive and perfect auxiliaries. It also captures the generalization that tense is shown on the first member of the verb group. We must now modify our schematic constituent structure representation for the verb group from that of Figure 45, to that shown in Figure 46:

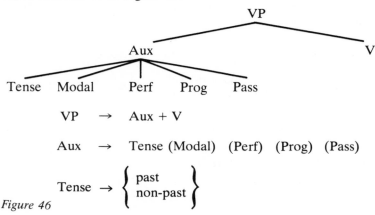

*Figure 46*

The constituent structure rules shown in Figure 46 state in the expansion rule for Aux that only Tense is an obligatory constituent: the other auxiliaries are optional. This explains the generalization that all verb groups are 'tensed', but not all groups contain an auxiliary. We can now show diagrammatically how we can deal with the verb groups in **24** and **25** in Figures 47–50. The reader can himself draw comparable structures for the verb groups in **21–3**.

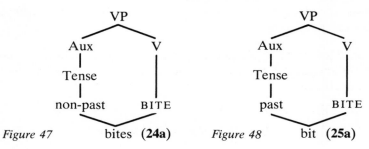

Figure 47      bites **(24a)**     Figure 48     bit **(25a)**

The structures in Figure 47 and Figure 49 are identical except for the introduction of the passive auxiliary – and similarly Figures 48 and 50.

One final remark on this analysis of auxiliaries: it introduces a degree of abstraction into the description absent from the simple constituent structure grammars we have considered hitherto. This abstraction arises because we no longer have a simple one-to-one relationship between the order of words, and parts of words, as they actually occur in sentences, and as we describe them in our grammar. Each of the elements we have labelled *-ing*, pp and Tense is not realized in the actually occurring sentences in the place we have described it in the grammar, but on the following constituent. We will see in chapter 14 how we can relate these abstract descriptions to the actually occurring word forms – at that time we will also consider a few residual features of the analysis of auxiliaries that we have ignored in this account, in particular the question of 'agreement' in 'number'

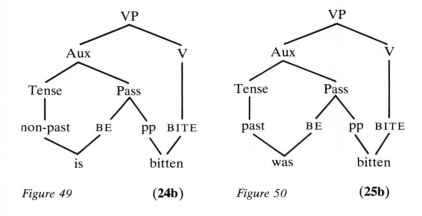

Figure 49       **(24b)**      Figure 50      **(25b)**

between subject expressions and auxiliaries (*The man* IS *going*, *The men* ARE *going*).

After this lengthy digression on auxiliaries, let us return to our description of the passive. We formulated the active : passive relationship as:

**26**  $NP_1 - Aux - V - NP_2$
$$\Leftrightarrow NP_2 - Aux + Pass - V - by + NP$$

This formula gives the correct analysis of passive verb groups. We noted before that the precise internal structure of the NPs is irrelevant (c.f. discussion of **6–7**); we can now observe that the precise internal structure of Aux is also irrelevant. It must consist minimally of Tense, but it does not matter which – if any – of the other auxiliaries are also present. In all cases the Pass auxiliary in the corresponding passive sentence appears as a right sister of the other auxiliaries, immediately preceding the main verb. This is illustrated in Figures 49 and 50, and the reader is invited to experiment with other active : passive pairs.

Let us now turn our attention to pairs of sentences like:

**27**  The cat has eaten the mouse
**28**  Has the cat eaten the mouse?

Once again there is both a syntactic and a semantic relationship. The most usual interpretation works from a semantic difference between **27** and **28**: **27**, the syntactic form called 'declarative', is most usually used to make a statement, whereas **28**, with the syntactic form usually called 'interrogative', is usually used to ask a question. However, the relationship of 'agent' (*the cat*) and 'patient' (*the mouse*) remains constant, as it did in the active : passive sentences discussed earlier: to this extent the pair of sentences has semantic material in common. As before we can diagram the syntactic relationship between the sentences:

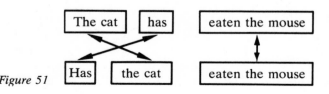

*Figure 51*

Once again we can generalize to other syntactically similar sentences:

**29a** The cat will eat the mouse
**29b** Will the cat eat the mouse?

**30a** The cat has been eating the mouse
**30b** Has the cat been eating the mouse?

**31a** John has left
**31b** Has John left?

**32a** Mary can sleep in the spare bedroom
**32b** Can Mary sleep in the spare bedroom?

**33a** The baby has always been fed at midnight
**33b** Has the baby always been fed at midnight?

In all the interrogative sentences, the **b** sentences, an auxiliary appears before the subject NP (*Will – the cat* ... (**29b**), *Has – the cat* ... (**30b**), etc.); it is always the same as the first auxiliary of the verb group of the corresponding declarative sentence. The rest of the sentence is the same. As a first approach to a formalization of the relationship between these pairs we can diagram them as in Figure 52:

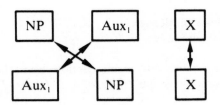

*Figure 52*

(By Aux$_1$ we mean 'the first auxiliary' and by X we mean 'anything that follows the first auxiliary'.) In our examples 'anything' includes the main verb (**29**), another auxiliary (**30**) and an adverb (**33**).

In terms of the description of the verb group given earlier this analysis cannot be quite right: the first auxiliary in our previous analysis was Tense, and clearly in the cases illustrated above one of the auxiliary verbs (WILL, HAVE, CAN) also appears before the subject NP. So let us examine the problem more closely: in Figure 53 each example is followed by an analysis in the terms already established.

In these examples, the tense auxiliary does indeed move round the subject, whether or not the tense auxiliary is itself further developed as past or non-past. The other element that follows Tense to a position before the MV is the item HAVE, BE or a Modal. The pp or -*ing* element is evidently 'left behind', as can be seen by inspection of the examples. These last two observations suggest we cannot simply talk in terms of Tense + Perf or Tense + Prog, etc, as being involved, since only part of Perf or Prog is involved.[2] Finally, observe that only Tense and HAVE or BE or Modal is involved. We can now reformulate Figure 52 as Figure 54. (X still stands for 'anything that follows the items specified in the second box', including the elements pp and -*ing* left behind when HAVE or BE follow Tense to a position in front of $NP_1$.)

There are other kinds of interrogative sentence where there is no overt auxiliary. Thus corresponding to the declarative sentences:

**37a**   John leaves (every morning at six o'clock)
**37b**   John left (yesterday)

there are the interrogative sentences:

**38a**   Does John leave . . . ?
**38b**   Did John leave . . . ?

In English the main verb itself cannot 'hop' the subject NP: there are no sentences like \**Left John?*, \**Leaves John?*

---

2 A minor advantage of formulating the rule as involving BE and HAVE rather than the progressive and perfective auxiliary, is that it will also catch BE and HAVE when they are 'main verbs'. BE as a main verb always forms interrogative sentences in the pattern:

*She is pretty*          *Is she pretty?*
*He is at home*        *Is he at home?*

HAVE is somewhat more problematical; its syntax varies to some degree from speech community to speech community. For some

*She has a car*          *Has she a car?*

are acceptable. Other communities treat HAVE more like a 'main verb', which we discuss next:

*She has a car*          *Does she have a car?*

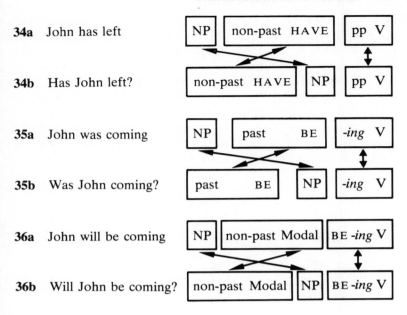

**34a** John has left

**34b** Has John left?

**35a** John was coming

**35b** Was John coming?

**36a** John will be coming

**36b** Will John be coming?

*Figure 53*

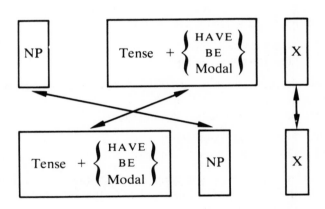

*Figure 54*

The tense distinction shown in **37a** and **37b**, where it is carried by the main verb (*leaves* : *left*), is still maintained in **38a** and **38b**, now carried by forms of the verb DO (*does* : *did*), and the main verb appears in its base form. The verb DO appears in the same structural position in **38** as do the auxiliaries *has*, *was*, etc. in **34–6**. Perhaps what has 'hopped' the subject NP in these cases is simply the tense auxiliary. We can now return to an earlier observation: the tense auxiliary cannot appear as a separate element all by itself; it needs a verb, as it were, to carry it. Since, under the analysis proposed, there is no verb available, DO is introduced as a 'dummy' verb, a 'carrier' of the tense. We can now add a further piece of description to Figure 54: this is shown in Figure 55:

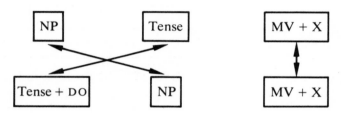

*Figure 55*

This relationship only holds when Tense immediately precedes the main verb (MV), since forms like:

**39**  *John do be leaving
    *Do John be leaving?

are not acceptable in standard English (though they are part of some regional varieties of English).

Let us consider next negative sentences:

**40**  The cat has eaten the mouse
**41**  The cat hasn't eaten the mouse

Once more there is a syntactic and a semantic relationship. Once again the semantic similarity lies in the fact that the agent is the same in both sentences, as is the patient: obviously the sentences differ in that **40** may be used to assert and **41** to deny that the cat ate the mouse. The syntactic relationship lies in the fact that both sentences have the same structure, except that there is a negative marker, *-n't* in the example, affixed to the first auxiliary. This, as the reader can easily check, is regular when there is an actual auxiliary verb present. Once again descriptive problems arise where there is no overt auxiliary:

**42a**   John leaves (every morning at six o'clock)
**42b**   John doesn't leave (every morning at six o'clock)

**43a**   John left (yesterday)
**43b**   John didn't leave (yesterday)

Again the DO verb appears, in this instance seemingly because the negative marker, (-*n't*) cannot be affixed to a main verb: there are no forms *John leaven't*, *John leftn't*, etc. The negative marker can only be affixed to an auxiliary verb; there is no auxiliary verb, so DO is supplied. But Tense is also carried by the DO verb: there are no forms *John doesn't left*, etc., where Tense appears on the main verb and the negative is carried by the DO verb. Both Tense and Negative must be marked on the same verb – as can be seen by considering negative questions:

**44**   Hasn't the cat eaten the mouse?
Won't John come back tonight?

and most strikingly:

**45**   Doesn't John like strawberries?
Didn't Mary come to your party?

We are now able to summarize in tabular form the affirmative : negative relationship:

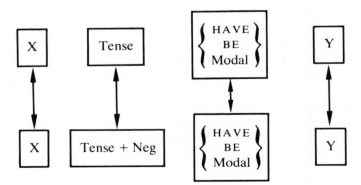

*Figure 56*

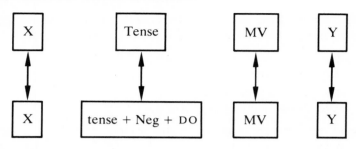

*Figure 57*

These tables again use the symbols X and Y to indicate 'any arbitrary constituents'. It doesn't matter what other constituents an affirmative sentence has: providing it has the constituents specifically named, there is a corresponding negative sentence with the analysis shown. In other words, for every affirmative sentence, there is a corresponding negative sentence.

Let us pause at this point and summarize. We have discussed three types of sentence relatedness illustrated in:

| | | |
|---|---|---|
| **46a** | The dog has bitten the cat | active |
| **46b** | The cat has been bitten by the dog | passive |
| **47a** | The dog has bitten the cat | declarative |
| **47b** | Has the dog bitten the cat? | interrogative |
| **48a** | The dog has bitten the cat | affirmative |
| **48b** | The dog hasn't bitten the cat | negative |

We can summarize the relevant structural relationships in terms of formulae rather than diagrams. In the formulae which follow we use the following conventions: the relevant constituents are separated by dashes (−); internal structure within a constituent is symbolized by a plus sign (+); the fact that the structures in question are systematically related is shown by using a double-headed arrow (⇔). Note also the use of square brackets: an item in square brackets on one side of the rule is to be matched with the corresponding item in the square brackets on the other side.

**49** Active $\Leftrightarrow$ Passive (cf. Figure 43)

$$NP_1 - Aux - V - NP_2$$
$$\Leftrightarrow NP_2 - Aux + Pass - V - by + NP_1$$

**50** Affirmative $\Leftrightarrow$ Negative (cf. Figures 56 and 57)

$$X - Tense - \begin{bmatrix} HAVE \\ BE \\ Modal \end{bmatrix} - Y$$

$$\Leftrightarrow X - Tense + Neg - \begin{bmatrix} HAVE \\ BE \\ Modal \end{bmatrix} - Y$$

$$X - Tense - MV - Y$$
$$\Leftrightarrow X - Tense + Neg + DO - MV - Y$$

**51** Declarative $\Leftrightarrow$ Interrogative (cf. Figures 54 and 55)

$$NP - Tense + \begin{bmatrix} HAVE \\ BE \\ Modal \end{bmatrix} - X$$

$$\Leftrightarrow Tense + \begin{bmatrix} HAVE \\ BE \\ Modal \end{bmatrix} - NP - X$$

$$NP - Tense - MV - X$$
$$\Leftrightarrow Tense + DO - NP - MV - X$$

All the **a** sentences in **46–8** are identical; it has long been traditional linguistic wisdom that there is something 'basic' about 'active, declarative, affirmative' sentences, like **52a** below, in comparison with, say, 'passive, interrogative, negative' sentences like **52b**:

**52a** The dog has bitten the cat
**52b** Hasn't the cat been bitten by the dog?

The description we have offered can perhaps go some way towards explaining why sentences like **52a** seem more basic than those like **52b**. There are two reasons.

In the first place, if the sentences in each pair in **46–8** are related, and if **46a**, **47a** and **48a** are identical as they are, then the corresponding **b** sentences must also be related. In each case the relationship is, as it were, mediated through the common **a** sentence. A distinct structural relationship between **46b** and **48b** *could* be established in the manner shown in Figure 58:

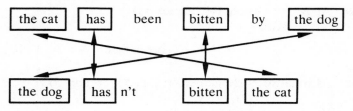

*Figure 58*

*Prima facie* there is no reason why this can't be done, but it seems more revealing to interpret the relationship as shown in Figure 59:

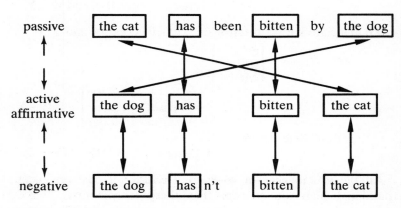

*Figure 59*

where one parameter of change is accommodated at a time: the intermediary is our basic sentence.

A second reason – which is implicit in the preceding account – is that the various relationships we have been discussing can be compounded. Thus, related to the basic sentence:

**53**  The dog has bitten the cat

is the corresponding passive:

**54**  The cat has been bitten by the dog

and related to this is the corresponding passive negative:

**55**  The cat hasn't been bitten by the dog

and related to this is the corresponding passive interrogative negative:

**56** Hasn't the cat been bitten by the dog?

The affirmative : negative relationship holds whether the sentence is active or passive; the declarative : interrogative relationship holds whether the sentence is active or passive, affirmative or negative. Breaking down these statements of sentence relatedness into 'elements', active : passive, affirmative : negative and so on, allows us to state the most basic relationships, and to combine these basic relationships to form more complex relationships. In doing so, the most 'basic' of all the sentences on which we can operate is the declarative, active passive.

Relationships of this kind are known as transformational relationships. They are relationships of one structure (with the constituent structure analysis shown on one side of the rule), to another structure (that has the constituent structure shown on the other side of the rule). This can be illustrated by the two analyses in Figures 60 and 61 on page 122. The rule that relates these two structures is, as we have seen (cf. **51**):

**57** $NP - Tense - MV - X \Leftrightarrow Tense + DO - NP - MV + X$

The following question now arises: in statements like **57**, or the other statements shown in **49–51**, are we to suppose that the structures are simply *related*, or is the one structure to be *derived* from the other? In formulating these rules, we have supposed that it is simply a *relation* between two structures: this has been symbolized by the use of the double-headed arrow $\Leftrightarrow$ which may be taken to mean 'any structure of the form found on one side of the rule can be matched by a structure found on the other side of the rule'. If you find a structure as shown on the left, you also find one as shown on the right; and vice versa, for any structure as shown on the right, there is a corresponding structure as shown on the left. This is a statement of *relatedness*. We can, however, reinterpret such rules with minor modification as rules of *derivation*, and symbolize the fact that the rules are derivational by using a single-headed arrow $\Rightarrow$. This we take to mean that, given the structure on the left-hand side of the rule, a structure can be formed as shown on the right-hand side of the rule by performing the changes noted in the rule. Thus in

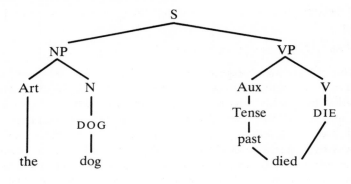

*Figure 60*                                    (declarative)

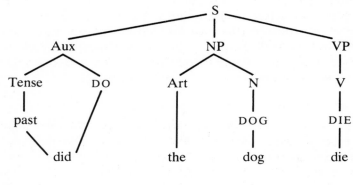

*Figure 61*                                    (interrogative)

the derivational sense we would say that Figure 61 could be formed from Figure 60 by (i) moving tense to the left-hand side of NP and (ii) inserting DO after Tense.

Most grammars that make use of transformational relationships formalized in the way that we have begun to formalize them are 'derivational' rather than 'relational': the rules are formulated using the symbol ⇒ (can be *changed* into the structure) rather than the symbol ⇔ (can be *related* to the structure). There are a number of reasons why. One is that it simplifies the associated constituent structure grammar. If we wish to use a relational type of rule, then the constituent structure rules must be able to generate all types of sentences directly, including passive sentences, interrogative sentences, negative interrogative sentences, and so on. To get a correct account of the constituent structure for all these diverse sentence types, together with all necessary co-occurrence restrictions, means a very complex set of constituent structure rules. For example, we need to allow for a negative element to be generated before the subject (for negative interrogative sentences) and for another negative element to be generated after the subject (for negative declarative sentences): but we need to specify that both negative elements cannot be present in one sentence to avoid nonsense like *Hasn't the man been't fishing?* Furthermore, the relational transformational rules will be a sort of 'addendum' to the grammar, rather than a fully integrated part of it.

If, however, we use a derivational type of rule, as in transformational grammars, then the constituent structure rules need to account only for the structure of the 'basic' sentences we discussed earlier. Other types of sentence are derived from these basic sentences by 'changing them into' some derived structure. Under this account the problem of the multiple negatives mentioned in the previous paragraph (and similar problems) simply does not arise. Furthermore, the transformational rules are fully integrated into the grammar, which then formally contains not only a statement of basic constituent structure patterns, but also a statement of regular relationships between sentences. Such a grammar consists of two components – a constituent structure component (or 'phrase structure component') and a transformational component. This book does not study transformational grammar in any more detail than is considered in this and the next chapter. In particular we do not discuss further the formalisms used in such grammars – the interested reader is referred to the books listed on pages 386–7. It is, however, useful to have a flavour of the way in which such grammars are presented, so we devote the remainder of this chapter to reformulating the rules already presented as a derivational transformational grammar.

First we need constituent structure (or phrase structure) rules to generate basic structures. The following will serve:

**58**    S → NP + VP
VP → Aux + V (+NP)
NP → Art + N
Aux → Tense (Modal) (Perf) (Prog)
Tense → $\begin{cases} \text{past} \\ \text{non-past} \end{cases}$
Perf → HAVE + pp
Prog → BE + -*ing*

This grammar is clearly only illustrative – it could be elaborated with some of the other rules we have discussed in previous chapters. Associated with these rules we also need a lexicon and a lexical insertion rule, as discussed in chapter 7. These two – the constituent structure, or phrase structure, rules and the lexicon – comprise what is referred to as the 'base component'. From the base component we can derive lexicalized trees which we call underlying structures.

The transformational component contains transformational rules that operate on these underlying structures to produce a derived structure. These rules may rearrange elements of the underlying structure, add elements to it, or delete elements from it. After the operation of all the relevant transformational rules we have a syntactic surface structure.

In some cases the underlying structure and the syntactic surface structure are almost identical. This is the case with active declarative sentences (the 'basic' sentences discussed on page 119), where we only need to use rules that account for the actual ordering of elements like past, -*ing* and pp which, as you will see, the grammar generates preceding the item to which they will eventually be affixed: we discuss machinery to accomplish this on pages 207–9. In other kinds of sentences a more radical restructuring occurs. An example is the passive. The rules in **58** derive elements in the order of active sentences only (the expansion of Aux contains, for instance, no provision for a passive auxiliary). The transformational rule re-orders the subject and object NPs and introduces a passive auxiliary. We discuss this immediately, but the reader may now like to consult Figure 62, which illustrates graphically the changes the passive transformation effects. The structure at the top of this figure is the underlying structure: the annotations show how this structure is 'changed' into the derived structure shown at the bottom of the figure. This derived structure still needs to go through the rules to re-order the elements past, *-ing* and pp mentioned above to produce the syntactic surface structure.

Since the transformational rules are to be derivational rather than relational, we need to amend our previous rules in various small ways. The way we formulate transformational rules in this and the following chapter is illustrated by considering the passive transformation:

**59**   Active $\Rightarrow$ Passive (optional)

$$SA: NP_1 - Aux - V - NP_2$$
$$SC: NP_2 - {}_{Aux}(Aux + {}_{Pass}(BE + pp))$$
$$- V - {}_{PP}(by + NP_1)$$

  **i**   $NP_2$ is moved to the front of the S, and adjoined as a daughter of S

 **ii**   A new constituent, Pass, expanded as BE + pp, is adjoined as a daughter of Aux, and the right sister of all other Aux constituents

**iii**   *by* is adjoined as left sister of $NP_1$ to form a new constituent PP, and this is adjoined as right sister of the VP.

SA is an abbreviation for 'structure analysis': it indicates that the rule only applies to trees that can be analysed into the constituents shown in the analysis. The relevant constituents are separated by $-$ as before. The abbreviation SC indicates 'structure change': it shows how the structure is to be changed. The notes below present, in ordinary language, an account of the relevant changes. We have also noted that the rule is optional – the passive does not have to apply whenever the structural analysis is met (otherwise we would find no active transitive sentence!). The additional detail in this formulation is an attempt to specify with some precision what the derived structure of the passive sentence will look like. This needs to be specified carefully since the passive structure may itself become the 'input' to a subsequent transformational rule (like that for forming a passive negative for example).

The effect of the rule is shown diagrammatically in Figure 62, which is annotated to show the relevant changes:

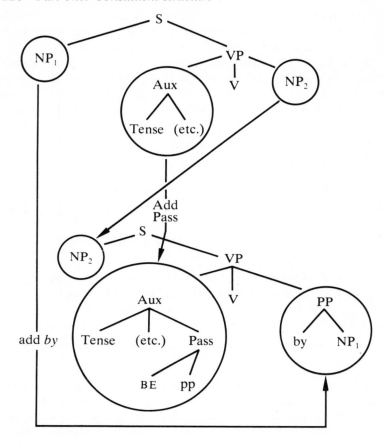

*Figure 62*

The other rules are amended as follows:

**50** Affirmative ⇒ Negative (optional)

$$SA: X - Tense - \begin{bmatrix} HAVE \\ BE \\ Modal \end{bmatrix} - Y$$

$$SC: X -_{Tense}(Tense + Neg) - \begin{bmatrix} HAVE \\ BE \\ Modal \end{bmatrix} - Y$$

$$SA: X - Tense - MV - Y$$

SC: $X - _{\text{Tense}}(\text{Tense} + \text{Neg}) - MV - Y$

i    X and Y are any arbitrary constituents.

ii   Neg is adjoined as a daughter of Tense, and a right sister of whatever is dominated by Tense.

**51**   Declarative $\Rightarrow$ Interrogative (optional)

$$SA: NP - \text{Tense} + \begin{bmatrix} \text{HAVE} \\ \text{BE} \\ \text{Modal} \end{bmatrix} - X$$

$$SC: \text{Tense} + \begin{bmatrix} \text{HAVE} \\ \text{BE} \\ \text{Modal} \end{bmatrix} - NP - X$$

SA: $NP - \text{Tense} - MV - X$

SC: $\text{Tense} - NP - MV - X$

i    X is any arbitrary constituent.

ii   Tense and HAVE, BE or any Modal verb are moved to the front of the sentence. If Tense is immediately followed by the main verb, Tense alone will move to the front of the sentence.

**52**   DO support (obligatory)

SA: $X - \text{Tense} - Y$

SC: $X - \text{Tense} + \text{DO} - Y$

i    X and Y are any arbitrary constituents or none (in the case of X), on condition that the left-most constituent of Y is not a verb, main or auxiliary.

ii   DO is introduced as a right sister of Tense when Tense is thus 'stranded' with no verb to its immediate right.

There are a number of small changes in these 'derivational' rules as compared with the corresponding 'relational' rules in **49–51**. Most of them are necessary precisely because these new rules are derivational, and we must specify the derived constituent structure in detail. Note that we have also formulated 'DO support' as a separate rule, rather than including it in the 'Negative' and 'Interrogative' rules as previously. This enables us to generalize about the circumstances that require 'DO support': whenever Tense is 'stranded' – i.e. separated from an immediately following verb, main or auxiliary – DO is supplied to 'carry' the tense marker. Making 'DO support' a separate rule means we can then use this rule (with some small further modification) for other circumstances in which DO occurs. For example, we find DO in negative imperative sentences:

**53a**  Go!
**53b**  *Do*n't go!

in some types of emphatic sentence (italics indicate stress):

**54a**  John is going (John's going)
**54b**  John *is* going

**55a**  John went
**55b**  John *did* go

and in 'Tag' questions:

**56a**  John is going, isn't he?
**56b**  John will go, won't he?
**56c**  John went, *did*n't he?

The description is clearly not yet complete (even in its outline form!). We need rules that relate the various elements we have been juggling with to actually occurring word forms or segments of word forms. This subject is tackled in Part Two, and we leave further discussion until then.

The discussion shows that transformational rules potentially form an important and powerful addition to our descriptive armoury. They enable us to relate together in a systematic fashion those sentences we perceive to be structurally related, and the relationship is formalized within the grammar itself.

We close this chapter by observing that we can call upon transformational rules to solve a descriptive problem noted on page 75, which we were not then able to account for – the alternative positions open to sentence adverbials. We saw that in sentences like:

**57a**  The dog bit the man yesterday
**57b**  Yesterday the dog bit the man

the time adverbial could occur either at the end of the sentence (its 'normal' position) or at the beginning. A constituent structure rule like:

**58**  $S \rightarrow (Adv_{time})\ NP + VP\ (+Adv_{time})$

allows us to generate an adverb either at the beginning or the end of the sentence. It also allows two adverbs, which we do not want:

**59**   *Yesterday the dog bit the man last week

To make a rule like **58** work we need additional notation to the effect that $Adv_{time}$ was to be chosen once only. A more illuminating solution is a constituent structure rule:

**60**   $S \rightarrow NP + VP (+Adv_{time})$

and then a transformational rule optionally fronting the adverb:

**61**   *Time adverb fronting* (optional):
    SA:   $NP - VP - Adv_{time}$
    SC:   $Adv_{time} - NP - VP$

Similar transformational rules will account for the distributional possibilities of the other adverbs discussed on pages 73–5.

## Technical terms

| | |
|---|---|
| active | negative |
| affirmative | passive |
| aspect | passive auxiliary |
| auxiliary verb | perfective auxiliary |
| base component | phrase structure |
| basic sentence | progressive auxiliary |
| declarative | structure analysis |
| derivation | structure change |
| derived structure | syntactic surface structure |
| DO support | tense |
| interrogative | transformation |
| main verb | underlying structure |
| modal auxiliary verb | verb group |

## Exercises

In these exercises, you are asked to proceed by stages.

The first stage is to examine some data that can be described in terms of a transformational rule insofar as there are formally describable structural relationships between sentences, and to attempt to formulate these relationships in ordinary language. This involves assigning the appropriate constituent structure to the data in question so that the statement can deal with structures of the maximum generality.

The second stage attempts to formulate the rules as transformational rules of the sort discussed in the preceding chapter. This usually involves having to decide on one structure as a 'basic' structure from which the other structures are to be derived: you need to find reasons why one rather than another structure is to be considered 'basic' and be prepared to justify them. Then you can write a constituent structure grammar which generates the basic structures.

Finally you need to formulate transformations that operate on the structures generated by the constituent structure grammar to produce the 'derived' structures.

## 1   *Dative movement*

Consider pairs of sentences like:

**1a**   Mary baked John a cake
**1b**   Mary baked a cake for John

**2a**   Jane sent Simon a Valentine
**2b**   Jane sent a Valentine to Simon

Describe the structural relationship between these sentences. Which sentence would you choose as 'basic'? (Hint: think of the problem of specifying the right preposition – *to* or *for*.)

Now consider the following extra data:

**1c**   *Mary baked John it
**1d**   Mary baked it for John

**2c**   *Jane sent Simon it
**2d**   Jane sent it to Simon

Describe the restrictions on 'dative movement' introduced by the pronominalization of *a cake* in **1**, etc. Does your original hypothesis about which sentence is 'basic' still hold?

Now write a grammar which generates the basic sentences (and others which operate syntactically like them) and an appropriate transformational rule. Write two grammars. In one suppose that pronouns (*it*, *him*, etc.) are introduced into structures by a constituent structure rule, perhaps of the following sort:

$$NP \rightarrow \begin{Bmatrix} Det + N \\ Pro \end{Bmatrix}$$

and consider what restrictions you must place on your transformation 'dative movement'. In the other grammar suppose that pronouns are introduced 'transformationally', so the constituent structure rules generates NPs by a rule like:

$$NP \rightarrow Det + N$$

(i.e. they do not introduce pronouns). There will be a transformational rule which we may informally describe as: 'replace some NP by an appropriate pronoun: *he*, if the replaced NP refers to a single male human; *she* if it refers to a single female human', etc. What restrictions do you now need to introduce on your rule of dative movement?

## 2 Phrasal verbs

Consider sentences like:

**1a** The woman rang up the policeman
**2a** The policeman stood near the hedge

Note that **1a** is related to sentences like:

**1b** The woman rang the policeman up
**1c** The woman rang him up
**1d** *The woman rang up him

and **2a** is related to sentences like:

**2b** *The policeman stood the hedge near
**2c** *The policeman stood it near
**2d** The policeman stood near it

Describe the structural relationships that hold between the different sets of sentences. Decide which sentence in each set you consider 'basic', and why. Describe the restrictions on 'particle movement' (as the transformation involved is usually called).

Write a grammar which generates these sets of sentences – and others like them (collect a set of verbs that operate in each structure). As with the previous exercise, you can write a grammar assuming that pronouns are generated either in the constituent structure rules, or are introduced by transformation.

### 3   Tag questions

Tags are constituents like those which follow the comma in the sentences below; we call the constituent that precedes the comma the main sentence:

1   You are coming, aren't you?
2   John has been stupid, hasn't he?
3   Mary will be coming, won't she?
4   You can't understand, can you?
5   Mary won't be coming, will she?
6   The shops haven't closed already, have they?

Assume that the main sentence is the basic form, and that a tag is derived by rule from the basic sentence. Formulate a rule for the derivation of tags. At this stage ignore sentences that do not contain an auxiliary verb (i.e. sentences like *Mary came*), or that contain an auxiliary verb other than HAVE, BE, WILL, WOULD, CAN, COULD, SHALL, SHOULD.

Now consider the formation of tags in sentences like:

7   He likes hamburgers, _____?
8   Your mother died in 1969, _____?
9   You don't like punk rock, _____?
10   John didn't break the window, _____?

Extend your first description to include such sentences.

In addition to the auxiliaries listed above, the following are often considered to be auxiliaries in English: MAY, MIGHT, OUGHT TO, USED TO, NEED TO, HAVE TO. How do these function in your dialect? (Dialects of English differ as to whether they categorize all or only some of these items as auxiliaries or as main verbs for the purposes of tag formation.) Incorporate your findings into your statement about tag-formation.

Now consider the formation of tags to sentences which contain HAVE as a possessive verb, or BE:

**11**   John has a big house, _____?
**12**   Mary is pretty, _____?

and incorporate this into your description.
    Next consider some other uses of HAVE, e.g.:

**13**   You had a good time at the party last night,
        _____?
**14**   Mary had a bath this morning, _____?

Now write a grammar including a transformational rule (or rules) to account for the tags you can form in your dialect of English (you will probably find it useful to use the analysis of auxiliaries developed in the preceding chapter).
    Your rules will not account for all possible types of tag. For instance, they will only handle 'reversed polarity' tags like those illustrated. (The system of negation, with the terms 'positive' and 'negative' is often referred to as one of 'polarity': the tags you have been looking at are all reversed polarity tags because the polarity of the main verb is reversed in the tag.) They will not handle non-reversed polarity tags like *I'll open the window, shall I?* Nor will they handle tags like *I think it's Monday, isn't it* (note that *\*I think it's Monday, don't I?* is deviant!).

# 9 Embedding and recursion

Sentences like:

1 Charlie married Mary
2 The rumour that Charlie married Mary is untrue
3 Fred believes that Charlie married Mary

can be analysed as in Figures 63–5.

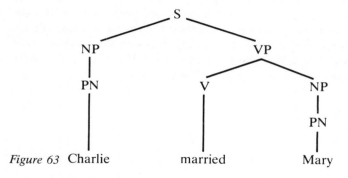

*Figure 63* Charlie married Mary

Figures 64 and 65 contain, as a constituent, a structure identical to the structure shown in Figure 63, with the same analysis as the independent sentence **1** but preceded by the 'complementizer' *that*. In Figures 64 and 65, the structure dominated by the topmost S is called the 'superordinate' or 'matrix' sentence, and the structure dominated by the lower S the 'subordinate' or 'embedded' sentence. Embedded sentences, then, are sentences which are themselves constituents of other sentences.

In the structures under discussion, the embedded sentences are analysed as constituents of an NP in the matrix sentence. This analysis can be supported by noting their distribution in transformationally related sentences, for example:

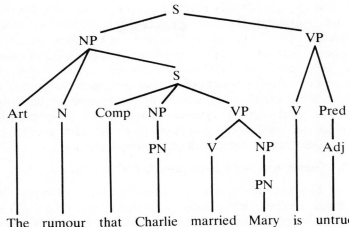

*Figure 64*

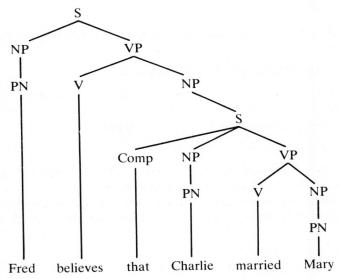

*Figure 65*

**4a** What is untrue is the rumour that Charlie married Mary

**4b** That Charlie married Mary is believed by Fred

In both **2** and **3** the embedded sentence is preceded by *that*.

We call such items 'complementizers' (Comp), as in the analysis: and the particular type of embedding illustrated is called 'complementation'. One of the functions of complementizers is to indicate that the sentence structure immediately following is a subordinate or embedded sentence. Two types of complementation are illustrated: Noun complementation, as in **2**, where the embedded sentence is the complement of the noun RUMOUR; and Verb complementation, as in **3**, where the embedded sentence is the complement of the verb BELIEVE. Not all nouns can co-occur with complement sentences:

>   **5**   *The house that Charlie married Mary is unsafe

and we can indicate which nouns can take complements by including an appropriate subcategorization frame (page 55) in the lexical specification of these nouns, like RUMOUR, STORY, FACT, INSINUATION, etc, as follows:

>   **6**   RUMOUR: N;__S

Similarly, not all verbs can take complement sentences; we do not find

>   **7**   *John killed that Charlie is married

For those verbs that do take complement sentences, like BELIEVE, EXPECT, THINK, SUPPOSE, etc., we can, once again, indicate this fact in the lexical specification:

>   **8**   BELIEVE: V; __ NP[S]

where the strict subcategorization frame __ NP[S] indicates that the object of BELIEVE can be a complement sentence.

To make the constituent structure rules account for sentences like those in Figures 64 and 65 we need rewrite rules of the form:

>   **9**   S → NP + VP
>   VP → V (+NP)
>   NP → $\begin{cases} \text{Art} + \text{N} \ (+\text{S}) \\ \text{S} \end{cases}$   (for structures like Figure 64)
>   (for structures like Figure 65)

In these rules the rule expanding NP reintroduces the initial symbol S. To expand this S we need to return to the beginning of the grammar and go through the rules a second time. This 'cycling' through the rules is known as recursion. Recursion in the grammar permits embedding. It will be noted that the rules in **9** do not account for the introduction of the complementizer *that*. For our immediate purposes we can suppose that this will be introduced by a transformational rule.

The subject of verb complementation in English is complex and we do not consider it in this book. Those interested in pursuing the subject are referred to any of the books on transformational grammar mentioned in 'Further reading'. Instead we now turn to consider a different embedded construction within the N P usually referred to as 'relativization'. This describes the formation of 'relative clauses'. These can be illustrated by

**10**   The woman *who you saw me with last night* is my wife

of which the italicized portion is the relative clause. The whole string *the woman who you saw me with last night* is an NP, as can be verified by checking it in appropriate transformations; and the relative clause is clearly a part of this. The relative clause cannot stand on its own as a sentence:

**11**   *who you saw me with last night

yet it clearly relates to the sentence:

**12**   You saw me with the woman last night

which has all the properties of an independent sentence. Let us suppose that the structure underlying **10** can be represented as in Figure 66. The structure to be related to the relative clause is represented as a sentence embedded within the N P. It has been generated by a constituent structure rule, which can be added to the rules in **9**:

**13**   $NP \rightarrow NP + S$

All relative clauses are derived from this rule. Note that this rule is distinct from the rule in **9** that introduces noun complement sentences. Since the syntax of noun complement sentences and relative clauses is different, we need a different rule for each type of structure. Rule **13** develops a structure as shown in Figure 66, the underlying structure (see page 124) for sentence **10**. We call the N P *the woman* in Figure 66 the 'head' of the construction and the S from which the relative clause derives the embedded or relative sentence.

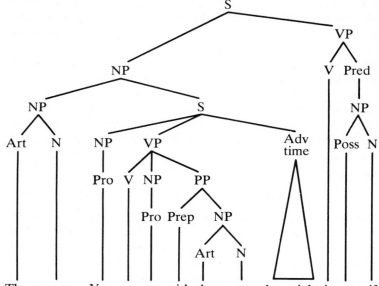

*Figure 66*

We can derive the sentence **10** by the rule shown in **14**. The rule is formulated as a derivational transformational rule.

**14**   Relative clause rule: (obligatory)

$$SA: \ _{NP}(NP \ _{S}(X - NP - Y))$$

$$SC: \ _{NP}(NP \ _{S}(\begin{bmatrix} rel \\ pro \end{bmatrix} - X - Y))$$

**i**   Identify the NP in the embedded S that is identical to the head.

**ii**   Move this NP to the front of the embedded S.

**iii**   Replace it by the appropriate relative pronoun.

The symbol $\begin{bmatrix} rel \\ pro \end{bmatrix}$ indicates 'the appropriate relative pronoun': *who* if the NP to be replaced contains a 'human' noun; *which* for all other nouns. X and Y, as before, indicate any arbitrary constituents, or none. In the case of 'subject relatives', X is null (i.e. the NP in the relative clause is the first constituent in its clause so X must be null); in the case of 'object relatives', X is not null (it includes the subject NP and the verb at least), but Y may be null, since the object NP may be the last constituent in the clause (the object need not, of course, be the final constituent, as it isn't in **10**: in that case neither X nor Y is null). Subject and object relative clauses are illustrated in **16**. The reader should try to derive the items in **16** using the rule **14**.

Applying rule **14** to the relevant string in Figure 66 gives:

**15**  Figure 66:  the woman (you saw me with the woman last night) is my wife

Rule **14 i**:  the woman (you saw me with *the woman* last night) is my wife

Rule **14 ii**:  the woman (*the woman* you saw me with last night) is my wife

Rule **14 iii**:  the woman (*who* you saw me with last night) is my wife

This produces the desired result. The rule **14** predicts the form of infinitely many relative clauses:

**16a**  The apples (*the apples* are ripe)
The apples which are ripe

**16b**  The man (*the man* lives next door)
The man who lives next door

**16c**  The girl (I love *the girl*)
The girl who I love

**16d**  The knife (she stabbed her lover with *the knife*)
The knife which she stabbed her lover with

**16e**  The girl (John gave the book to *the girl*)
The girl who John gave the book to

etc. The rule applies whether the NP which is identical to the head is the subject (**16a,b**), the object (**16c**), the indirect object (**16e**), an NP in an 'instrumental phrase' (**16d**), etc.

We can now go a stage further. In **16d,e** the NPs in the embedded S that are identical with the head are constituents of a PP (*with the knife*; *to the girl*). In the examples shown the NPs have been lifted out of their PPs and moved to the front of the embedded S. It is, however, possible to take the preposition as well:

**17**  The knife with which she stabbed her lover
The girl to whom John gave the book

This suggests that we should amend **14** as follows:

**14′**   Relative clause rule: (obligatory)

$$\text{SA: }_{NP}(NP\ _S(X - NP - Y))$$

$$\text{SC: }_{NP}(NP\ _S(\begin{bmatrix} rel \\ pro \end{bmatrix} - X - Y))$$

$$\text{SA: }_{NP}(NP\ _S(X - \ _{PP}(Prep - NP) - Y))$$

$$\text{SC: (a) }_{NP}(NP\ _S(Prep - \begin{bmatrix} rel \\ pro \end{bmatrix} - X - Y))$$

$$\text{(b) }_{NP}(NP\ _S(\begin{bmatrix} rel \\ pro \end{bmatrix} - X - Prep - Y))$$

  **i**   Identify the NP in the embedded S that is identical to the head.

 **ii**   Move this NP to the front of the embedded S (and, optionally, if the NP is in construction with a preposition in a PP, also move the preposition).[1]

**iii**   Replace the NP by the appropriate relative pronoun.

---

1 We need to include the restriction that this rule applies only to cases where the preposition is part of a PP in order to avoid producing nonsense when we deal with 'phrasal verbs'. Phrasal verbs are items like RUN UP in the sense 'amass, accumulate' or PUT DOWN in the sense 'kill'. We describe these as having a structure verb stem + particle. We can then distinguish between items like UP and DOWN when they are used as particles (in phrasal verbs) and when the 'same' items are used in prepositional phrases like *up the hill, down the drain*, etc. For example, given the structure:

the cat (we put down the cat last week) was very old

we want to avoid producing:

*the cat down which we put last week was very old

while still allowing for the acceptable:

the cat which we put down last week was very old

The distinction between a 'phrasal verb' and a verb + PP string can be observed in the following·

the bill (John ran up the bill) was enormous    RUN UP = 'amass'
the bill which John ran up was enormous
*the bill up which John ran was enormous

the hill (John ran up the hill) was enormous    RUN + PP
the hill which John ran up was enormous
the hill up which John ran was enormous

We can go further still. In sentences **16c,d,e** the relative pronoun can be omitted without affecting the acceptability of the sentences in question:

**18**  the girl (who) I love
the knife (which) she stabbed her lover with
the girl (who) John gave the book to

The relative pronoun cannot be omitted in **16a,b**:

**19**  the apples which are ripe (need to be picked)
*the apples are ripe (need to be picked)
the man who lives next door (is the Lord Mayor)
*the man lives next door (is the Lord Mayor)

nor can it be omitted in the NP in **17**:

**20**  The knife with which she stabbed her lover
*The knife with she stabbed her lover.

The general principle which governs the omission of the relative pronoun may be formulated as:

**21**  Relative pronoun deletion rule: (optional)

$$\text{SA:} \quad _{NP}(NP \, _S(\begin{bmatrix} rel \\ pro \end{bmatrix} - NP - X))$$

$$\text{SC:} \quad _{NP}(NP \, _S(NP - X))$$

The relative pronoun, *who* or *which*, may be deleted, optionally, if
**i**  it directly follows the head noun
*and*
**ii**  it immediately precedes the subject NP of the embedded S.

Both of these conditions are satisfied in the sentences in **18**, so the relative pronoun can be deleted. In the sentences in **19** the first condition is met, but the second is not, since the relative pronoun has replaced the subject noun. In sentences **20** the second condition is met, but the first is not.

There are a number of reasons why it is attractive to derive relative clauses in the way suggested by rules **14′** etc. It accounts for the fact that relative clauses, although not independent sentences, seem to have many of the characteristics of full sentences: we can show this by supposing that they are derived from full sentences, but that the rules alter them in various ways. It explains why the pronoun *who* in **16b** is a 'subject relative pronoun' and the 'same' pronoun in **16c** an 'object relative pronoun' – they derive from the subject and object respectively of the embedded sentence. It also accounts for the fact that even though a verb like LOVE is a 'transitive verb' (i.e. one that requires an object NP) no object NP appears following the verb in the actual structure of a sentence like **16c**. Without this way of accommodating that information, a constituent structure grammar must specify, for example, that LOVE is a transitive verb, and must therefore co-occur with an object NP, except when it is found in a relative clause in which the relative pronoun is understood to be the object relative pronoun. Our derivation is more straightforward, and in addition accounts for a variety of facts about relative clauses.

Let us now continue some lines of investigation that the account so far suggests.

Consider the sentences:

**22a**   The man (the man is scratching his head)
**22b**   The man who is scratching his head
**22c**   The man scratching his head

These sentences seem systematically related in a way that can be matched by numberless other sentences of a similar kind:

**23a**   The music (the music is on the piano)
**23b**   The music which is on the piano
**23c**   The music on the piano

**24a**   The man (the man was run over by a bus)
**24b**   The man who was run over by a bus
**24c**   The man run over by a bus

In each case the **c** sentences omit the relative pronoun and a form of the verb BE. We make a rule to cover this case:

**25**   *Relative clause reduction rule* (optional):

$$\text{SA:}\ _{NP}(NP\ _S(\begin{bmatrix} \text{rel} \\ \text{pro} \end{bmatrix} - \text{Tense} - \text{BE} - Y))$$

$$\text{SC:}\ _{NP}(NP\ _S(Y))$$

i  Optionally, the relative pronoun, tense and an
immediately following form of BE may be deleted.

It does not appear to matter whether the BE in question is the
BE found in a 'locative' sentence like **23**; the BE which is the
'progressive' auxiliary as in sentences like **22**; or the 'passive'
auxiliary BE as in sentences like **24**. Note also that the rule only
deletes a form of BE – in **22c** for example the *-ing* in *scratching*,
which derives from the progressive BE + *-ing* (as we noted
earlier, pages 107–8) is not affected by the rule: there is of
course no NP like *\*the man scratch his head* where both the BE
and the *-ing* have been deleted.

As formulated, the rule also applies to the copula BE in NPs
like:

**26**  The apples (which are ripe)

For many adjectives, there is a relation between an adjective in
a relative clause, and the same adjective in a simple NP:

**27**  The ripe apples
The apples which are ripe

We can maintain that rule **25** does apply to these, and that an
extra rule is needed which would reverse the order of noun and
adjective. The derivation is as follows:

**28a**  The apples (the apples are ripe)
**28b**  The apples (which are ripe) (by rule **14**)
**28c**  The apples ripe (by rule **25**)
**28d**  The ripe apples

The step between **28c** and **28d** is accounted for by postulating
the rule:

**29**  *Adjective shift rule: (obligatory)*
SA: $_{NP}(\ _{NP}(Art - N)\ _S(Adj)\ )$
SC: $_{NP}(\ Art - Adj - N)$

i  Obligatorily, in a structure of the form N + Adj reverse
order of these two constituents.

Handling the derivation of adjectives in this way has descriptive advantages over the constituent structure account of adjectives we discussed on pages 76–9, but it is not without

problems. The rules do make interesting generalizations about systematic structural relationships between sets of sentences. They also go some way towards explaining their paraphrase relation – they derive from a common underlying structure, later obscured by transformational rearrangements. A further advantage is that the rules simplify the account, however it is handled, of co-occurrence restrictions between adjectives and nouns. Instead of having to state that, say, RIPE can modify a noun like APPLE both when it precedes it (*the ripe apple*) and when it follows it in a relative clause (*the apple which is ripe*), a single statement suffices. If *the apple is ripe* is semantically well formed, then so too is *the ripe apple*. By contrast, if *the apple is careless* is ill formed, then so too is *the careless apple*. Yet another advantage is to simplify further the constituent structure rules. We can replace rule **30a** by **30b**, since both adjectives and prepositional phrases within the N P are derived from 'reduced' relative clauses.

**30a**   $NP \rightarrow Art (+Adj)^* + N (+ PP)$

       (*see rule illustrated in Figure 31, page 80*)

**30b**   $NP \rightarrow \begin{Bmatrix} Art + N \\ NP + S \end{Bmatrix}$

We do, however, have to 'pay for' this simplification. To begin with there is the additional machinery of transformational rules. We also note that not all adjectives go through the derivation proposed. Some do not appear in relative clauses:

**31a**   The major difficulty
**31b**   *The difficulty which is major
**31c**   The same problem
**31d**   *The problem which is same

and conversely some can appear in relative clauses but not preceding nouns:

**32a**   *The alike girls
**32b**   The girls who are alike
**32c**   *The ablaze building
**32d**   The building which is ablaze

We could perhaps handle such cases by marking items like MAJOR in the lexicon as obligatorily having to undergo rules **25** and **29**, and items like ABLAZE as being unable to go through these rules, but this seems a somewhat *ad hoc* solution.

A wide range of structures in English involve embedding. We do not have space to examine more in detail, but some are worth mentioning. We find embedded sentences in temporal adverbials:

**33** When you go to London you should visit the National Gallery

in place adverbials:

**34** You will find your book where you put it down last night

in manner adverbials:

**35** He walks in a manner that reminds me of his father

in adverbial clauses of reason and purpose:

**36** You cannot have another glass of wine because the bottle is empty
He emigrated to Australia in order to escape from his mother-in-law

and in conditional clauses:

**37** You should go and live in France if you want to learn to speak French well

We can also use the approach outlined in this chapter to explain certain sorts of ambiguity. We noted on page 83 that the ambiguity in sentences like:

**38** The shooting of the hunters was disgraceful

cannot easily be accounted for in terms of simple labelling and bracketing. The ambiguity arises from the fact that *the shooting of the hunters* can have a 'subjective' interpretation (*the hunters shot 'something'*) or an 'objective' interpretation (*'somebody' shot the hunters*). If we derive 'nominalizations' like *the shooting of the hunters* from sentence-like structures of the sort indicated, then we have a systematic account of such ambiguities.

Embedding is one of the most remarkable features of language. It enables a speaker to construct not only simple sentences, but also sentences of considerable syntactic complexity.

Our grammar, however it is formulated, needs to be able to capture this potential. Transformational grammar claims that it enables the grammarian to capture this 'creative' power in a language. The constituent structure rules cannot only generate simple sentences; they can also, by the use of recursive rules (which enable us to cycle again and again through the same small set of rules) generate sentences containing complex embedding. A small set of transformational rules, operating on these embedded sentences as many times as is necessary will produce the complex sentences we wish to account for.

## Technical terms

| | |
|---|---|
| 'adjective shift' | recursion |
| complementation | relative clause |
| complementizer | relative clause reduction |
| constituent sentence | relative clause rule |
| creativity | relative pronoun deletion rule |
| embedding | subordinate sentence |
| head matrix sentence | superordinate sentence |
| noun complementation | verb complementation |

## Exercise

### Relative clauses in English

We noted in the text that relative clauses can be regarded as being derived by a set of rules from an underlying structure which contains a 'full' sentence. We looked at four such rules. To save space we can represent the effect of these rules in terms of bracketed strings which 'chart' the derivation of an NP. Thus the derivation of **16a** can be shown as:

|  |  |
|---|---|
| *Underlying structure:* | The apples (the apples are ripe) |
| *Relative clause rule:* | The apples (which are ripe) |

**18** can be charted as:

|  |  |
|---|---|
| *Underlying structure:* | The girl (I love the girl) |
| *Relative clause rule:* | The girl (who I love) |
| *Rel. Pro. deletion rule:* | The girl (I love) |

and **28** can be represented by:

| | |
|---|---|
| *Underlying structure:* | The apples (the apples are ripe) |
| *Relative clause rule:* | The apples (which are ripe) |
| *Rel. Cl. reduction rule:* | The apples (ripe) |
| *Adjective shift:* | The ripe apples |

Check that these derivations are correct in terms of the description in the text.

Note that some of the other transformations looked at on pages 102–33 can be applied to the embedded sentence before it undergoes the relativization rules. Thus, for example, consider the following derivation:

| | |
|---|---|
| *Underlying structure:* | The man (a bus ran over the man) |
| *Passive to embedded S:* | The man (the man was run over by a bus) |
| *Relative clause rule:* | The man (who was run over by a bus) |
| *Rel. Cl. reduction rule:* | The man (run over by a bus) |

Write derivations like the above for the following N Ps:

   **i**   The music on the piano
  **ii**   The girl who won the tennis match
 **iii**   The book I bought yesterday
  **iv**   The criminal imprisoned by the authorities
   **v**   The guilty man
  **vi**   The knife father cut the turkey with
 **vii**   The woman to whom he is married

The text discussed relative clauses formed with the relative pronouns *who* and *which*. In addition we encounter relative clauses with the 'genitive' relative pronoun *whose*:

the man whose leg was broken
the man whose dog I rescued from the river

If we derive these also from underlying structures containing a full sentence, then they have underlying structures like this:

The man (the man's leg was broken)
The man (I rescued the man's dog from the river)

Write a rule like those in the text which will derive such sentences, and then write derivations for the following N Ps:

    **viii**   the woman whose dog died
    **ix**   the boy whose mother I gave it to
    **x**   the people whose cars have been stolen

In most forms of English, in addition to relative clauses formed with a relative pronoun (*who*, *which* etc.), you find relative clauses formed with *that*:

    The girl that I love
    A man that I would like to meet

The rules for *wh-* and *that* relative clauses are slightly different, and to indicate this we distinguish between a '*Wh*-rel rule' and a '*That*-rel rule'

    *Underlying structure:* The girl (I love the girl)
    *That-rel rule:*        The girl (that I love)

See if you can formulate the differences between the two types of relative clause forming rules by considering the different relative clauses you can form from the following underlying structures:

    **xi**   The girl (I gave the book to the girl)
    **xii**  The man (I envy the man's cellar)

# 10   The sentence

Lyons defines the sentence as the maximum unit of grammatical analysis: 'A grammatical unit between the constituent parts of which distributional limitations and dependencies can be established, but which can itself be put into no distribution class' (1968, 173), and we adopt this definition. In other words, formal statements can be made about the distribution of sentence constituents, but not about sentences as wholes. Thus, we can talk about the distribution of NP (in environments like __VP; V__; Prep __ etc.) but no comparable distributional statements can be made with respect to the sentence itself, except, perhaps, that a text consists of a series of sentences S & S & S . . . .[1]

Lyons's definition implies that the sentence has a certain sort of unity: it is grammatically complete; it can stand on its own independent of context; and it has a degree of semantic independence. This is largely true of the units so far identified as sentences and used as examples. What, however, of the relationship between such units and, say, the orthographic sentences out of which this chapter is composed? Lyons suggests that no distributional statements can be made about such units – a text it is suggested consists of a series of sentences S & S & S . . . . Consider, for example, the three orthographic sentences that form the preceding paragraph. The second and third begin with *In other words* and *Thus*, expressions which tie the relevant sentences to their predecessors. *In other words* indicates that the

1 This is a well-established descriptive viewpoint with a long history. Consider the following quotation from *Hermes*, by James Harris (1751): 'The Extensions of Speech are quite indefinite, as may be seen if we compare the Eneid to an Epigram of *Martial*. But the *longest Extension* with which Grammar has to do is the Extension here considered, that is to say a SENTENCE. The greater Extensions (such as Syllogisms, Paragraphs, Sections and complete Works) belong not to Grammar but to Arts of a higher order; not to mention that all of them are but Sentences repeated.'

sentence is a rephrasing of the point made in the sentence before: *Thus* introduces an example of the point just made. We call such expressions 'binding expressions' since they bind sentences together into text. Without the binding expressions the three sentences could be rearranged in some other order – 3–2–1; 1–3–2; 2–1–3, etc. – with no substantial difference to the message conveyed, and with few other consequential amendments to the text (other binding expressions, or none, would be needed). Furthermore, if we disregard the binders, each sentence can stand on its own as a grammatically complete unit, and forms, in some sense, a complete message.

Orthographic sentences in texts are not always capable of such ready permutation. Consider, for instance, the following (read it as a text – the numbers are for reference):

> **1** When John and Mary got back home, they found the front door had been left open. **2** John accused Mary. **3** She denied it. **4** John asked her to shut it. **5** She wouldn't.

The first sentence is grammatically and semantically capable of standing as an isolate, but none of the others is. If the second sentence were found as an isolate, one might reasonably enquire: 'What did John accuse Mary of?' In an isolate sentence ACCUSE requires a sentence frame NP __ NP PP, where the subject NP is the 'accuser', the object NP is the 'accused' and the PP contains the 'accusation'. In connected text, however, ACCUSE permits the ellipsis or omission of the 'accusation', providing the 'accusation' is recoverable from the context, as in the example. Similarly if **3** were found as an isolate, we might enquire: 'Who denied what?'. The proforms *she* and *it* are understood in context as, respectively, 'Mary' and 'that she left the door open'. **4** further illustrates the use of proforms. **5** is another example of ellipsis – here understood as 'Mary wouldn't shut the door'.

The sentences **2–5** cannot stand alone. They are to a greater or lesser degree either grammatically and semantically incomplete or both: grammatically incomplete insofar as constituents have been elided; and semantically incomplete inasmuch as the sentences can only be understood with reference to their context. In both cases, these 'sentence fragments' are only fully understood by reference to some 'understood' fuller form, where the items that have been elided, reduced to proforms, etc., are restored:

**6a** John accused Mary of leaving the door open
**6b** Mary denied that she had left the door open
**6c** John asked Mary to shut the door
**6d** Mary wouldn't shut the door

The amount of grammatical and contextual interpretation necessary can be appreciated if we consider, for example, **5**. Only in this particular context is it understood as **6d**. In another context it might be understood as 'Mary wouldn't feed the cat'; 'Jane wouldn't give up smoking'; etc.

Strings like **2–5** are entirely appropriate and natural in a text. By contrast the series of sentences **1,6a–d** do not form a text under any normal interpretation of text. On the other hand each of **1,6a–d** can stand alone as a well-formed grammatical sentence, and each is semantically self-contained. These sentences can be re-ordered to form a different text, perhaps:

**7** John accused Mary of leaving the door open when they got back home and found it like that. **8** She denied it, but wouldn't shut it when John asked her to.

This time the 'accusation' is restored to ACCUSE: it is hardly possible in this context to elide this constituent since there is now no context from which it would be recoverable. *Wouldn't* has, this time, lost its subject, but gained its main verb, *shut*, the object of which now turns up as a proform; and *asked* has lost its complement which must now be recovered from the context. Different arrangements of the 'understood' sentences have different consequences in terms of elision, pronominalization, etc., and these processes produce sentence fragments, incapable of standing alone as sentences and relying for their interpretation on context and on the ability of the reader to reconstruct the 'understood' sentences to which they relate.

Such processes can create sentence fragments that relate to almost any part of a sentence. Consider, as well as the examples in **2–5**, **7–8**, the relevant strings from the examples below, which are to be understood as exchanges between two speakers:

**9a** Nobody wants to go to the pictures
**9b** Except John

**10a**   Anybody remember to feed the cat?
**10b**   Yes, Kate did

**11a**   What has John done now?
**11b**   Broken another plate

**12a**   Gill adores pastrami
**12b**   Not adores, just likes

All of these might be appropriate exchanges, and the **b** fragments comprehensible and appropriate in context; all of them rely for their interpretation on the hearer's reconstructing the understood forms to which they relate.

The question arises: What is the status of sentence fragments? If our grammar generates these directly as expansions of the initial S symbol, that leads to an incoherent grammar, and destroys the very foundations of the grammar. We can postulate two sets of rules: firstly grammatical rules which generate full sentences like **1, 6a–d** and a set of 'text formation rules' which produce, *inter alia*, sentence fragments. The rules allow for the ellipsis of contextually recoverable constituents, for inter-sentential proform formation, for the insertion of binding expressions, and so on. Text formation rules depend on linguistic and non-linguistic context. The rules for the formation of sentences, by contrast, are in principle independent of such constraints.

This is an attractive proposal, but it is far from clear whether it can be accomplished in any straightforward fashion. Let us look at the problems. We may begin by drawing a distinction between simple and complex sentences. Suppose simple sentences are those sentences that contain a single main verb, sentences with the sort of structure examined in earlier chapters:

**13**   The dog frightened the cat
       The man put the lamp on the table

Complex sentences are those sentences that can be analysed as consisting of a number of simple sentences. We have already considered (page 134) a sentence like:

**14**   John believes that Bill has married Mary

as having a constituent sentence (*Bill has married Mary*) embedded in a matrix sentence (*John believes NP*). The constituent sentence is traditionally called a subordinate sentence, and the general structure of complex sentences involving

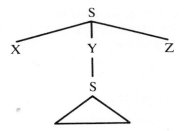

*Figure 67*

subordination can be shown schematically as in Figure 67, where the constituents of the matrix sentence are represented as X, Y, Z and the subordinate sentence is shown as a constituent of one of these constituents.

Many subordinate sentences bear overt markers of subordination. Thus, complementizers like *that* in **14** are markers of subordination, as are items like *when* and *after* in:

**15a** *When Mary came into the room*, John stood up
**15b** *After entering the room*, John took off his coat
**15c** John wanted *Bill to go*
**15d** I don't like *your smoking so much*

In **15** the strings deriving from embedded subordinate sentences are italicized. There are not only overt markers of subordination in complementizers (*that*) and subordinating conjunctions (*when*, etc.), but also grammatical constructions only open to subordinate strings: the 'infinitive construction' (*Bill to go*), and the 'gerund construction' (*your smoking so much*) (the derivation of these constructions is not considered further in this volume.

The distribution of these subordinate constructions can be accounted for in terms of the distribution of the sentence constituent into which they are embedded. Thus NPs with sentences embedded in them operate much like other NPs (see page 135; similarly temporal subordinate sentences (e.g. **15a,b**) form a class with adverbs of time and are distributed like them (cf. page 74).

Subordinate sentences may be important for the strict subcategorization of various lexemes – we have already noted that nouns like RUMOUR and verbs like BELIEVE are subclassified precisely in terms of the fact that they can occur with complement sentences.

Finally, complex subordinate sentences cannot typically be resolved into a string of separate sentences without doing some violence to the dependency relations between the various constituents involved in a single sentence. This is obviously the case with complex sentences like:

**16**  John wanted Bill to go

which do not resolve into anything like:

**17**  *John wanted. Bill was to go

or even

**18**  John wanted something. Bill was to go

since this breaks the relation of dependence: in these forms it is not necessarily the case that 'what John wanted' was for 'Bill to go'. The same argument can be applied, though with perhaps less force, to examples like:

**19a**  Mary left the room because John started talking politics
**19b**  Mary left the room. John started talking politics
**19c**  John started talking politics. Mary left the room

In **19a** the causal relation is explicit. In **19c** the relationship may be causal, but it may equally well not be. In **19b**, even if the relationship is considered causal, and it need not be, the causality is 'reversed'.

The discussion leads to a number of conclusions. Our grammar needs to account for the formation of such sentences as those in **15** – it is not satisfactory to derive them by the use of text formation rules of any sort. The grammar must contain rules that account for strings that often resemble sentence fragments: a point we will return to.

First, however, consider another type of complex sentence, illustrated by:

**20a**  Mary came into the room and John stood up
**20b**  Jane doesn't buy books, but Mary buys a book whenever she passes a bookshop

Such sentences are 'co-ordinate complex sentences', and forms like *and* and *but* are 'co-ordinating conjunctions'. The structure of co-ordinate sentences can be shown schematically as in Figure 68. Comparison with Figure 67 shows ˌthat in subordinate

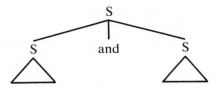

*Figure 68*

constructions the subordinate sentence is embedded in the matrix sentence, but in co-ordinate constructions, the co-ordinate sentences are sisters: one sentence is not subordinate to the other. In principle, then, each of the conjunct sentences should be grammatically independent. Disregarding the conjunctions, this is true of the sentence in **20**, which can be resolved into two separate sentences:

**21** Mary came into the room. John stood up

Now this is not the case for all co-ordinate sentences. Consider, for example, the following:

**22a** John wanted Harry to come and Bill to go
**22b** John uses a fountain pen when writing to his mother and when writing letters to the press
**22c** John asked Mary to shut the door but she wouldn't

In each of these the second conjunct is a string identical to the sort of string seen earlier in the chapter as sentence fragments.

We now find ourselves on the horns of a dilemma. One uncomfortable horn prods us into allowing that sentences like **22** should be generated by our grammar, so the grammar will have rules for producing sentence fragments. The other equally uncomfortable horn goads us into proposing that co-ordinate sentences are formed by text formation rules and not by rules of the grammar at all!

The former position entails an initial rule for the grammar of the sort:

**23** S →S*

(where S* is to be understood as allowing expansions S, S & S, S & S & S, etc.: a similar rule for adjectives was proposed on page 78). This rule enables sentences to be generated of infinite length, identical to texts, except that where texts are typically subdivided into orthographic units the units are simply conjoined by conjunction. Children often produce texts of this sort (*We went to the seaside last Sunday and we played on the sands and Daddy bought us an ice cream and . . .*). This approach also allows us to treat binding expressions (of the sort discussed at the beginning of this chapter) as a form of conjunction, which in many cases they are! But the approach does have problems. We cannot make distributional statements about constituent sentences produced by such a rule since the rule produces no distinct environments we can use. We also need to postulate some set of rules to accommodate sentential sequence, and these rules must take account of matters that go beyond the simple sentence as we have so far considered it. Rules relating to various matters of word order are taken up again in Part three.

The arguments in the preceding paragraph lead to the conclusion that conjoined sentences are not to be considered part of the grammar at all, but are derived by text formation rules. This conclusion is not wholly comfortable, but the logic of the argument seems to force us into this position. It at least has the advantage that it permits us to adopt the definition of the sentence with which we began the chapter: the sentence is an abstract unit, established in order to account for distributional regularities of its constituents. The question of whether there are further distributional regularities between sentences in some larger unit, say the paragraph, is discussed in Part three.

**Technical terms**

co-ordinate sentence

co-ordinating conjunction

sentence

sentence fragment

text formation rules

subordinate sentence

subordinating conjunction

**Exercises**

The Introduction suggested that much of the data actually used by linguists to establish grammar is 'regularized'. In informal conversation we do not typically speak in units that can easily be recognized as grammatical sentences. Here is an extract from a transcription of part of a radio phone-in discussion on police pay. The speaker is a serving policeman. The items in brackets indicate interpolations from the Chairman of the programme.

The symbol + indicates a pause. The symbols *eh um* indicate 'filled pauses'.

> First of all + I would say that + I don't think any    (1)
> policeman wants a + wants a medal for + for eh the
> profession which he's in + (No) every person + eh
> decides + how his eh life is going to + be run (um hum)
> We we'd work seven days shifts we'd be going to have    (5)
> our two days off (Yes) + and + I don't think + eh +
> the people realize about shift allowance in England we
> will receive no shift allowance for this (um hum) um I
> feel that the press eh eh in a lot of cases give us a bad
> publicity (Yes) +eh the article in fact that you have    (10)
> written + you + read this morning about the + the
> Strathclyde eh (Yes) the press reported that + the +
> this would + mean a loss of wages about the overtime
> + about thirty five pounds a week (Yes) well in our
> local force here in the county area + eh we're not    (15)
> actually allowed to be paid for overtime we're told that
> if we want to do overtime then we must + take time
> off for it.

*1*

Make a transcription of the text for publication in a periodical. You should make sure that your transcription follows the usual orthographic conventions about punctuation, etc. and that you write what, in the orthography, are considered to be grammatical sentences.

*2*

Make a note of what sort of things you have left out of your 'cleaned up' version (pauses, filled and unfilled; repetitions; false starts; . . .) and of the sort of things you have found it necessary to add. See if you can formulate these as a set of instructions to a secretary who was asked to do a similar task.

*3*

What is the relationship between the sort of units that are usually held to be sentences and any sort of unit you can discern in the text?

Part two

# Morphology

# 11 Words and morphemes

Hitherto the word has been the smallest constituent with which we have been concerned. It is clear, however, that many words are susceptible to further analysis. Thus in the sentence:

1 The cats attacked the dog

the words *cats* and *attacked* can usefully be further analysed as *cat-s* and *attack-ed*. In other words, words themselves appear to have a constituent structure.

The study of the internal structure of words is called morphology. We do not, however, regard morphology as an independent study, but rather as a bridge between the syntax of a language and its phonology. It is part of syntax insofar as the syntactic study of a language involves the labelling and bracketing of sentence constituents. Since we have regarded words as constituents, the study of the constituent structure of words is logically part of the study of syntax: there is, in principle, no difference between the analysis of the structure of the noun phrase, and the analysis of the structure of the noun. This chapter extends our grammatical description beyond the level of the word, down to the smallest constituents a grammar seeks to account for. On the other hand, morphology is connected to a phonological study of a language insofar as it involves a study of the phonological shapes of words. In this sense morphology cannot be regarded as an independent study, but rather as a bridge between syntax and phonology.

Why, then, should morphology be treated separately? This question has to do with the status of the word as a linguistic unit. Literate people in western cultures do not in general have any difficulty in recognizing the words in their language. Children as they learn to read quickly come to recognize the established practice of the orthography, and for adults the word seems to represent a 'natural' unit. To be sure there are marginal difficulties. In some cases it is not clear whether we should write one word or two (*all right* or *alright?*); in the case of 'compound words' like *windmill, water-mill, flour mill* there is some indeterminacy as to whether these should be written as a single orthographic unit, a hyphenated unit or as two discrete units – an indeterminacy reflected in the practice of dictionary compilers. On the whole, however, literate societies do not find word divisions a great difficulty. In illiterate societies, speakers seem capable of segmenting their utterances into 'word-sized' units; when such languages are eventually reduced to writing there is generally, once more, agreement about the size of the unit established as a word. These facts seem to indicate the unit has some linguistic reality. It is not, however, easy to lay down the criteria by which words are to be identified.

Three sorts of criteria are commonly called on – semantic, grammatical and phonological. A semantic criterion would be that a word is 'a unit of meaning'. This belief is widely held, but how can the definition be made to apply in any straightforward way? For example, *reheat* is a word, yet it appears to have at least two relatively independent units of meaning. The first is the meaning attached to the prefix *re-*, perhaps something like 'again', and found in other words like *rewrite* and so on; the second is the meaning associated with the stem *heat*, and also found as a component of words like *heater*. So if *reheat* is a unit of meaning, is not the string *heat again* also a unit of meaning, though it is agreed to be a sequence of two words? The word *heat* itself seems to have a meaning we can represent as 'make hot', but *make hot* again is a string of two words. Clearly the semantic criterion by itself cannot be made to stand up. On the other hand, the notion that words do have a kind of intuitive semantic unity is not totally to be discarded, particularly for compound words. A *blackboard*, as used in the classroom, is often a piece of 'board' which is 'black' (though with modern technology this is less and less the case!), but the meaning of *blackboard* as a unit word is more than a simple conjunction of the meanings of the two stems from which it is composed, and is different from *black board*, in the sense 'a piece of board which is black'. We shall not call upon a semantic criterion for defining words, but it is not possible, and probably not desirable, to eliminate semantic considerations altogether.

Phonological criteria are more satisfactory. A common

criterion is that of 'potential pause': there is the potentiality for pause between word boundaries, but not within a word. This criterion indicates those points within an utterance where it is possible to insert a 'filled pause' – of the form usually represented orthographically as *er* or *um*. In general this works. The reader should test it by reading, say, this paragraph in this fashion. In most cases it is difficult to conceive of an *er* being interpolated into what are orthographically represented as words – *poss-er-ible* or *fill-er-ed* are unlikely. On the other hand the criterion is not infallible. One may well find, say, *un-er-grammatical*, particularly if a speaker were hesitating between *un-grammatical* and *un-acceptable*. There is no suggestion, of course, that speakers do in fact pause between words in normal speech. On the contrary, particularly in rapid speech, words are 'run together'. This is sometimes recognized in the orthography, regularly in forms like *can't, isn't,* and also in forms like *dunno* (don't know) *wanna* (want to). It is a feature of those humourous books dealing with particular accents of English (*Jew asbestos to believe . . . Do you expect us to believe . . .*). Cases of this sort are usually recognized as instances of two or more words being 'fused' together by quite regular processes in rapid colloquial speech (see the discussion in Brown (1977)). The notion of potential pause tries to capture the generalization that if speakers are to pause within their utterances, they are most likely to pause between what we recognize as words. However, another difficulty is raised: it suggests that the recognition of places at which a pause is possible rests on a prior knowledge of word boundaries. This is a valuable clue to the recognition of word boundaries, but is not in itself criterial.

In some languages other phonological features correlate with word units. Thus in some languages the placement of accent is related to word structure. In Spanish, words ending with a consonant are typically accented on the final syllable (*avión* 'aeroplane'; *generál* 'general'; etc.), and words ending with a vowel are typically accented on the penultimate syllable (*muchácho* 'boy'; *blánco* 'white'; etc.). Other languages have different patterns of accent placement (Czech words are normally accented on the initial syllable; Turkish words on the final syllable; etc.). Some languages have rules of 'vowel harmony', usually associated with word units: in such languages the vowels are divided into two or more 'sets' and in any word all the vowels are chosen from one set: Akan and Turkish are instances. In these cases, however, the criteria for deciding the extent of the unit over which the rules (of accent placement, or of vowel harmony, or whatever) hold is not a simple phonological decision – grammatical criteria also come into consideration (the affixation of suffixes to a word, for example). Such criteria, then, like potential pause, are useful indications, but do not by themselves suffice to identify words.

The most satisfactory criteria are syntactic criteria, among them the 'internal cohesion', and 'external distribution' of a word, and its ability to stand alone as a 'minimal free form'. Together these criteria show that a word has a unity that justifies its treatment as a unit. Consider, for example, the structure of a word like *uninterruptability*. It is probably agreed that we can segment this word as *un-interrupt-abil-ity*. The basis of this segmentation is the recognition that each of these segments can recur in other words, words given a related meaning by the common segment (note that meaning slips in here – it is hard to exclude!): thus we find UN-*intelligent*; *corrupt*-ABIL-ITY; *stupid*-ITY, etc., and the form *interrupt* can itself stand as a word. As far as the 'internal cohesion' of the word is concerned, it is not possible to interpolate any other segments between the segments we have isolated, nor is it possible to rearrange the order of the segments we have isolated. In other words the item is bound together into a unit. This is not generally the case with strings of words – where it is almost always possible to add new items or rearrange the items within the sentence and still maintain a grammatical string. We can see this if we compare *black hat* (*black top hat*, *hat which is black*, etc.) with *blackcap* (in the sense 'type of bird'): and we can compare *blackcap* with *black cap* (*black corduroy cap*, *cap which is black*, etc.).

Similarly in its external distribution a word operates like a unit. Either the whole word must be moved round the sentence or none of it can be moved round the sentence – you cannot move part of a word about. Thus, as the example *black hat* shows, each word is capable of a certain amount of independent movement, but in the case of *blackcap* either the whole word is moved or nothing is moved.

These two criteria are reflected in the ability of a word to stand on its own as an isolate – the definition of a word as a 'minimal free form', which derives from Bloomfield. So, *uninterruptability*, our example, is as an appropriate one-word response to some such request as *Name a syntactic criterion for the identification of a word*. It is impossible to think of a comparable question which yields *abil* as a response (except perhaps *Can you give an example of a segment of a word that cannot stand as an isolate?*). This leads to a distinction between 'free' and 'bound' forms explored further on page 176).

These criteria are in general satisfactory for an identification of words in English. Like all linguistic criteria, they apply to a greater or lesser extent with individual items. For the most part forms that we wish to classify as verbs, nouns, adjectives and adverbs meet the criteria outlined. Some cases are less determinate, particularly compound words like *water-mill*. Other form classes do not so readily fulfill all these criteria. This is particularly the case with articles like *the* or *a*, as Bloomfield himself recognized; these are not usually found as isolates, and they are not usually detachable from the nouns with which they are in construction in an NP (as noted on pages 24–5). On the other hand they are not, in English, bound to their nouns in the way that a prefix like *un-* is bound: we can, for instance, interpolate other items (THE *great grey green greasy Limpopo* RIVER : *the river*). For this reason they are usually considered separate words. Having isolated those units that do fulfill all the criteria noted, other segments, which may fulfill only some of the criteria, must also be treated as words.

The foregoing discussion suggests a certain indeterminacy about the definition of a word: this is indeed the case. On the other hand it does seem to be a unit that is unavoidable, and on to which a number of criteria converge.

At this point we leave discussion of criteria for words, and consider another problem about the use of the term word itself. As Lyons points out (1968, 196 ff.), the word is used in a number of different senses. We need to distinguish between them.

One use is to refer to the actually occurring physical forms. In this sense of the term we can say that in the sentence:

2   John loved Mary once, but he doesn't love her any more

there are eleven words. We shall use the term word form for

this usage: thus we shall say there are eleven word forms in 2.

From time to time it is convenient to make the further distinction between a phonological and an orthographic word form. Orthographic word forms, when used for exemplification are italicized; phonological word forms will be represented in 'phonemic brackets' e.g. *word forms*, /wɜd fɔmz/.

A different usage is illustrated by saying that in 2 *loved* and *love* are different forms of the word LOVE. This use of the term 'word' applies when we say we are going to look up the meaning of a particular word in the dictionary: we do not expect to find an entry for each of the different inflectional forms such as *loved*, *loves*, *loving*, etc. We use the term lexeme to distinguish this usage of the term word. To distinguish lexemes from word forms we always use small capital letters to refer to lexemes, a usage silently followed in previous chapters.

The status of these two terms is rather different. Word forms can, in some sense, be regarded as substantial units, as actually occurring forms; the words written on this page are word forms. The notion of lexeme, on the other hand, is an abstract notion. Word forms like *love*, *loves*, *loved* and *loving* can all be related to the lexeme LOVE, but none of them can be considered actually to be the lexeme LOVE. If we associate the head word of a dictionary entry with the notion lexeme, the lexicographer must choose some word form by which to represent the lexeme in question; the choice of word form is a matter of convention in different languages. In English dictionaries, typically, verbal lexemes are represented by the 'infinitive' form: i.e. LOVE is represented by *love*. The same is true in French and Spanish, so we find *aimer* in a French dictionary and *amar* in a Spanish dictionary. In Latin or Greek dictionaries, however, verbal lexemes are typically represented by the 'first person singular present indicative' form of the verb; thus we find *amo* rather than *amare* (the 'infinitive' form) in a Latin dictionary, and φῐλέω in a Greek dictionary.

We might also note instances of 'homography': when two different words (= lexemes) are orthographically represented by the same word (= word form). Thus the same word form *mace* may realize either the lexeme MACE (1) with the sense 'spice' or the lexeme MACE (2) with the sense 'staff of office' – a fact usually recognized in dictionaries by according each lexeme a different entry.

The difference between these two senses of word is clearly at issue if the question is asked: 'How many different words are there in this chapter?' If we mean word in the sense of word form, then we count each instance of word forms like *is*, *are*, *be*, *was*, *were*, as 'different words', and each instance of word forms like *word* as 'the same word'. If, on the other hand, we mean word in the sense of lexeme, then all the forms *is*, *are*, etc. are different forms of the same word (= lexeme) BE, and we need to distinguish between WORD (1) (= word form) and WORD (2) (= lexeme). It is by no means always clear in word counts which of the two senses is at issue, but they need to be distinguished.

There is, finally, yet a third use of the term 'word' that it is sometimes useful to distinguish; it can be illustrated by comparing the forms *I wrote* and *I have written* with the forms *I laughed* and *I have laughed*. Viewed as word forms, *wrote* and *written* are different word forms, but *laughed* and *laughed* are instances of the same word form. However, from a different point of view, we can describe *wrote* as the 'past tense of WRITE' and *written* as the 'past participle of WRITE' and analogously, the first instance of *laughed* as the 'past tense of LAUGH' and the second instance of *laughed* as the 'past participle of LAUGH'. Syntactic descriptions such as these can be useful; they are called morphosyntactic words. Typically, but not invariably, a morphosyntactic word consists of a lexeme and some associated grammatical description, as in 'past tense of LAUGH', and there is a direct correspondence between a morphosyntactic word and the word form by which it is realized, as in the examples given.

So now we have identified three different senses: in different circumstances we say that *laughed* and *laughed* in the examples given are the same word (= word form); are different forms of the same word (= lexeme); or are different words (= morphosyntactic word)! Unless the context makes it clear which sense is at issue, we need to make a terminological distinction between these three senses of word.

This brings us to another difficulty. The forms *laughed* and *wrote* may, as morphosyntactic words, be described as, respectively, the 'past tense of LAUGH' and the 'past tense of WRITE'. And from a strictly syntactic point of view we wish to be able to describe them in this way. However, whereas *laughed* may, without disagreement, be segmented as *laugh-ed*, no comparable segmentation is possible for the form *wrote*. Furthermore, in the case of *laugh-ed* the segment *laugh* can be identified with the lexeme LAUGH and the segment *-ed* with the description 'past tense'. The principle that permits us to do this is that other word forms can be related to the lexeme LAUGH; for example in *laugh*, *laugh-s*, *laugh-ing* we find the same segment *laugh*; and other past tense forms contain the segment *-ed*, e.g. *kill-ed*, *walk-ed*, *attack-ed*. This suggests the constituent structure analysis of *laughed* shown in Figure 69.

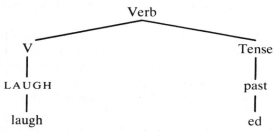

*Figure 69*

But what now do we do with *wrote*? For syntactic description it is clearly advantageous to postulate a similar structure, as in Figure 70

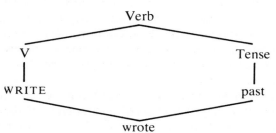

*Figure 70*

since this enables us to account in a systematic way for syntactic descriptions like 'past'. But there is no very satisfactory way to identify part of the word *wrote* as realizing the lexeme WRITE and some other part of the word as realizing the syntactic description 'past tense': rather, the whole form *wrote*, as a unity, realizes the description 'WRITE + past'. For such reasons we will find it advantageous to identify two different sorts of units: one is a set of abstract units, like LAUGH, WRITE and past, which we need for syntactic descriptions, and one a set of units, like *laugh*, *write*, *wrote* and *-ed*, which we need to account for the actual structure of word forms.

To distinguish between these two different sorts of units, we call the grammatical units morphemes, and the word forms, or segments of word forms, morphs as shown in Figure 71.

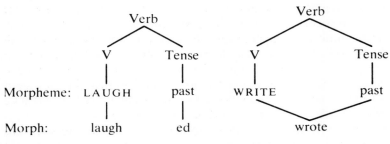

*Figure 71*

The relationship between morpheme and morph is called realization. Thus, the string of morphemes {WRITE + past} is realized by the single morph *wrote*; the morpheme {LAUGH} is realized by the morph *laugh*; and the morpheme {past} is realized (except in cases like those mentioned above) by the morph *-ed*.

The morpheme is an abstract unit, a unit that is part of the syntactic description; from the point of view of the syntactic description it matters little whether a single morpheme is realized by a single morph, as is the case of the relationship between {LAUGH} and *laugh*; or whether a string of morphemes is realized as a single morph, as is the case of the relationship between {WRITE + past} and *wrote*.

The morph, on the other hand, is a substantial unit, a word or part of a word form. When a word form can be segmented into smaller units, which cannot in their turn be segmented, these smaller units are morphs. Within words we show morph boundaries by using hyphens (e.g. *laugh-ed*). Thus word forms may either consist of single morphs (as *wrote*, which we consider to be unsegmentable) or of a string of morphs (as *laugh-ed*).

In these terms a morpheme is not part of a word form at all: it is an abstract element whose distribution is determined by the syntactic description: the relationship between a word form, or the morph(s) that compose it, and a morpheme or string of morphemes, is one of realization: a morph realizes a morpheme or a string of morphemes. To distinguish morph from morpheme in discussion we enclose morphemes in curly brackets, and we show morphs, like word forms, of which they may be part, by italic letters: thus the morpheme {past} and the morph *-ed*.

Further reasons for this distinction will emerge. We may offer here a number of examples that show the general principle: that the morpheme is a unit that is accounted for in the syntactic description, and that the morph is a unit that accounts for the formation of words; that the morpheme is an abstract and the morph a substantial unit. This enables us to free syntactic descriptions from an unnecessarily close identification with word forms or morphs, and allows us to postulate in the syntactic descriptions those units, morphemes, that are useful for a syntactic description. Conversely it allows us to study the structure of words without necessarily seeking a syntactic correlation for every morph we may wish to postulate.

We have already discussed examples like:

   **3**   walk-ed; laugh-ed; ran; wrote; went

Syntactically speaking they all represent the past tense of the verbal lexeme concerned – {WALK + past} ... {GO + past} – irrespective of the fact that in the first two examples the morphemes concerned correspond directly with one of the morphs we wish to identify; whereas in the last three examples the words are not readily segmentable.

Next consider the forms:

|  |  |  |
|---|---|---|
| **4a** | large | larg-er |
| **4b** | bad | worse |
| **4c** | foolish | more foolish |

Forms like those in the left-hand column have traditionally been called the 'simple' forms of the adjectives concerned (LARGE, BAD, FOOLISH), and the forms in the right-hand column the 'compared' forms. Simple adjectives have a different distribution from compared adjectives:

   **5a**   My house is large, but yours is larger than mine
   **5b**   My essay is bad, but yours is worse than mine
   **5c**   My opinions are foolish, but yours are more foolish than mine

It would not be possible to interchange the simple and compared forms:

6   *My opinions are more foolish, but yours are foolish than mine

From a syntactic point of view we describe all of the compared forms as having the same structure – let us say {comp(ared) + Adj} although in word formation all three forms are different: *larg-er* consists of two morphs, *worse* is a single unsegmentable word form, and *more foolish* is two separate word forms – and furthermore the morph realizing {comp} in this case precedes the adjective stem, whereas in the case of *larg-er* it follows. For syntactic description we need one type of statement, but for word formation we need another type.

This brings us to our final example for the present. Consider the word *foolish* in example 5c. *foolish* itself may be considered as segmentable into morphs *fool-ish* on the analogy of other forms, like *fool*, *fool-hardy*, on the one hand, and *boy-ish*, *girl-ish* on the other. This brings us to a distinction often drawn between 'derivational' and 'inflectional' morphology. Derivational morphology is concerned with those rules by which new lexemes can be formed; thus from the noun *fool* we can derive the adjective *foolish* by the addition of the morph *-ish*; similarly, from the noun *morpheme* we can derive the adjective *morphemic* or the verb *morphemicize* (= to analyse into morphemes). Typically each of these forms is represented by a separate dictionary entry – FOOL, FOOLISH, MORPHEME, MORPHEMIC, MORPHEMICIZE – and for this reason we consider them separate lexemes, and derivational morphology to be the set of rules by which new lexemes can be formed. Inflectional morphology, on the other hand, is concerned with the syntactic rules by which a lexeme and its associated grammatical morphemes are realized. Thus inflectional morphology relates the lexeme FOOL to the forms *fool* and *fools*, the lexeme MORPHEMICIZE to the forms *morphemicizes*, *morphemicizing*, *morphemicized* and so on. Typically, as we have observed, these latter forms are not found in a dictionary, and we do not consider them lexemes. But to return to *foolish*. From the point of view of the syntax, it is irrelevant whether *foolish* is a simple, underived, adjective, like *large*, or whether it is derivationally a complex form *foolish*. For syntax we only need to know that *foolish* is an adjective, since the syntax can then assign to it the additional morpheme {comp} to yield the appropriate compared form. This last example, then, is a word which can quite legitimately be analysed further into morphs, but where this morphological analysis is irrelevant to the syntactic description. In other words, *foolish* realizes the single morpheme FOOLISH. Its compositional analysis into *fool-ish* is a matter for the derivational morphology and not for the syntax. (We discuss the status of word forming morphs like *-ish* on pages 222–7.)

We conclude that the compositional structure of words is to some degree independent of the syntactic description of a sentence. It is thus necessary to distinguish between the morpheme – an abstract unit whose distribution is accounted for by the syntax – and the morph – a substantial unit whose distribution is not wholly accounted for by the syntax.

**Technical terms**

| | |
|---|---|
| derivational morphology | morphosyntactic word |
| homographs | orthographic words |
| inflectional morphology | phonological words |
| lexeme | potential pause |
| morph | realization |
| morpheme | word form |

# 12  Morphemes and morphs

## Morphemes

In the preceding chapter we described the morpheme as an abstract unit whose distribution is accounted for in the syntax. We described strings such as {LAUGH + past}, {BOY + plur} and {LARGE + comp} as strings of morphemes. There are two distinct types of morpheme: items like {LAUGH}, {BOY}, and {LARGE}; and items like {past}, {plur}, and {comp}. The former type we call lexical morphemes, or lexemes, and the latter grammatical morphemes. There is an important distinction between them.

Lexical morphemes, lexemes, are listed in the lexicon, and are inserted into syntactic derivations by a lexical insertion rule, in the manner described on page 94 (though these rules need some amendment now that we have embarked on a morphological description). Lexical morphemes, we have seen, are inserted in tree diagrams under terminal nodes labelled Noun, Verb, Adjective, etc. Terminal nodes of this sort are called lexical category nodes, since lexemes are inserted beneath these nodes, and, as we have seen, lexemes can be categorized into classes of Noun, Verb, etc. Classes like Noun, Verb, etc. we call lexical categories; in the lexicon each lexeme needs to be characterized in terms of the lexical category to which it belongs.

Lexical categories are, in principle, open; it does not seem possible to list exhaustively the membership of any major lexical category, since it is always possible to introduce new items. Thus, in English, the category of Noun can be extended by the addition of new members as cultural needs dictate; a new artifact, for example, is often given a name, and this name, syntactically, is a noun. Nor is it the business of a syntactic description of a language to determine the total distribution of a particular lexeme: other considerations are important, particularly semantic restrictions of the sort discussed (pages 85–8) as selection restrictions. Thus, while the syntax determines the distribution of the category Noun, the total distribution of a particular noun is only in part determined by the syntax.

Grammatical morphemes, items like {past}, {non-past}, {sing}, {pl}, etc., are somewhat different. These morphemes too can be grouped into categories, such as tense or number, which we call grammatical categories. The important distinction between lexical and grammatical categories is twofold. The first distinction is that whereas the membership of a lexical category is in general open, the membership of a grammatical category is closed: it is possible to list exhaustively the membership of grammatical categories. Thus, in English, the category number has two terms – we shall refer to members of grammatical categories as 'terms' in the particular category at issue – singular and plural. These two terms are established by the fact that there is, in English, just this opposition possible in this category and no other. It is not a necessary characteristic of any language that there should be just two terms in the category number; some languages have a third term, dual, characteristically applied to objects that occur typically in pairs. Thus in classical Greek we find:

| *Singular* | *Dual* | *Plural* |
|---|---|---|
| ὁ πούς | τώ πόδε | οἱ πόδες |
| 'the foot' | 'the (2) feet' | 'the feet' |

Note the formal contrast between the noun forms, echoed by the concordial forms of the article (ὁ – τώ – οἱ). Such a formal contrast is not available in English, so we say that English has only two terms in its number system. The number of terms in a grammatical category is determined by formal characteristics of the language in question and cannot be assumed in advance.

The second distinction between grammatical morphemes and lexemes is that the distribution of purely grammatical categories is, in principle, describable purely within the syntax. This distinction can best be illustrated by the following fragment of a grammar:

*Constituent structure rules:*

$$S \rightarrow NP + VP$$

$$VP \rightarrow V + NP$$

$$V \rightarrow Verb + Tense$$

$$Tense \rightarrow \begin{cases} past \\ non\text{-}past \end{cases}$$

$$NP \rightarrow Art + N$$

$$N \rightarrow Noun + Number$$

$$Number \rightarrow \begin{cases} sing \\ pl \end{cases}$$

*Lexical rules:*

Noun → {BOY, DOG, CAT, HOUSE, . . .}

Verb → {FRIGHTEN, AMUSE, . . .}

In this grammar the distribution of morphemes like {past} or {sing} is totally determined by the constituent structure rules. On the other hand, whereas the distribution of the class Noun or Verb is determined by the constituent structure rules, the distribution of an individual noun – HOUSE, say – is determined in part by the distribution of the class Noun, but also by semantic considerations which are external to the syntax proper.

Having drawn this distinction, we can observe that in many languages certain grammatical categories are typically associated with certain lexical categories. In English the category of tense is typically associated with verbs. So the morphs associated with the morpheme {past}, orthographically realized as *-ed* are found in verb words (*kill-ed*, *walk-ed*, etc.) not in noun words. Conversely the grammatical category of definiteness is realized in English by articles, which, although they are not affixed to nouns, only occur in association with nouns, (*the man*, *a walk*, etc.).

A further distinction commonly used in grammatical discussions is between grammatical and lexical words. Grammatical words are those words that realize only grammatical morphemes; lexical words are those items whose stems realize lexemes. This is why it is possible to recognize in nonsense poetry the fact that the poem is, in some sense, in English:

> 'Twas brillig and the slithy toves
> Did gyre and gimble in the wabe.

The grammatical words are all clearly English – *and*, *the*, *did* – it is the lexical words that have 'nonsense' stems – *tove*, *gyre*, *gimble*, *wabe*. Take *slithy* for instance; it is in the syntactic position for an adjective (Art Adj N), and it has the morph -*y*, a common marker of a derivational process deriving adjectives from nouns (cf. *slime*: *slimy*; *grime*: *grimy*, etc.). There are lexical classes truly open to new membership. On the other hand it would probably be impossible to interpret 'nonsense' where the lexical stems were related to 'regular' English lexemes, but where the 'grammatical' words were nonsense.

### Morphs

When a word form can be analysed into smaller forms, which cannot themselves be analysed into yet smaller forms, the smaller forms are morphs. A morph is thus a word form or part of a word form. Word forms that can be analysed into a string of two or more morphs we call morphologically complex. Word forms that consist of a single morph we call morphologically simple: *walk-ed* is morphologically complex; *went* or *ran* is morphologically simple.

A morph that can stand alone as a word is a free morph: *boy*, *tea*, *time*, *half*, *back*, *happy*, *long* are free morphs. A morph incapable of standing alone as a word is a bound morph: -*ish*, *un*-, -*ed*, -*ness* in *boy-ish*, *un-happy*, *walk-ed*, *good-ness* are bound morphs. We show bound morphs preceded or followed by a hyphen, e.g. -*ish*, -*un*.

By definition a morphologically simple word must consist of a single free morph. A morphologically complex word may consist of a free and a bound morph (*boy-ish*, *un-happy*, *good-ness*, etc.), two free morphs (*tea-time*, *half-back*, etc.), or any appropriate combination of free and bound morphs.

In discussing morphologically complex words it is convenient to have some terminology for various different types of constituent. That part of a word form to which derivational or inflectional affixes can be added is a *stem*. A stem may be morphologically simple or morphologically complex; a morphologically simple stem is often called a *root*. An *affix* is an inflectional or derivational morph added to a stem. Affixes which precede their stem are *prefixes*; affixes which follow their stem are *suffixes*; and affixes inserted within their stem are *infixes*.

So, for example, in the forms *duck*, *duck-ling* and *duckling-s*: *duck* consists of just a simple root; *duck-ling* consists of the stem *duck*, which is also a root, and the derivational suffix *-ling*; and *duckling-s* consists of the stem *duckling*, which is not a root because it is morphologically complex, and the inflectional suffix *-s*.[1]

Prefixes and suffixes can easily be illustrated in English. *im-*, *un-* and *pre-* are prefixes in the words *im-possible*, *un-likely* and *pre-fix*; *-ed*, *-ment* and *-ly* are suffixes in *walk-ed*, *conceal-ment* and *ungentleman-ly*. Infixes do not regularly occur in English, though one might consider *im-bloody-possible* as a peculiar example of infixation. Infixation does, however, occur in children's 'secret' languages. A quite widely spoken secret language, sometimes called "aigy-paigy", is formed by infixing the syllable *aig* (pronounced /eig/ as in the proper name C*r*aig) before every vowel nucleus of 'regular' English: *Thaigis aigis haigow yaigou taigalk saigecraigetlaigy* − th-is -is h-ow y-ou t-alk s-ecr-et-ly. In this language *aig* is an infix in a word like th-is, yielding th-aig-is. Many semitic languages are analysed as containing infixes: in modern Arabic, a root like k-t-b 'write' appears in words like *katab* 'he wrote', *kita:b* 'book', and, with prefixes, *ma-ka:tib* 'places for writing, studies', *ma-ktab* 'places for writing, study', *je-ktab* 'he is writing'; similarly the root g-l-s appears in *galas* 'he sat', *ga:lis* 'sitting person', *ma-ga:lis* 'councils' *ma-glas* 'council' (Bloomfield 1935, 243–4).

Hitherto many of our examples have been recorded in the traditional orthography; we should, however, also consider examples involving phonological as well as the orthographic form. Consider the following plural forms in English:

---

1 Sometimes a further terminological distinction is drawn between stems to which inflectional elements can be added, which are called stems, and stems to which derivational elements are added, which are called bases. Thus *duck* in *duck-ling* is a base, since *-ling* is a derivational affix; and *duckling* in *duckling-s* is a stem, since *-s* is an inflectional affix.

| buses | /bʌs-ɪz/ | hats | /hat-s/ | hags | /hag-z/ |
|---|---|---|---|---|---|
| cheeses | /tʃiz-ɪz/ | sacks | /sak-s/ | bags | /bag-z/ |
| bushes | /buʃ-ɪz/ | maps | /map-s/ | knobs | /nɒb-z/ |
| garages | /garɑʒ-ɪz/ | proofs | /pruf-s/ | eaves | /iv-z/ |
| patches | /patʃ-ɪz/ | moths | /mɒθ-s/ | lathes | /leið-z/ |
| judges | /dʒʌdʒ-ɪz/ | | | bees | /bi-z/ |
| | | | | paws | /pɔ-z/ |

Three distinct morphs realize plural in English: /-ɪz/, /-z/ and /-s/. When a particular morpheme is realized by a series of different morphs, the alternative realizations are called allomorphs. In the example above the distribution of these allomorphs is determined by phonological characteristics of the stem final segment, thus:

/-ɪz/    occurs after stems ending in /s, z, ʃ, ʒ, tʃ, dʒ/ i.e. after stems ending in a sibilant, voiced or voiceless
/-z/    occurs after stems ending in a voiced segment other than a sibilant
/-s/    occurs after stems ending in a voiceless segment other than a sibilant

When the distribution of allomorphs can be described in phonological terms, the allomorphs are said to be phonologically conditioned.

In the example quoted there is some phonological similarity between the appropriate allomorph and the stem to which it is affixed: /s/ and /z/ are voiceless and voiced alveolar fricatives, affixed to stems ending in voiceless and voiced segments. There is no need for phonological conditioning to involve phonological similarity. Thus in the following data from Tsotsil (taken from Nida 1949) we find dissimilation – i.e. the affixes are phonologically dissimilar in a regular fashion from the stem vowels:

| 1 | -k'uʃ | *wedge* | 1a | -k'uʃi | *to put a wedge in* |
|---|---|---|---|---|---|
| 2 | -ʃik' | *prop used beneath an object* | 2a | -ʃik'u | *to put a prop under* |
| 3 | -ʃon | *prop used against an object* | 3a | -ʃoni | *to put a prop against* |
| 4 | -vov | *crazy* | 4a | -vovi | *to go crazy* |
| 5 | t'uʃ | *wet* | 5a | -tuʃi | *to become wet* |

The suffix is /-i/ (a front vowel) when the stem vowel is /u/ or /o/ (both back vowels), and /-u/ (a back vowel) when the stem vowel is /i/ (a front vowel). There may indeed be no phonological similarity at all between stems and phonologically conditioned affixes (Tojolabal data from Nida 1949):

| 1 | -man | *to buy* | 7 | -al | *to say* |
|---|------|----------|---|-----|----------|
| 2 | hman | *I buy* | 8 | awal | *you (sg) say* |
| 3 | -il | *to see* | 9 | -lap | *to dress* |
| 4 | kil | *I see* | 10 | -slap | *he dresses* |
| 5 | -k'an | *to want* | 11 | -u | *to drink* |
| 6 | ak'an | *you (sg) want* | 12 | yu | *he drinks* |

Given this limited amount of data the affixes appear to be as follows:

| '1st person' (examples **2, 4**) | /h-/ preceding consonants |
| | /k-/ preceding vowels |
| '2nd person' (examples **6, 8**) | /a-/ preceding consonants |
| | /-aw-/ preceding vowels |
| '3rd person' (examples **10, 12**) | /s-/ preceding consonants |
| | /y-/ preceding vowels |

If this analysis accurately represents the situation in the language as a whole, we see that in the case of the '1st' and '3rd' person pronouns there appears no obvious phonological similarity between the preconsonantal and prevocalic allomorphs: the distribution, however, is clearly phonologically conditioned.

The selection of allomorphs is not always phonologically conditioned. There may be other conditioning factors. Consider the following data, from English:

| house | /haus/ | houses | /hauz-iz/ |
|-------|--------|--------|-----------|
| calf | /kɑf/ | calves | /kɑv-z/ |
| elf | /ɛlf/ | elves | /ɛlv-z/ |
| sheaf | /ʃif/ | sheaves | /ʃiv-z/ |
| wife | /waif/ | wives | /waiv-z/ |
| bath | /bɑθ/ | baths | /bɑð-z/ |
| path | /pɑθ/ | paths | /pɑð-z/ |

The distribution of the plural affixes (in the right-hand column) is entirely regular, and follows the rules for English plurals given above. The stem in this case shows allomorphic variation: /haus/ : /hauz-/ etc. There appears to be no phonological reason for this alternation, since comparable forms are entirely regular:

| piece | /pis/ | pieces | /pis-iz/ | not | */piz-iz/ |
|-------|-------|--------|----------|-----|-----------|
| reef  | /rif/ | reefs  | /rif-s/  | not | */riv-z/  |

and indeed the 'possessive' forms are entirely regular:

| wife  | /waif/ | wives  | /waiv-z/ | wife's   | /waif-s/ |
|-------|--------|--------|----------|----------|----------|
| youth | /juθ/  | youths | /juð-z/  | youth's  | /juθ-s/  |

If you check, the allomorphs for the possessive (e.g. *wife's*), are identical to those for plural.

We are thus forced to say that with items like (HOUSE) the allomorph /hauz-/ is chosen in the environment {__ plural}. When the selection of the appropriate allomorph is determined by circumstances which cannot be described phonologically, then these allomorphs are said to be grammatically conditioned.

Grammatically conditioned affixes in English include the plural affixes -*im* and -*en* in:

| kibbutz | kibbutz-im |
| seraph  | seraph-im  |
| ox      | ox-en      |

These irregular forms include loans (kibbutzim) and linguistic 'fossils' (oxen).

Occasionally morphs may be in free variation: in such cases it does not matter which of two (or perhaps more) allomorphs is chosen. Thus the forms *burned* and *burnt* seem to be free variants.

| I burned . . .      | I burnt . . .      |
| I have burned . . . | I have burnt . . . |

If this is the case, then /-d/ and /-t/ are in free variation as realizations of the morphemes past and past participle in construction with {BURN}.

The grammar may sometimes have a morphemic distinction when there is no overt marker of this particular distinction in actual word forms. In such cases a 'zero' morph or allomorph is sometimes postulated. This is usually represented by Ø. Zero allomorphs are often postulated when the structure of a series of related forms is such that there is a 'significant absence' of a formal marker at some point in the series: e.g., with English noun plurals we find:

boy – boys; dog – dogs; ox – oxen, etc.

but

sheep – sheep; salmon – salmon; grouse – grouse, etc.
cf.
I shot two dogs yesterday
I shot two grouse yesterday
*I shot two grouses yesterday

We can postulate that the plural form of GROUSE is *grouse-∅*.

Zero morphs are sometimes postulated when the general structure suggests a zero element. For example, in Totonac the subject pronouns are as follows:

| k- | first person singular | -tit | second person plural |
|----|----------------------|------|---------------------|
| -wi | first person plural | ∅- | third person singular |
| -ti | second person singular | -'qu | third person plural |

The third person singular is never indicated overtly; i.e. it has no obvious form. The absence of some other form indicates the third singular. Structurally this is a type of significant absence (Nida 1949, 46).

Zero should be used sparingly since it can lead to abuses. Consider the following ways of looking at the structure of English singular and plural nouns.

1   Suppose we analyse the singular forms of nouns as consisting of the simple stem with no marker at all: then we may say that *boy* differs from *boys* in that the former represents the single morpheme {BOY} and the latter the two morphemes {BOY + pl}: *boy* consists of a single morph, and *boy-s* of two morphs. Under this analysis *grouse* (singular) represents the single morpheme GROUSE and *grouse* (plural) the two morphemes {GROUSE + pl}: *grouse* (singular) consists of a single morph, and *grouse* (plural) of the two morphs *grouse-∅*.

2   Suppose now that we consider the absence of a marker of singular in nouns as a form of 'significant absence' (cf. above).

We might then say that the form *boy* represented the two morphemes {BOY + sing}: and the form *boys* the morphemes {BOY + pl}. Now {sing} is represented by the morph $\emptyset$. Thus *boy* consists of the two morphs *boy-$\emptyset$*, and *boys* of the two morphs *boy-s*. Analogously *grouse* (singular) consists of the two morphs *grouse-$\emptyset$* and *grouse* (plural) of the two morphs *grouse-$\emptyset$*. In the former case $\emptyset$ is the invariant morph representing {sing} and in the latter case $\emptyset$ is an allomorph of {pl}!

### Realization rules

The relationship between morpheme and morph is described as 'realization'. Thus in the form *walk-ed*, *walk* realizes the lexeme WALK and *-ed* realizes the grammatical morpheme {past}. This entails a new set of rules, 'morphological realization rules'. These are those rules that realize the various morphemes, lexical and grammatical, introduced by the grammar.

Our total description now has three sets of rules:

**i** Constituent structure rules. These develop constituent structures as far as the terminal symbols of the grammar. The terminal symbols are either lexical category symbols (N, V, Adj, etc.) or terms from grammatical categories (past, sing, pl, etc.).

**ii** Lexical rules, or a lexical insertion rule and an associated lexicon. We have already noted that, in the grammars we are dealing with, these produce the same effect, but that we would prefer to use a lexical insertion rule. In the example which follows, however, it is convenient (for lack of space) to use a lexical rule.

**iii** Morphological realization rules. These rules introduce the appropriate morphs that correspond to the grammatical or lexical morphemes introduced in **i** and **ii**. Realization rules can be formulated either as rules which introduce phonologically specified items (i.e. items specified in phonological terms) or orthographically specified items. We use both kinds at various stages of our account. The rules that follow, to exemplify the principle, are formulated as rules which introduce phonologically specified morphs.

The data we will seek to account for represents the formation of some singular and plural, and possessive forms of English nouns. Our data is as follows:

|                  | BOY    | CAT    | BUS     | GROUSE   |
| ---------------- | ------ | ------ | ------- | -------- |
| N                | bɔi    | kat    | bʌs     | graus    |
| N + poss         | bɔiz   | kats   | bʌsɪz   | grausɪz  |
| N + pl           | bɔiz   | kats   | bʌsɪz   | graus    |
| N + pl + poss    | bɔiz   | kats   | bʌsɪz   | grausɪz  |

|                  | SHEEP  | WIFE   | DWARF   |
| ---------------- | ------ | ------ | ------- |
| N                | ʃip    | waif   | dwɒf    |
| N + poss         | ʃips   | waifs  | dwɒfs   |
| N + pl           | ʃip    | waivz  | dwɒvz   |
| N + pl + poss    | ʃips   | waivz  | dwɒvz   |

*Constituent structure rule:*

1  N → NS (+ pl)(+ poss)          NS = Noun stem
                                          pl = plural
                                          poss = possessive

*Lexical rule:*

2  NS → {BOY, CAT, BUS, GROUSE, SHEEP,
            WIFE, DWARF, . . .}

*Morphological realization rules:*

| 3  | DWARF  | → | /dwɑv-/  | in the environment __ pl |
|    |        |   | /dwɒf/   | elsewhere |
| 4  | WIFE   | → | /waiv-/  | in the environment __ pl |
|    |        |   | /waif/   | elsewhere |
| 5  | SHEEP  | → | /ʃip/    | |
| 6  | GROUSE | → | /graus/  | |
| 7  | BUS    | → | /bʌs/    | |
| 8  | CAT    | → | /kat/    | |
| 9  | BOY    | → | /bɔi/    | |
| 10 | pl     | → | Ø        | in the environment /graus/__ |
|    |        |   |          | or /ʃip/__ |
| 11 | poss   | → | Ø        | in the environment pl__ |
|    |        |   | /-ɪz/    | in the environment sibilant C__ |
|    |        |   | /-s/     | in the environment voiceless C__ |
|    |        |   | /-z/     | elsewhere |
| 12 | pl     | → | /-ɪz/    | in the environment sibilant C__ |
|    |        |   | /-s/     | in the environment voiceless C__ |
|    |        |   | /-z/     | elsewhere |

*Some typical derivations:*

| Rule | | Rule | |
|---|---|---|---|
| **1** | NS + pl + poss | | |
| **2** | BOY + pl + poss | **2** | WIFE + pl + poss |
| **9** | /bɔi/ + pl + poss | **4** | /waiv/ + pl + poss |
| **11** | /bɔi/ + pl | **11** | /waiv/ + pl |
| **12** | /bɔi-z/ | **12** | /waiv-z/ |

*Rule*
**2**   GROUSE + pl + poss
**6**   /graus/ + pl + poss
**10**  /graus/ + poss
**11**  /graus-ɪz/

Rules **3**, **4** and **10–12** introduce allomorphs: where the environment is specified in phonological terms these are phonologically conditioned allomorphs; where the environment is grammatically conditioned they are grammatically conditioned allomorphs.

Rules **10** and **11** introduce zero elements.

Rules **3–9** introduce bases.

Rules **11**, **12** introduce suffixes.

You might like to think of the rules as formulaic statements of ordinary language statements, with which we hope you agree, like: **3** DWARF has two stems /dwɒv-/, which is a bound form, occurs in plural forms, and /dwɒf/, which is a free form, elsewhere; **11** the genitive is not marked separately in the plural form of nouns (except with nouns like GROUSE, SHEEP, which have no plural marker accounted for by rule **10**); where it is marked the marker is an affix /-ɪz/, /-z/ or /-s/ as appropriate.

Note that the rules must be applied in the order stated. For instance rules **10–12** must be in this order. Try using them as in the derivations above in the reverse order – you will get wrong answers:

**1**   NS + pl + poss
**2**   BUS + pl + poss
**7**   /bʌs/ + pl + poss
**12**  /bʌs-ɪz/ + gen
**11**  /bʌs-ɪz-ɪz/

SHEEP + pl + poss
**5**   /ʃip/ + pl + poss
**12**  /ʃip-s/ + poss
**11**  /ʃip-s-ɪz/
(rule **10** cannot apply since the environment in which it ought to have applied is gone)

**Technical terms**

| | |
|---|---|
| allomorph | lexical morpheme |
| base | lexical word |
| bound morph | morph |
| category | morpheme |
| derivational affix | morphological realization rule |
| derivational morphology | morphologically complex |
| free morph | morphologically simple |
| free variation | phonological conditioning |
| grammatical category | prefix |
| grammatical conditioning | realization rule |
| grammatical morpheme | root |
| grammatical word | stem |
| infix | suffix |
| inflectional morphology | term (in a grammatical category) |
| lexical category | zero |

# 13   The analysis of words

We have distinguished between the morpheme (a distributional unit of the syntax) and the morph (a distributional unit connected with word formation). The relationship between the two we have called realization, and we have seen that the relationship between morpheme and morph is not always one-to-one. In this chapter we look at how the sort of analysis we establish can be accommodated in a grammar containing the three types of rules discussed in the last chapter: constituent structure rules, lexical rules, and morphological realization rules.

Our data will be extremely limited, but are sufficient to illustrate the problems. The data are the forms of the nouns and verbs in simple sentences like

    **1a**  The boy yawned
    **1b**  The boys yawned
    **1c**  The boys yawn
    **1d**  The boy yawns

Note that we must consider these forms in sentences, rather than in isolation since the morpheme, as a syntactic unit, has implications that go beyond purely word formation.

Let us first consider the apparently straightforward description of the singular and plural forms of English nouns. The 'regular' paradigm for English nouns is illustrated in such pairs as:

    **2**  *singular*    *plural*
       boy        boys
       girl       girls

The paradigm is called regular since it applies to the vast majority of English nouns, and applies to all new borrowings (e.g. *sputnik* : *sputniks*). For simplicity we shall take our examples from the written rather than the spoken form of the language and do not consider questions of allomorphy: so we consider the regular plural morph to be simply *-s*. Since we have distinguished between morph and morpheme, in analysing forms such as those in **2** we need to distinguish a morphological analysis (= analysis into morphs) from a morphemic analysis (= an identification of the morpheme or morphemes realized by a particular morph).

The principal criterion for a morphological analysis is a formal difference between a set of words. *Boy* and *boys* differ in that the former lacks and the second contains the morph *-s*. This formal distinction is shared by other nouns (*girl* : *girl-s*; *cat* : *cat-s*, etc.) and leads us to analyse *boys* into two morphs *boy-s*, and *boy* into a single morph *boy*. The formal analysis also has a semantic justification: the form *boy* is found in sentences appropriately applied to situations describing a single young male human; and the form *boys* in sentences appropriately applied to situations describing more than one young male human. Since *boy* is common to both words, we assume that this is the form associated with the semantic notion of 'young male human'; and since *boys* contains the additional morph *-s* we assume that this can be associated with the semantic notion of 'more than oneness'. The semantic criterion reinforces our formal analysis. It is convenient to refer to *boy* as a lexical stem and *-s* as the 'plural marker'.

As far as a morphemic analysis (= an identification of the relevant morphemes) is concerned, we again find formal and semantic criteria. The *boy* part of either word can be related to the lexeme BOY. The alternation between the simple form *boy* and the complex form *boy-s* is accounted for by postulating a category of number with the two terms {sing(ular)} and {pl(ural)}, such that *boy* realizes the morphemes {BOY + sing}, and *boys* realizes the morphemes {BOY + pl}. The formal identification of these morphemes, however, can involve considerations beyond those which apply to single words, since there are wider considerations involving the structure of whole sentences. We note, for example, that in sentences like **1c, 1d** the difference in form between *boy* and *boys* is matched by a difference in form between the verbs *yawns* and *yawn*. This difference is systematic in that it is replicated in other similar pairs of sentences (*the cat walks*; *the cats walk*, etc.); the systematic difference between the subject nouns is matched by a difference in the verb word. We shall later identify this too as an alternation in number, and it is convenient to have the same system operating in the verb as in the noun. To facilitate this, it is covenient to match morphemes in both words. This lends additional support to the analysis of *boy* as realizing the morphemes {BOY + sing}, and *boys* as realizing the morphemes {BOY + pl}. As far as semantic considerations are concerned, with the particular pairs of items in **2** we have no further observations to add to those made for the morphological analysis since we need to account for the same distinction.

Using our analysis, we can formalize our description into the following little grammar for the NP:

**3**  *Constituent structure rules:*

$$\text{NP} \rightarrow \text{Art} + \text{Noun}$$
$$\text{Noun} \rightarrow \text{N} + \text{Number}$$
$$\text{Number} \rightarrow \left\{ \begin{matrix} \text{sing} \\ \text{pl} \end{matrix} \right\}$$

*Lexical rule:*
N → {BOY, GIRL . . .}

This grammar generates the trees in Figures 72 and 73.

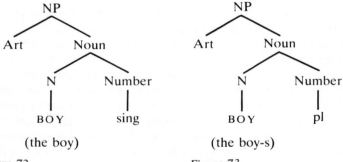

| (the boy) | (the boy-s) |
|-----------|-------------|
| *Figure 72* | *Figure 73* |

Already there is a problem. In Figure 73 each of the morphemes can be related to a single morph (Art: *the*; BOY: *boy*; pl: *-s*) but what about Figure 72? We appear to have too many morphemes.

Before we examine this problem further, consider some of the 'irregular' noun forms in English:

**4**  | *sing* | *pl* |
|-------|------|
| man   | men  |
| mouse | mice |
| goose | geese |

There appears to be no acceptable segmentation of the plural forms here: i.e. no morphological analysis is possible. A morphemic analysis, however, is clearly possible, and exactly the same considerations that applied to the morphemic analysis of **2** applies to the forms in **4**. We want to say that *man* realizes the morpheme string {MAN + sing} and *men* the morpheme string {MAN + pl}. This implies that we can expand our lexical rule in **3** to:

**5**  N → {BOY, GIRL, MAN, MOUSE, GOOSE, . . .}

Let us now turn to morphological realization rules. Consider first the plural forms. As far as the rules for forms like *boys* are concerned, no great problem arises. We can have quite straightforward rules of the form:

**6**  BOY → *boy*
  pl → *-s*

Informally we call rules of this sort 'agglutinative' rules: such rules have a single morpheme on the left-hand side of the rule matched to a single morph on the right-hand side. As far as rules for forms like *men* are concerned, we can, since we have decided that these forms are unsegmentable, have rules of the form:

**7**  MAN + pl → *men*

We call rules like this 'fusional': fusional rules have two morphemes on the left-hand side of the rule matched to a single morph on the right-hand side. A rule like this seems to capture well the fact that *men* is unsegmentable, and that it realizes two morphemes.

Rules like **7** are no longer simple 'rewrite' rules, as defined on pages 40–3, since there are two items on the left-hand side of the rule. A rule like this is in fact a transformational rule. We shall find that morphological realization rules are of a 'mixed' nature, but this will not detain us here.

Let us now turn to the singular forms. There are a number of possible solutions. We can suggest a fusional type of realization rule here too:

**8**  BOY + sing → *boy*

We might alternatively say that BOY corresponds to *boy* and that there is no singular morph: the absence of any marker is in itself distinctive (you will remember the story where Sherlock Holmes perceived the significance of the fact that the dog did *not* bark). We can adopt an analysis involving the use of a 'zero' morph, as discussed in the preceding chapter. However, postulating zero morphs brings problems (and if we follow this solution we will need a lot of zero morphs to account for the relevant facts of English, even in this small area). Instead, we propose the following rule:

**9**   N + sing → N

This rule can be understood to mean: for any string {N + sing}, the morpheme {sing} has no realization. In other words singular nouns occur in their simple stem form. We call rules like this 'null realization rules': note that this type of rule is not a rewrite rule either. Note too that the implications of this type of rule are different from the use of zero. Zero implies a realization, but that the realization is ∅. Null realization rules imply no realization at all.

Another solution is more radical. Since only plural forms have a marker, we might consider plural to be an optional category; singular forms have no mark of number either at the morpheme or at the morph level. This implies that the constituent structure rules shown in **3** need to be amended to:

**10**   NP  →  Art + N
         N   →  N (+ pl)

These rules yield the tree diagrams of Figures 74 and 75:

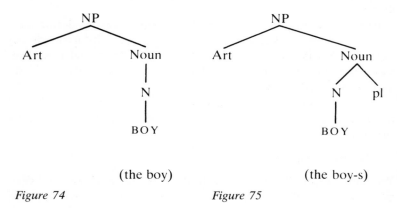

(the boy)                (the boy-s)

*Figure 74*                *Figure 75*

Consider each solution in turn. The last solution, **10**, has the attraction that we need only postulate morphemes when we find morphs that correspond to them: but we have already seen that this is unsatisfactory for all forms, e.g. the irregular plurals. A much greater problem lies in the fact that with rules like those of **10** the grammar does not systematically account for the category of number: this is a drawback at a theoretical level since we expect our grammar to give a systematic account of such categories; even at a practical level a systematic account of the category of number makes easier the description of the facts of such grammatical characteristics as number agreement between subjects and verb (illustrated in (**1c,1d**).

The solution of **8** is perfectly possible; its drawback is that listing every possible noun in a rule of this sort makes the grammar extremely cumbersome and anyway misses a proper generalization about the language: that singular nouns appear in the base form alone. This leaves solution **9**: it has the advantage of being able to postulate a morpheme {sing} and allows us to state the correct generalization that singular nouns are never marked by any morph: they occur in their simple stem form. We can summarize our rules as:

**11** *Constituent structure rules:*

$$NP \rightarrow Art + N$$
$$N \rightarrow N + Number$$
$$Number \rightarrow \begin{Bmatrix} sing \\ pl \end{Bmatrix}$$

*Lexical insertion:*

$$N \rightarrow \{BOY, GIRL, MAN, MOUSE, \ldots\}$$

*Morphological realization rules:*

$$MAN + pl \rightarrow men$$
$$MOUSE + pl \rightarrow mice$$
$$N + sing \rightarrow N$$
$$MAN \rightarrow man$$
$$MOUSE \rightarrow mouse$$
$$BOY \rightarrow boy$$
$$GIRL \rightarrow girl$$
$$pl \rightarrow \text{-}s$$
$$Art \rightarrow the$$

Note that the morphological realization rules must be ordered as we saw in the last chapter; or at least partially ordered: clearly the first rule shown must precede the fourth and the rule realizing plural as -*s*: otherwise we shall produce forms like *mans* (children indeed sometimes produce such forms).

Consider now the analysis of the verb forms in the sentences:

**12a**   The boy yawns
**12b**   The boys yawn
**12c**   The boy yawned
**12d**   The boys yawned.

The verb forms shown are often called the 'regular' forms of the verb, since these forms are most common, and are used with new borrowings or coinings. As far as a morphological analysis is concerned, there are three distinct word forms, which can be analysed as *yawn, yawn-s* and *yawn-ed*. The formal identification of these morphs can be reinforced by semantic criteria. The forms **12c, 12d** are appropriately applied to a situation which happened at some time previous to the time of utterance, whereas the forms **12a, 12b** are more appropriately applied to a situation describing either a general truth or habit (it is the habit of boys to yawn, etc.) or possibly to a situation actually happening at the moment of utterance – rather in the fashion of a commentary.

Let us characterize this distinction as one between past **12c, 12d** and non-past time, **12a, 12b**. A morphemic analysis (an analysis into morphemes) needs to postulate the same distinction, which we can, following tradition, identify as the category of tense, as we have already noted.

Now consider the pair of forms *yawns* and *yawn* in **12a, 12b**. We have already identified the distinction between *boy* and *boys* as involving the grammatical category of number: we now note that the distinction between *yawn* and *yawns* correlates with this. We find sentences like **12a, 12b**, but we will not find:

**13**   *the boy yawn
       *the boys yawns

and this relationship is, of course, shared by other different sentences similar to **12a, 12b**:

**14**   the cat yawns; the cats yawn
       the boy walks; the boys walk

The selection of the appropriate verb form depends on the number of the subject N P: if the subject is singular, then the verb has an -*s* suffix; if the subject is plural, then the verb has no affix. This suggests we should characterize the distinction in the verb forms too as one of number. Agreement between subject N P and verb form is called concord.

Note at this point that the criteria for setting up these morphemes of number in the verb involve syntactic considerations (i.e. the need to account for concord) that go beyond strict morphological considerations (i.e. an analysis into morphs).

We are now able to postulate that the morphemes realized by the forms *yawns* and *yawn* are:

**15a** *yawns*: {YAWN + non-past + sing}
**15b** *yawn*: {YAWN + non-past + pl}

This morphemic analysis might be represented in constituent structure trees of the form shown in Figures 76 and 77.

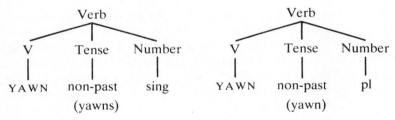

*Figure 76*          *Figure 77*

Note the same problem as was encountered with respect to the analysis of the noun: we have too many morphemes for the number of morphs we can identify. Once again a number of possible solutions suggest themselves. We can have fusional rules of the form

**16**   YAWN + non-past + sing → *yawns*
        YAWN + non-past + pl   → *yawn*

but this is open to the same objection as the comparable rule for the singular forms of nouns discussed in **8**: it misses an obvious generalization. More realistically we could have a rule for the lexeme YAWN:

**17**   YAWN → *yawn*

and then consider realization rules for the grammatical morphemes. Here a fusional rule may seem appropriate for the singular form:

    **18**   non-past + sing → -*s*

but what of the plural form? Neither {non-past} nor {pl} have any realization. We can have a rule:

    **19**   V + non-past + pl → V

analogous to rule **9**: i.e. a 'null realization' rule. Yet another solution is to say that {non-past} has no realization in either the singular or plural forms, that singular is realized by -*s* and plural has no realization. This suggests rules like:

    **20**   V + non-past → V
              sing    → -*s*
       V + pl     → V
         YAWN  → *yawn*

We provisionally adopt this last solution as the best, though we shall have cause to return to examine it later. Before leaving these rules, observe that the rules in **17–19** and those in **20** make somewhat different generalizations about the forms in question. The first set of rules, **17–19**, asserts that -*s* is a marker of both tense and number, i.e. that it is a singular tense marker. The second set of rules, **20**, assert that there is no marker of tense and that -*s* is merely a singular marker.

Now consider the morphemic description of *yawned* in **12c, d**. These forms have already been characterized as being {past} in comparison with the forms in **12a, 12b** which are {non-past}. We need to consider whether *yawned* in **12c** is {sing} and yawned in **12d** is {pl}, paralleling the singular/plural description of *yawn* and *yawns*. We may take either of two opposite positions. We can assert that verb forms always agree, or concord, with their subject nouns in number, but that in past tense forms there is no overt marker of this agreement: *yawned* in **12c** realizes {YAWN + past + sing}, and *yawned* in **12d** realizes {YAWN + past + pl}. Alternatively, we can say that verbs only concord with the subject NPs in the non-past, as suggested by **20**, and there is no concord at all in the past. So *yawned* in both **12c** and **12d** simply realizes {YAWN + past], and the question of number agreement is irrelevant, since verbs in the past do not concord.

A problem for either of these analyses is just how to capture the relevant generalization in terms of rules. There are two problems: one related to the realization of the tense morphemes and the other related to the number of morphemes. Let us consider them in turn.

Tense is a category that, in English, is associated with the verb. We have suggested that this category has two terms: {past} and {non-past}. We have further hypothesized that {past} can be associated with the morph *-ed* and {non-past} has a null realization. It may be argued then that we can dispense with a morpheme {non-past} altogether. But this raises the same sort of objections as we raised to a comparable situation with singular nouns, discussed with respect to **10**: it misses an important generalization about English verb groups. Furthermore we find the morphemes {past} and {non-past} useful for other purposes, for example co-occurrence restrictions with adverbs of time, which can be accounted for, at least in part, in terms of co-occurrence restrictions with tense morphemes: the tense morphemes have a syntactic function irrespective of the fact that one of them need not be realized by any overt morph. We therefore retain tense morphemes in the verb.

Number morphemes pose a different problem. We can argue, for English, that number is primarily a category associated with the noun, only secondarily a category associated with the verb: the subject noun controls the number morpheme on the verb. For example, the verb cannot be in the singular form if the subject noun is plural (*the boys yawns*). In traditional terms this relationship is called concord and the noun considered to be the 'controller' of the concord. But does the subject noun always require the verb to show concord? As we have seen, this question can be answered in two ways. We can say that the verb always agrees in number with the subject (i.e. always has a number morpheme) but that this agreement is not always marked with an overt morph of number agreement. This solution can be diagrammed, informally, as:

**21**  {N + sing}− {V + non-past + sing} (*yawns*)
             {V + past + sing}    (*yawned*)
   {N + pl}  − {V + non-past + pl} (*yawn*)
             {V + past + pl}     (*yawned*)

At the other extreme, we can say that the verb only concords with the subject in number when the subject is singular and the verb is non-past. This solution we can diagram as:

**22**  {N + sing}— {V + non-past + sing}  (*yawns*)
            {V + past}              (*yawned*)
  {N + pl}  — {V + non-past}        (*yawn*)
            {V + past}              (*yawned*)

As far as morphology is concerned, the solution shown in **22** is simpler in that we have fewer morphemes to account for that have no overt realization: the solution shown in **21** leaves us with a number of morphemes with no overt realization. Solution **22** also enables us to say that a form like *yawned* is simply the past tense form of YAWN (there being no number agreement in the past), where the solution **21** entails our having to say that *yawned* is either the past tense singular form of YAWN or the past tense plural form of YAWN. A further advantage of **22** is that it enables us to make clear in the grammar that number is primarily a category of the noun, and that it is a verbal category only secondarily, and by concord.

How, then, can we express this generalization in terms of rules? Constituent structure rules for these phenomena suffer two drawbacks: firstly, they are extremely clumsy to write (the reader is invited to try), but more importantly they do not express the generalization so clearly. More appropriate is to formulate a transformational rule that has the effect of copying the morpheme of number from the NP subject on to the verb. This means that in the constituent structure we only need to develop number as a category of the noun (which is what we want); the transformational rule then copies it on to the verb (also what we want). The rules in **23** do this.[1]

Constituent structure and lexical rules develop the tree shown in Figure 78 opposite.

---

1 In the rules of **23** we treat tense as a category of the verb, and further as a category that follows the verb. On page 110 we made a different proposal: that tense should be treated as an auxiliary and that auxiliaries should be considered a category of the VP rather than of the verb. The more straightforward analysis is preferred at this point, since we shall then not have the further complication of re-ordering Tense + Verb to Verb + Tense, to accommodate the facts of morph order. The analysis adopted does not affect the argument in any way.

**23** *Constituent structure rules:*

$$S \rightarrow NP + VP$$
$$VP \rightarrow V$$
$$NP \rightarrow Art + N$$
$$N \rightarrow N + Num$$
$$Num \rightarrow \begin{Bmatrix} sing \\ pl \end{Bmatrix}$$
$$V \rightarrow V + Tense$$
$$Tense \rightarrow \begin{Bmatrix} past \\ non\text{-}past \end{Bmatrix}$$

*Lexical rules:*

$$V \rightarrow \{YAWN, \ldots\}$$
$$N \rightarrow \{BOY, GIRL, \ldots\}$$
$$Art \rightarrow the$$

*Subject–verb concord:*

SA: $_{NP}(Art + N + sing) - {}_{Verb}(V + non\text{-}past)$

SC: $_{NP}(Art + N + sing) - {}_{Verb}(V + non\text{-}past + sing)$

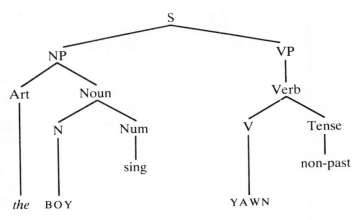

*Figure 78*

The concord rule operates on this structure. The structure meets the structural analysis specified in SA: there is a singular N followed by a non-past verb. The structural change (SC) specifies that we must add a morpheme {sing} to the verb. The resultant structure is shown in Figure 79:

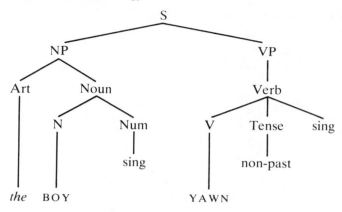

*Figure 79*

Realization rules operating on Figure 79 yield *The boy yawns*.

Consider the advantages of the analysis proposed. To begin with, we have identified the categories of number and tense as being primarily categories of, respectively, the noun and the verb: this is shown by the constituent structure rules. We have identified the category of number as only secondarily a category of the verb (shown by the fact that it is derived by the concord rule) and then only a category under certain conditions (i.e. when the verb is non-past and singular).

Before closing the discussion of the morphology of the verb, note that, just as we find irregular noun plurals in English (e.g. *goose: geese*), so too we find irregular past tense forms of verbs – *run: ran*; *think: thought*, etc. It is clear that the relevant past tense forms can be analysed as realizing morpheme sequences such as {RUN + past}, {THINK + past}, etc.

Morphological realization rules for the verb forms discussed are shown in **29** below. In form they are similar to those introduced for the noun forms discussed at the beginning of the section.

At this point it is sensible to illustrate the operation of concord rules with a further example. Consider the following NPs:

**24a**   the boy
**24b**   the boys
**24c**   a boy
**24d**   some boys

The opposition *the* : *a* has been traditionally described as one of definiteness, the category of definiteness having the terms definite and indefinite. This is done on the grounds that in uttering a sentence like:

25   I want the boy to come and see me this evening

the speaker typically has some particular individual in mind, whereas in uttering a sentence like:

26   I want a boy to come and see me this evening

no particular boy is in the mind of the speaker and any boy will serve. This characterization suffices for our present purposes, and we postulate morphemes {def(inite)} and {indef(inite)} to account for the distinction. What then of the plural forms **24b** and **24d**? Consider first the forms **24a, 24b**. The article morph is the same in both cases: *the*. We encounter the problem discussed with respect to agreement in the verb: do we wish to analyse *the* in the **a** sentence as 'the singular form of the definite article' and *the* in the **b** sentence as 'the plural form of the definite article'. This analysis suggests that the forms correspond, respectively, to morpheme strings {def + sing} and {def + pl}. Alternatively we can say that *the* is simply the definite article, realizing the morpheme {def} and no question of number arises. This seems a more satisfactory solution since, as before, it leads us to postulate fewer morphemes that have no overt realization.

In the forms of **24c, 24d**, it is possible to argue that the forms *a* and *some* are, respectively, 'the singular form of the indefinite article' and 'the plural form of the indefinite article'. Evidence for such an analysis is shown if we compare **26** with:

27   I want some boys to come and see me this evening

In **26** we can assert that the speaker has no particular boy in mind and any boy will serve – the speaker clearly has only a single boy in mind; in **27** the speaker has a number of boys in mind, but no particular number and no particular boys. The opposition appears to be between a single unspecified individual and a number of unspecified individuals. This leads us to postulate that *a* and *some* realize, respectively, the morpheme strings {indef + sing} and {indef + pl}.

If we accept this analysis, we need to consider how it can be incorporated in our grammar; and once again a concord rule seems to be an appropriate mechanism. The following will serve:

**28**  *Constituent structure rules:*

$$NP \rightarrow Art + N$$
$$N \rightarrow N + Num$$
$$Num \rightarrow \begin{Bmatrix} sing \\ pl \end{Bmatrix}$$
$$Art \rightarrow \begin{Bmatrix} def \\ indef \end{Bmatrix}$$

*Article–Noun concord:*

$$\text{SA: } _{NP}(_{Art}(indef) - N - \begin{bmatrix} sing \\ pl \end{bmatrix})$$

$$\text{SC: } _{NP}(_{Art}(indef + \begin{bmatrix} sing \\ pl \end{bmatrix}) - N - \begin{bmatrix} sing \\ pl \end{bmatrix})$$

The concord rule is understood exactly as the previous rule, except that here we have an additional notational convention: an item in one pair of square brackets is matched with the corresponding item in the other pair of square brackets. For example the constituent structure rules generate the trees in Figures 80 and 81:

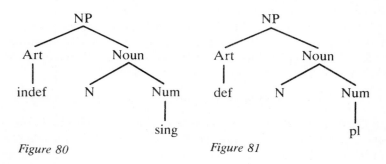

Figure 80                    *Figure 81*

The concord rule now operates on the first of these strings to yield the derived tree shown in Figure 82. Note that the rule cannot operate on the second of these trees (Figure 81) since it does not meet the structural analysis: this corresponds to our observation that the definite article does not concord with the noun in number.

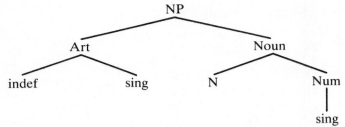

*Figure 82*

We can summarize the rules we have proposed and add appropriate realization rules:

**29**  *Constituent structure rules:*

$$S \rightarrow NP + VP$$
$$VP \rightarrow Verb$$
$$NP \rightarrow Art + N$$
$$N \rightarrow N + Num$$
$$Num \rightarrow \left\{ \begin{matrix} sing \\ pl \end{matrix} \right\}$$
$$Art \rightarrow \left\{ \begin{matrix} def \\ indef \end{matrix} \right\}$$
$$Verb \rightarrow V + Tense$$
$$Tense \rightarrow \left\{ \begin{matrix} past \\ non\text{-}past \end{matrix} \right\}$$

*Lexical rules:*

$$N \rightarrow \{\text{BOY, GIRL, MAN, GOOSE,} \ldots\}$$
$$V \rightarrow \{\text{YAWN, WALK, RUN,} \ldots\}$$

*Concord rules:*

Subject–verb concord:

SI: $_{NP}(Art + N + sing) - {}_{Verb}(V + non\text{-}past)$

SC: $_{NP}(Art + N + sing) - {}_{Verb}(V + non\text{-}past + sing)$

Article–noun concord:

SA: $_{NP}(_{Art}(indef) - N - \begin{bmatrix} sing \\ pl \end{bmatrix})$

SC: $_{NP}(_{Art}(indef - \begin{bmatrix} sing \\ pl \end{bmatrix}) - N - \begin{bmatrix} sing \\ pl \end{bmatrix})$

*Morphological realization rules:*

| | | |
|---|---|---|
| **1** | MAN + pl | → *men* |
| **2** | GOOSE + pl | → *geese* |
| **3** | N + sing | → N |
| **4** | BOY | → *boy* |
| **5** | GIRL | → *girl* |
| **6** | MAN | → *man* |
| **7** | GOOSE | → *goose* |
| **8** | pl | → *-s* |
| **9** | RUN + past | → *ran* |
| **10** | V + non-past | → V |
| **11** | RUN | → *run* |
| **12** | YAWN | → *yawn* |
| **13** | WALK | → *walk* |
| **14** | sing | → *-s* |
| **15** | past | → *-ed* |
| **16** | def | → *the* |
| **17** | indef + sing | → *a* |
| **18** | indef + pl | → *some* |

This grammar produces trees like Figures 83 and 84.

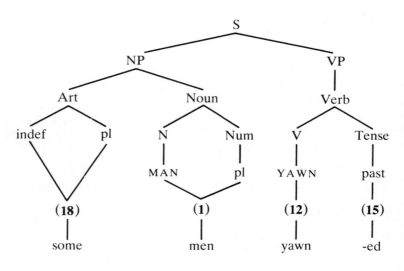

*Figure 83*                    (some men yawned)

1 Subject–verb concord does not operate since verbs only concord in number, according to our rule, when they are non-past, and when the subject is singular: neither condition is satisfied in our tree.

2 Article–noun concord does operate since the article is indefinite and the noun is plural – article concord is shown in the tree.

3 The relevant morphological realization rules are identified in the tree by the number of the rule that has operated.

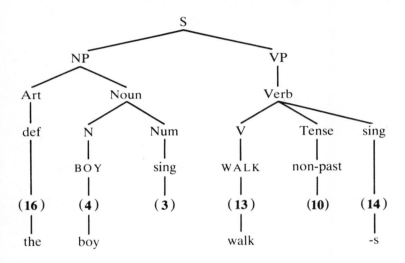

*Figure 84*                 (the boy walks)

1 Subject–verb concord has operated since the subject N P is singular and the verb non-past.

2 Article–noun concord has not operated since this rule only applies to indefinite articles, and the article here is definite.

3 The relevant morphological realization rules are identified by the number of the rule that has operated. Note that {sing} in the NP (rule **3**) and {non-past} in the V (rule **10**) have no realization.

Before closing this chapter it is useful to point out some implications of our grammar. There is nothing 'given' about our model: it is the result of analytic decisions taken about various aspects of the structure of sentences and their constituents. Different decisions would have resulted in a different grammar. Note also that the formalization of the grammar makes totally overt those analytic decisions we have made: for instance our observations on the scope of concordial relations, and to which category the categories of number and tense 'primarily' apply.

**Technical terms:**

| | |
|---|---|
| agglutinative rules | null-realization rules |
| concord | rule ordering |
| fusional rules | tense |
| number | |

# 14   The order of morphs and the order of morphemes

Hitherto we have assumed that we should represent the morphemes in a morphemic description in the same order as the morphs which realize them. Thus we have represented the morphemes realized by a form like *walked* as {WALK + past}. Morphs need to be ordered in the sequence in which they actually occur, since in a form like *walk-ed* the morphs always appear in that order, never in the impossible order *ed-walk*. However, if the morpheme is an abstract unit, why should we not order the morphemes in a way that makes our grammatical statement most revealing and economical? Thus in the grammar we may order the morphemes that are realized by *walked* as {past + WALK} if there seems good reason to do so: we have already seen that there is good reason in the discussion of pages 110–11. The realization rules that relate morphemes to morphs ensure that the morphs occur in the correct order. We will look at the morphology of English verb forms in a moment. First let us consider a different, and more straightforward example. Consider the verb forms in the following Akan sentences.[1] The second word in each sentence is the verb word, which has been morphologically analysed. The verb stem is *fura* (FURA 'wrap round, put on, wear'). The descriptions to the left of each sentence are the names used to refer to the various verb forms, and we suppose that we can regard these as descriptions of the relevant morphemes: for example in 1 we regard the verb word as realizing the morphemes {hab + FURA}.

1   hab(itual)      Kofi fura ntoma      'Kofi wears a cloth'
2   prog(ressive)   Kofi re-fura ntoma   'Kofi is putting on a cloth'

---

1 The sentences are represented in the orthographic form. Tone markings have been omitted, although these are also relevant to a complete description of the verbal system. This does not affect the point at issue.

| **3** | fut(ure) | Kofi be-fura ntoma | 'Kofi will put on a cloth' |
| **4** | pret(erite) | Kofi fura-a ntoma | 'Kofi put on a cloth' |
| **5** | perf(ect) | Kofi a-fura ntoma | 'Kofi has put on a cloth' |

The habitual verb form has no affix; there is simply the bare root *fura*. For all the other forms there is an affix; it is a prefix in all cases except the preterite, where it is a suffix. Also note that all these affixes are mutually exclusive: no form can have more than one of these affixes – there are no forms *\*a-re-fura*, *\*be-fura-a*, etc. It appears that we have here a five-term category, which we call the category of Aspect. It is clearly most illuminating to have a rule of the following kind:

**6**   Verb → Asp + V      (Aspect)

$$\text{Asp} \rightarrow \left\{ \begin{array}{l} \text{hab} \\ \text{prog} \\ \text{fut} \\ \text{pret} \\ \text{perf} \end{array} \right\}$$

This rule places the {pret} morpheme before V. We therefore need a rule to reorder these two morphemes into the correct order for the realization of the relevant morphs. Such a rule might be:

**7**   *Preterite hopping:*
   pret + V → V + pret

It is not easy to devise a set of simple rewrite rules that would achieve the correct ordering, and still maintain the generalization that all five terms belong to the same category of Aspect: the reader is invited to try. The rules we have proposed, on the other hand, allow us to make the correct generalization in the grammar **6**, with a subsequent rule **7** to accommodate the facts of morph order in the actual structure of word forms.

The principle is to enable the grammar to make the appropriate generalizations about the classification of various grammatical morphemes into appropriate categories, in this case that {hab, prog, pret, . . .} are all members of the category of Aspect, independent of the quirks of word formation.

Let us now consider the morphology of English verb forms. We have already discussed some aspects of this (pages 105–11). There we established the description shown schematically in Figure 85.

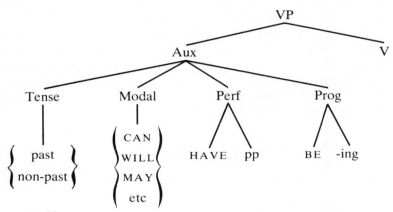

*Figure 85*

Of the auxiliaries, only Tense is obligatory (since all verb groups in simple sentences are tensed) and this category has two terms {past} and {non-past}. The other auxiliaries are optional, but if they occur they must occur in the order shown. The category Modal can be realized by any one of the modal auxiliaries (a form of CAN, WILL, MAY, etc.). The category Perf is realized by a form of HAVE, which form depending on what other auxiliary immediately precedes it, and is followed by a verb in the past participle form: this we represented by the notation pp. Similarly the category Prog is realized by a form of BE, which form depending on what precedes, and it is followed by a verb in the *-ing* form. The realization of Perf and Prog is thus discontinuous: they are realized by two non-contiguous morphs. We can represent this, diagrammatically, as in Figure 86, for the verb group *has been walking*.

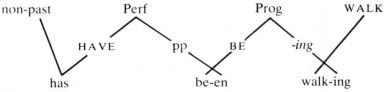

*Figure 86*

*has* is formed by the fusion of non-past + HAVE. *been* and *walking* are formed agglutinatively by the suffixation of *-en* and *-ing* to the stems *be* and *walk*. Perf is realized discontinuously by (*has . . . -en*), and Prog by (*be . . . -ing*).

The most economical grammar to deal with these facts supposes that a constituent structure rule introduces those elements that are later to be discontinuous as a single constituent; the discontinuity is handled by a later reordering rule. Let us see how this might be managed for the examples we already have. We propose the rules in Figure 87 below:

*Constituent structure rules:*

$$S \rightarrow NP + VP$$
$$NP \rightarrow Art + N + Num$$
$$Num \rightarrow \begin{Bmatrix} sing \\ pl \end{Bmatrix}$$
$$VP \rightarrow Aux + V + NP$$
$$Aux \rightarrow Tense \ (+Modal) \ (+Perf) \ (+Prog)$$
$$Modal \rightarrow \{CAN, \ WILL, \ MAY, \ . . .\}$$
$$Tense \rightarrow \begin{Bmatrix} past \\ non\text{-}past \end{Bmatrix}$$
$$Perf \rightarrow HAVE + pp$$
$$Prog \rightarrow BE + \text{-}ing$$

*Lexical rule:*

*Figure 87*    $V \rightarrow \{WALK, \ . . .\}$

These rules produce strings like:

**8a**    past + WALK
**8b**    past + Perf + WALK: past + HAVE + pp + WALK
**8c**    past + Perf + Prog + WALK: past + HAVE + pp + BE + -ing + WALK
**8d**    non-past + Modal + Prog + WALK: non-past + WILL + BE + -*ing* + WALK etc.

To account for the discontinuities we propose a rule:

**9**    *Affix hopping:*

Any affix which is found to the left of a verb is to be moved to the right of that verb. An affix may hop a verb only once. past, non-past, pp and -*ing* are affixes; any modal HAVE, BE and any item categorized as V and introduced by a lexical rule are verbs.

Applying this rule to the strings in **8** we get:

**10a**  past + WALK ⇒ WALK + past (*walk-ed*)

**10b**  past + HAVE + pp + WALK ⇒ HAVE + past + WALK + pp (*had walk-ed*)

**10c**  past + HAVE + pp + BE + -*ing* + WALK ⇒ HAVE + past + BE + pp + WALK + -*ing* (*had be-en walking*)

**10d**  non-past + WILL + BE + -*ing* + WALK ⇒ WILL + non-past + BE + WALK + -*ing* (*will be walk-ing*)

(Since **9** is formulated as a transformational operation, we have used the symbol ⇒ in the structures in **10**.)

We now need morphological realization rules. For the data we have been considering we can propose rules of the following sort (which are formulated as 'orthographic rules'):

**11**  

| | | |
|---|---|---|
| HAVE + past | → *had* | |
| HAVE + non-past | → *have* | |
| BE + past | → *was* | |
| BE + non-past | → *is* | |
| BE + pp | → *been* | |
| HAVE | → *have* | |
| BE | → *be* | |
| CAN + past | → *could* | (and similarly for |
| CAN + non-past | → *can* | WILL and MAY) |
| pp | → -*ed* | |
| past | → -*ed* | |
| WALK | → *walk* | |

Our examples now become:

**12a**  *walk-ed* (the past form of WALK)
**12b**  *had walk-ed* (the past perfective form of WALK)
**12c**  *had been walking* (the past perfective progressive form of WALK)
**12d**  *will be walking* (the non-past modal (WILL) progressive form of WALK)

The reader is invited to try other combinations as permitted in the rules.

We now try to accommodate within this type of description the facts of number agreement between subject and verb. We have discussed some aspects of this problem already, pages 186ff., but two amendments are needed to bring our account into line with our new model. The first is needed to deal with number agreement as it affects all the verbal auxiliaries (our previous account dealt only with verb groups with a single verb, past or non-past – forms like *walk*, *walks*, *walked*). The second has to do with the order of morphemes: our previous account supposed that tense was introduced following the verb, and we have now decided to place it as the first auxiliary: the changes that this new analysis requires are relatively trivial.

The facts of English number agreement are complex and can, as we have seen, be analysed in a number of different ways. In line with our previous discussion, we will suppose that verbs only agree in number when there is an overt marker of number on one of the auxiliaries or on the main verb. With this assumption, the facts can be summarized as follows:

**i** Number agreement is only shown on the first item in the verb group, whatever that is:

> **13**  The man walks/the men walk
> The man is walking/the men are walking
> The man has walked/the men have walked

Note that the first item in the verb group is also the item that shows tense. Tense and number go together, even in interrogatives:

> **14**  Does the man walk/do the men walk?
> Is the man walking/are the men walking?
> Has the man walked/have the men walked?

We say that tense and number are cumulated, i.e. realized together, on the first verb in the verb group.

**ii** Modal verbs never show number agreement:

> **15**  The man can go/the men can go
> The man could go/the men could go

**iii** With non-past verb forms, when the subject is singular, HAVE, BE and the main verb show number agreement:

**16** The man has gone
The man is going
The man goes

**iv** With non-past verb forms, when the subject is plural, only BE shows number agreement (but not HAVE or the main verb, which are in their stem forms)

**17** The men have gone
The men are going
The men go

**v** With past verb forms, only BE shows number agreement in both singular and plural:

**18** The man was going/The men were going
The man had gone/The men had gone
The man went/The men went

We can summarize these facts in terms of the three rules:

**19** Verb Number agreement (obligatory)

**19a** SA: $X - N - sing - non\text{-}past - V - Y$

SC: $X - N - sing - {}_{Tense}(non\text{-}past + sing) - V - Y$

(on condition V is not a modal)

**19b** SA: $X - N - pl - non\text{-}past - BE - Y$

SC: $X - N - pl - {}_{Tense}(non\text{-}past + pl) - BE - Y$

**19c** SA: $X - N - \begin{bmatrix} sing \\ pl \end{bmatrix} - past - BE - Y$

SC: $X - N - \begin{bmatrix} sing \\ pl \end{bmatrix} - {}_{Tense}(past + \begin{bmatrix} sing \\ pl \end{bmatrix}) - BE - Y$

The summary **i–v** above is expressed in these rules as follows. **i** is shown by the fact that the number morpheme is adjoined as a sister to tense (and dominated by tense) showing that the two are cumulated. The generalization is expressed like this so that in formulating the question rule we can say that tense hops over the subject NP, and tense brings number along with it (cf. **14**). **ii** is shown by the fact that modals are specifically excluded from the scope of any of the rules proposed. **iii–v** are directly represented in the rules **19a–19c** respectively.

The number agreement rule, expressed this way, simplifies our morphological realization rules, though it clearly leads to a complex statement of the number agreement rule. It is possible to state the number agreement rule in a different way. We can, for instance, assert that *all* verbs agree in number with their subjects: but this complicates the morphological realization rules since we then must say, of for example modals, that whereas they agree in number with their subjects (as stated by the rule), number agreement is never realized in any way. It seems preferable to formulate the rules as we have done in **19** so number agreement is only held to occur when there is an overt marker of this agreement.

We can also accommodate in this description the facts of interrogative and negative sentences as discussed on pages 112–18. There we proposed (cf. discussion on page 127) that the morpheme {neg} should be adjoined to the tense morpheme. Note that just as number cumulates with tense, so too does the negative morpheme; as can be seen most clearly in interrogative negative sentences.

> **20**　The man hasn't gone/the men haven't gone
> The man doesn't go/the men don't go
> Didn't the man go?

Finally observe that the introduction of a passive auxiliary by a passive transformation of the sort envisaged in chapter 8 (cf. page 126) falls quite naturally within the scope of our rules. We can consider this by the derivation of the sentence:

> **21**　Weren't the dogs bitten by the cat?

We start from the active structure (corresponding to *the cat bit the dogs*) shown in Figure 88 (some details are omitted). From this we derive the passive structure (by the passive rule page 125) corresponding to *the dogs were bitten by the cat*, as shown in Figure 89. From this we derive the negative structure (by the rule on page 126) corresponding to *the dogs weren't bitten by the cat*, shown in Figure 90.

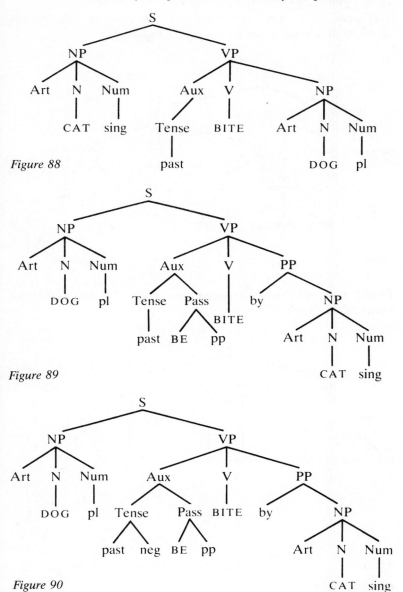

*Figure 88*

*Figure 89*

*Figure 90*

We apply the number agreement rule **19c** (the one that applies here) to derive the structure shown in Figure 91:

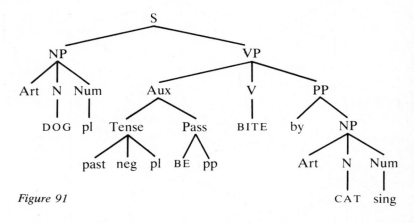

*Figure 91*

Finally we apply the interrogative rule (page 127) and derive the structure in Figure 92:

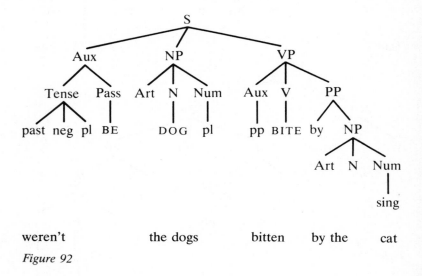

*Figure 92*

The effect of the morphological realization rules is shown below the structure in Figure 92.

**Technical terms**

affix hopping
cumulation
number agreement

**Exercises**

*1 Noun classes in Luganda (a language from Uganda)*

In Luganda, as in other Bantu languages, nouns can be analysed as having the structure prefix + stem (e.g. *omu-kazi*). The alternation between singular and plural is shown by different prefixes (e.g. *omu-kazi* 'woman', *aba-kazi* 'women'). Nouns can be assigned to 'gender classes' depending on the form of the singular and plural prefixes. Four different noun classes are illustrated in the data. They have been assigned arbitrary numbers for ease of reference.

| | *singular* | *gloss* | *plural* | *stem* |
|---|---|---|---|---|
| **1** | omu-kazi | woman | aba-kazi | -kazi |
| | omusajja | man | abasajja | -sajja |
| | umuntu | person | abantu | |
| | omwana | child | abaana | |
| | omwezi | sweeper | abeezi | |
| | omwozi | washerman | aboozi | |
| **2** | eŋkoko | chicken | eŋkoko | -koko |
| | eŋgo | oil | eŋgo | |
| | ente | cow | ente | |
| | endiga | sheep | endiga | |
| | embogo | buffalo | embogo | |
| | emmese | rat | emmese | |
| **3** | omugga | river | emigga | |
| | omuggo | stick | emiggo | |
| | omwaka | year | emyaka | |
| | omwezi | moon | emyezi | |
| **4** | ekisolo | animal | ebisolo | |
| | ekintu | thing | ebintu | |
| | ekyalo | village | ebyalo | |
| | ekyenyi | forehead | ebyenyi | |

Segment the words into morphs. Write the stem form in the right-hand column above. Fill in the matrix below with the prefix forms. When a prefix is realized by two or more allomorphs, there is a space for each allomorph. State the appropriate environment that conditions the allomorphs. Make your statements as general as possible. In the worked example, __C means 'in the environment preceding a consonant' and __V means 'in the environment preceding a vowel'.

| class | singular | | plural | |
|---|---|---|---|---|
| | | *in the environment* | | *in the environment* |
| 1 | omu- | __ C | | |
| | omw- | __ V | | |
| | / | / | | |
| 2 | | | | |
| | | | | |
| | | | | |
| 3 | | | | |
| | | | | |
| 4 | | | | |

## 2   *The verb word in Luganda*

In Luganda the verb word is usually marked with a prefix which represents the subject, and with a morph which shows the 'tense' of the verb; it may also, in certain circumstances, be marked with a morph which represents the object. Each of the verb words below could stand as an independent sentence, with the meaning glossed. In this exercise you are asked to analyse the verb words below:

| | | |
|---|---|---|
| 1 | ndigenda | I shall go |
| 2 | yagenda | He went |
| 3 | nkyagenda | I am going |
| 4 | twagenda | We went |
| 5 | aligenda | He will go |
| 6 | wagenda | You(sg) went |
| 7 | baligenda | They will go |

| 8  | mukyagenda  | You(pl) are going            |
|----|-------------|-----------------------------|
| 9  | mwagenda    | You(pl) went                |
| 10 | tukyagenda  | We are going                |
| 11 | baagenda    | They went                   |
| 12 | nnagenda    | I went                      |
| 13 | akyaŋkuba   | She is beating me           |
| 14 | baamukuba   | They beat him               |
| 15 | bakyakulaba | They are looking at you(sg) |
| 16 | yatukuba    | She beat us                 |
| 17 | ndibagoba   | I shall chase them          |
| 18 | akyandaba   | He is looking at me         |
| 19 | tukyabalaba | We are looking at them      |
| 20 | olitugoba   | You(sg) will chase us       |
| 21 | twabalaba   | We saw you(pl)              |
| 22 | tulibalaba  | We shall see you(pl)        |
| 23 | nnabakuba   | I beat them                 |
| 24 | mulindaba   | You(pl) will see me         |

(a) Give the morphs associated with the following translation meanings: where a given morpheme is realized by two allomorphs, state the environment (i.e. what conditions the choice of one allomorph rather than another).

| *subject pronouns* | | |
|--------------------|--|------------------------|
|                    |  | *in the environment*   |
| *I*                |  |                        |
|                    |  |                        |
| *you(sg)*          |  |                        |
|                    |  |                        |
| *he/she*           |  |                        |
|                    |  |                        |
| *we*               |  |                        |
|                    |  |                        |
| *you(pl)*          |  |                        |
|                    |  |                        |
| *they*             |  |                        |
|                    |  |                        |

| object pronouns | | |
|---|---|---|
| | | *in the environment* |
| *me* | | |
| | | |
| *you(sg)* | | |
| *him/her* | | |
| *us* | | |
| *you(pl)* | | |
| *them* | | |

| tense/aspect affixes | | |
|---|---|---|
| | | *in the environment* |
| *future* | | |
| | | |
| *past* | | |
| *progressive* | | |

| Verb stems | | |
|---|---|---|
| | | *in the environment* |
| 'go' | | |
| 'beat' | | |
| 'chase' | | |
| 'see /look at' | | |

(b) What is the order of affixes within the word?

(c) Supply the probable forms for the following meanings:

I shall beat them      You (pl) saw me

## 3 Syntactic analysis

Here is an extensive morphological and syntactic exercise. The data comes from a Xhosa (a Bantu language of Southern Africa) folk tale. The data are presented in three lines. In the first line is the language text; the second line is a fairly literal 'word-by-word' gloss into English; the third line contains a more idiomatic English translation. You should beware of taking the glosses literally, since the grammatical structure of the language differs from English and a full word-by-word translation is not possible without a lot of further explanation.

Following the text are a number of questions designed to help you towards an analysis. You will not be able to make an exhaustive grammatical description of Xhosa on the basis of the amount of data you have here. The texts do, however, have enough data to give some idea of the structure of the language as a whole.

**Amasela** (*Thieves*)

1 Ngenye imini, udyakalashe nomvolufu babona   inqwelo yeentlanzi
   *One      day      Jackal         and Wolf   they saw a wagon of fishes*
   *One day Jackal and Wolf saw a wagon of fish*

2 Kwa oko udyakalashe wathi   "Mvolufu, ndilambile. Ndifuna intlanzi."
   *Then      Jackal      he said  Wolf    I hungry    I want    a fish*
   *Then Jackal said, "Wolf, I am hungry, I want a fish."*

3 Mvolufu wathi   "Uya kuzifumana  njani iintlanzi?" Udyakalashe
   *Wolf    he said You will find them how   the fishes  Jackal*
   *Wolf said, "How are you going to find the fish?" Jackal*

4 wathi   "Uya kubona". Udyakalashe yena wabaleka waya     kulala
   *he said You will see  Jackal       he   he ran    he went to lie down*
   *replied, "You will see." Jackal, he ran and lay down in the road*

5 endleleni   phambi kwenqwelo. Umqhubi wasibona esi silo
   *in the road in front of the wagon Driver   he saw this   creature*
   *in front of the wagon. The driver saw this creature*

6 wacinga    ukuba sifile. Wasiphakamisa ke   wathi   "Ndiya kumhlinza
   *he thought that   it dead He picked it up then he said  I will flay him*
   *and thought it was dead. Then he picked it up and said, "I will flay*

7 lo   dyakalashe ekhaya. Ndiya kwenza umnweba ngesikhumba.
   *this Jackal       at home I will make    a caross   with the skin*
   *this Jackal at home and make a caross with the skin*

8 ndiwuthengise, ndifumane imali." Kwa  oko
   *I sell it          I find     money Then*
   *and sell it to make money."*

9  wamphosa    enqwelweni  waya    kuhlala    esihlalweni sakhe
   *he threw him on the wagon he went to sit down on the seat of him*
   *Then he threw him on the wagon, went and sat down on his seat*

10 waqhuba inqwelo.    Wavuka  udyakalashe, wathatha iintlanzi
   *he drove the wagon He got up Jackal      he took   the fishes*
   *and drove on. Jackal got up and took the fish*

11 waziphosa      phantsi emva kwenqwelo, watsiba    ke  enqwelweni,
   *he threw them down    behind the wagon he jumped then from the wagon*
   *he threw them down behind the wagon. Then he jumped off it*

12 wahlala phantsi, watya.  Umvolufu wayibona le     nto.  Wabaleka
   *he sat   down   he ate Wolf      he saw it  this thing He ran*
   *and sat down and ate. Wolf saw this happening and ran*

13 kudyakalashe, wafika    wathi  "Dyakalashe, nam ndilambile".
   *to Jackal      he arrived he said Jackal, I      also I hungry*
   *to Jackal. On arrival he said, "Jackal, I am hungry too."*

14 Waphendula udyakalashe wathi  "Mvolufu, ukuba ulambile, yiya
   *he answered Jackal       he said Wolf      that you hungry you go*
   *Jackal answered, "Wolf, if you are hungry, go*

15 kulala      phaya endleleni.  Umqhubi uya kucinga ukuba ufile.
   *to lie down there in the road The driver he will think that   you dead*
   *and lie down there in the road. The driver will think that you are dead.*

16 Uya kukuphakamisa, akuphose     enqwelweni  aye kuhlala esihlalweni
   *He will pick you up  he throw you on the wagon he go to sit  on the seat*
   *He will pick you up, throw you on the wagon and go and sit on his seat*

17 sakhe aqhube inqwelo.   Wena ke uya kuvuka,    uthathe iintlanzi,
   *of him he drive the wagon You then you will get up you take the fishes*
   *and drive the wagon. Then you get up and take the fish*

18 uziphose      phantsi, utsibe  ke  enqwelweni,   uhlale phantsi,
   *you throw them down    you jump then from the wagon you sit down*
   *and throw them down. Then you jump down from the wagon, sit down*

19 utye.   Umvolufu walithatha eli cebo,  wabaleka waya    kulala
   *you eat Wolf     he took it  this advice he ran     he went to lie down*
   *and eat. Wolf took this advice, and ran and went and lay down*

20 endleleni.  Kodwa umqhubi waqonda      ezi zilo
   *in the road But    the driver he understood these creatures*
   *in the road. But the driver now knew that these creatures*

21 zamqhatha.          Wambetha kakhulu umvolufu emzimbeni.
   *they were cheating him He beat him hard    Wolf      on the body*
   *were cheating him. So he beat Wolf hard on his body.*

22 Umvolufu wakhala,    wavuka, wabaleka.    Udyakalashe sisilo
   *Wolf      he cried out he got up he ran away Jackal      it a creature*
   *Wolf cried out, got up and ran away. Jackal is a creature,*

23 nomvolufu sisilo         naye. Zizilo        zonke. Kodwa udyakalashe
   *and Wolf  it a creature too  They creatures both   But   Jackal*
   *and so is Wolf. They are both creatures. But Jackal*

24 uhlakaniphile, umvolufu sisidenge.
   *he clever       Wolf    he stupid.*
   *is clever and Wolf is stupid.*

(a) Make a list of all the verb stems in the data, and gloss each item (e.g. *bona* 'see'). List the stems in the form in which they occur, or in which you think they would occur, in the simple past tense form. Do not try to account for forms which are translated in the free English translation by 'I am —', 'They are —', 'I want —', etc.: i.e. forms with the 'present' tense (e.g. *ndilambile* **2**, *ndifuna* **2** and the forms in **22–4**).

(b) Diagram the structure of past tense verb forms in terms of the morphs that obligatorily and optionally occur. Make a list of subject and object morphs, and gloss them in some way so that the relevant concordial relationships are clear.

(c) Diagram the structure of those verb forms that are apparently (judging from the glosses provided) used to refer to future events etc. Note that there are two types of form (e.g. in sentence beginning line 16). Describe their distribution.

(d) There appear to be three different types of locative expression (they translate such phrases as 'on the road', 'in front of the wagon', etc.). Diagram their structure. (Note the following nouns: *umzimba* 'body'; *isihlalo* 'seat'; *indlela* 'road'.)

(e) Make an analysis of the sentence *Uya kukuphakamisa . . . aqhube inqwelo* (lines **16–17**) into morphs. Separate the morphs in each word by hyphens (e.g. *u-dyakalashe*) and identify each morph (e.g. Personal name class prefix-jackal). Ignore the word *sakhe*.

# 15   Lexical morphology

On page 171 a distinction was drawn between lexical or derivational morphology and inflectional morphology. Processes for the formation of new words, in the sense of new lexemes, is the field of lexical or derivational morphology. Thus from *write* we can derivationally derive *writer* and *rewrite*. On the other hand the formation of forms like *writes, wrote* is a matter of inflectional morphology. In these terms the word *writing* is a derivational formation in the sense 'handwriting' (*Your writing is illegible*), but an inflectional formation when it is part of a verb group (*He is writing a letter to his girl friend*). Inflectional morphology is a matter for the grammar as we have seen, but we shall argue that derivational morphology is not. The boundary line between the two is not entirely clear-cut but in this brief account we will assume that a distinction of the sort drawn above can be made.

It is obvious that many lexemes are morphologically complex, as *writ-er, re-write* above. It also seems to be the case, as noted on page 171 that, from the point of view of the grammar, we need to treat items like this as units. This suggests that we should not treat *-er* and *re-* in the examples as morphemes, in the sense in which we have defined morpheme. We call them lexical formatives. The stem to which lexical formatives are affixed we call a lexical stem. Lexical stems may be morphologically simple, as in *write*, or may themselves be complex, for example the stem in *un-realistic*. The derivational process by which this latter example is formed proceeds as follows: to the adjective stem *real*, which is a root, and morphologically simple, we affix the derivational suffix *-ist* to form the noun *realist*. To this stem, which is complex, we affix the derivational suffix *-ic* to form the adjective *realistic*. Finally we prefix the derivational affix *un-* to form the adjective *unrealistic*. This suggests that the word has the internal constituent structure represented in Figure 93.

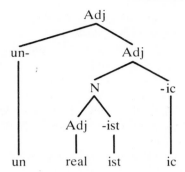

*Figure 93*

The fact that words can be analysed as having an internal constituent structure of the sort shown in Figure 93 suggests some general 'word formation rules', of this form:

| **1a** | Adj + *-ist* | ⇒ N | real-ist |
|---|---|---|---|
| **1b** | N + *-ic* | ⇒ Adj | angel-ic |
| **1c** | *un-* + Adj | ⇒ Adj | un-real |
| **1d** | N + *-ish* | ⇒ Adj | girl-ish |
| **1e** | Adj + *-en* | ⇒ V | rip-en |
| **1f** | V + *-al* | ⇒ N | refus-al |
| **1g** | V + *-ion* | ⇒ N | confus-ion |
| **1h** | N + *-hood* | ⇒ N | man-hood |

Rules of this sort need to be supplemented by further rules relating to the phonological and orthographic changes that accompany them. Phonological changes can be illustrated by **1b** and **1g**. The noun *angel* is stressed on the first syllable, but in the corresponding adjective, *angelic*, the stress has 'shifted' to the second syllable. The final segment of the verb *confuse* /kənfjuz/ is 'changed' from /z/ to /ʒ/ in the noun *confusion* /kənfjuʒn/. Orthographic changes can be illustrated by **1e–1g**. In these cases the stem form loses its final *-e* before the affix is added: *refuse:refus-al*. Many such phonological and orthographic 'changes' are subject to rules, but we shall not explore these here.

Rules of the sort shown in **1** capture some valuable generalizations about the structure of lexical items. We have not formulated the rules as rewrite rules, which rules do not here seem appropriate. A rewrite rule of the sort:

**2**   N → Adj + *-ist*

captures the wrong generalization: we do not want to say that a noun has the constituents Adj + -*ist* (which is not generally true) but rather that in appropriate cases a noun may be formed from an adjective stem by the suffixation of -*ist*: the generalization captured in rule **1a**. We consider rules like those in **1** as rules of word formation belonging to the lexicon (i.e. they are rules for forming new lexical items) rather than rules that belong to the grammar as we have previously considered grammar. There are a number of reasons for this.

In the first place, formation rules like **1** are of limited rather than general productivity. By productivity we mean the general applicability of a rule. Inflectional rules are of general productivity – the rule that affixes {past} to a verb stem is one that can apply to all verb stems. On the other hand rules like **1f** or **1g** are of limited productivity, because it is not the case that any V undergoes these rules. The rules are, however, productive insofar as they apply to a range of stems (*arrival, rebuttal, perusal, acquittal*, . . .; *expectation, action, procession, edition*, . . .). Not only are such rules of limited productivity, but they also apply to lexical stems in a somewhat arbitrary fashion. While rule **1f** applies to many verb stems (*arrive, rebut* etc.), it clearly does not apply to all (there are no forms *expect*:\**expectal*; *act*:\**actal*). Stems like *expect* and *act* must instead derive nouncs by rule **1g** (*expectation, action*). In general, if a verb stem undergoes one formation process (like *refuse*), then an alternative process is not open to it (\**refusion*). In a few cases both forms are available (*remit, remittal, remission*) – and here we note that each of the derived forms has a different sense. Different rules are productive to different degrees. The suffixation of -*y* (*length-y, fox-y*) is still an active productive process, as in contemporary spoken forms as *trendy*, or *a very linguisticy sort of solution*. So too is the suffixation of -*ish*, established in words like *girlish, bookish*, and also found in spoken forms like *five o'clockish, a very smokerish reaction* ('the typical reaction of a smoker'), etc. Conversational forms like *smokerish, linguisticy* suggest that a rule like **1d** is an active part of some speaker's word formation rules. By contrast the derivational process that relates *long* and *length* (Adj + -*th* ⇒ N (with appropriate vowel change) – *strong* : *strength*; *wide* : *width*) seems no longer productive.[1]

1 In some cases words appear to have been derived by a productive process,

Word formation rules, then, are of limited rather than general productivity; some are still productive, other fossilized; and they have a somewhat arbitrary application to particular stems. In all of these respects they contrast with the centrally grammatical rules, such as the rule forming noun plurals, which are generally productive and of wide application.

We have already noted a second reason (page 171): from the point of view of the grammar, the process by which a lexeme is formed is not relevant. For the adjectives STUPID and FOOLISH in the environment *a__ boy*, it is not relevant that STUPID is a root and FOOLISH a derived form. No grammatical rules need to have access to the information that FOOLISH is derived from a noun root. Thus in Figure 93 grammatical rules operate only on the topmost Adj node: the subordinate N and Adj nodes are not subject to grammatical rules. The rule ascribing number to a noun cannot apply to the string *realist* when it is part of the adjective *realistic* (there is no form *'*realistsic*), nor can the string *realistic* be compared when part of the form *unrealistic* (*unmorerealistic*). Indeed it is only confusing the grammar to include such information in a string to which grammatical rules apply, since we would need to put special restrictions on our rules. For example, we would need to state that the rule ascribing number to a noun does not apply when a particular noun stem is itself dominated, as in Figure 93, by an Adj node. This observation is confirmed by the fact that grammatical affixes are usually more 'peripheral' to a word than 'derivational' affixes. Schematically, we find strings like GA + DA + STEM + DA + GA (where GA = grammatical affix and DA = derivational affix) but not strings like *DA + GA + DA + STEM + GA + DA, where the grammatical affixes are less peripheral than the derivational affixes. In English, for instance, we find *morph-eme-ic-iz-ed* (STEM + DA + DA + DA + GA) but not say *morph-eme-s-ic-iz-ed* (STEM + DA + GA + DA + DA + GA) where the number affix (*-s*) is sandwiched between two derivational affixes. This generalization appears true of many, perhaps all, languages, and demonstrates the point: grammatical and word formation rules need to be

when this is not in fact the case. Thus we have *aggression*, but no *aggress*; *butler* and *vicar*, but no *buttle* or *vic* (though in fact all of the starred forms can be found – the latter two in novels by P. G. Wodehouse). The derivational process by which they are assumed to have been formed is called 'back formation': the analogy of *think :thinker* suggests the comparable *vic :vicar*.

separate. The grammatical rules are part of the grammar, and it is not relevant to the grammar whether a given lexeme is a root or a derived form. It seems more appropriate to put the lexical derivation rules in the lexicon.

Thirdly, some of the rules in **1** involve recategorization. Thus, **1a, 1b, 1d–g** take a stem of one category and produce a lexeme that is assigned to another category: so the 'class changing' rule **1a** derives nouns from adjectives. Others of the rules, like **1c, 1h**, are 'class maintaining': the derived category is the same as the original category. We do not in general wish to have rules like this within the grammar that change items from one major lexical category to another.

A fourth reason has to do with the semantic properties of rules such as those in **1**. A derived lexeme generally has some semantic relation to the lexeme from which it is derived, usually through the root which both lexemes share. It is not clear, however, what generalizations can usefully be made about which aspects of the meaning of the stem are reflected in the derived form – compare forms like *boy*:*boyhood*; *knight*:*knighthood*; *sister*:*sisterhood* etc. Similarly the derivational affix often has some general meaning, but any statement of the meaning of an affix will have to be stated in extremely general terms, to which there are exceptions. For example, nouns formed by rule **1h** are typically abstract (*man*:*manhood*) the connotations of *-hood* being 'state, quality or rank' (Partridge 1958, 848), but Partridge also notes the "resultant secondary senses, 'concrete instance' – as in *falsehood*, and, from the nuance 'rank', 'collectivity' as in *brotherhood* and *sisterhood*". A similar example is *remit*:*remission*:*remittal*, noted earlier in the chapter. The two noun forms clearly share some aspect of the meaning of the corresponding verb, but the particular aspects of shared meaning differ in the pairs *remit*:*remission* and *remit*:*remittal*. Such changes of meaning are more appropriately accounted for in the lexicon than in the grammar.

The examples considered so far have been examples of word formation, where a lexical formative has been affixed to a lexical stem. Another common source of new lexemes is composition or compounding, illustrated by words like *bookmark*, *teatime*, *halfback*. The distinction between compounding and derivation rests on the fact that each part of the compound is itself a lexical stem, and is typically a free morph – as is the case with *book*, *mark, bookmark*. By contrast, formatives are always bound morphs.

In compounding there is often a considerable problem about word division, and orthographic conventions offer little help: sometimes compounds are written as a single word (*waterfall*), sometimes hyphenated (*water-drop*), sometimes as two words (*water bottle*) – the examples are all from the *Shorter Oxford English Dictionary*. A recent history of English (Strang 1970, 39) treats as 'morphological units': *middle distance, market research, cost effectiveness, standing ovation*. The criteria used have been discussed (pages 162–4): typically no further item can be inserted between the two elements; they cannot be transformationally separated; one element cannot be pronominalized or be taken as the antecedent for pronominalization; etc. However, there is little clarity as to what counts as a compound word and what is a modifier-head construction where the modifier is a noun. Thus it is curious that in the *Shorter Oxford English Dictionary*, of the forms *field mouse* and *harvest mouse* only the latter has an entry (under *harvest*)! Compounding is an extremely productive source of new lexical items in English, even though its boundaries are unclear.

As a final consideration, we may ask how far one would wish to carry the process of derivational analysis within words. Clearly the basis for analysis is the fact that words share common phonological material and a common element of meaning. Thus *strawberry* is analysed as *straw-berry* on the analogy of *dew-berry, logan-berry, rasp-berry*, etc. One can easily justify the *berry* morph, and in the case of *strawberry*, the *straw* morph: *logan-* and *rasp-* are more difficult and it would perhaps be best to consider *loganberry* and *raspberry* as simple non-derived forms. Another problem area involves 'phonaesthemes' (formatives with phonaesthetic properties) in onomatopoeic words. Some analysts have wished to make an analysis of such words. Thus Bloomfield (1933, 245) sees 'intense, symbolic connotations' associated with the 'prefixes' and 'affixes' in such words as:

3  *fl-* 'moving light': flash, flare, flame, flicker, . . .
   *gl-* 'unmoving light': glow, glare, gloom, glint, . . .
   *sl-* 'smoothly wet': slime, slush, slip, slide, . . .
   *-are* 'big noise or movement': blare, glare, flare, . . .
   *-ash* 'violent movement': bash, crash, flash, slash, . . .

An analysis of this sort can, with some ingenuity, be made quite extensive. A similar and more problematical area involves the etymology of words. Thus in the following set of words:

4   re-ceive    re-cur    *re-duct    re-duce
    de-ceive    *de-cur   de-duct     de-duce
    con-ceive   con-cur   con-duct    con-duce
    *in-ceive   in-cur    in-duct     in-duce,

some analysts recognize 'etymemes' (formatives with etymological relevance). As with phonaesthemes, the problem with this sort of analysis is how far to go; the analyst with a background in the historical study of a language might well wish to go further than an analyst without such a background. For ordinary speakers of the language there is no perception of the etymology of many words (*orchard* deriving from Old English *ort-ȝeard*, the first element probably deriving from Latin *hortus* 'garden'; *caterpillar* said to derive from Old French *chate* 'cat' + *piller, pilour* 'pillager'!). Probably no one would wish to analyse such extreme examples as these. Items like *receive* are more problematical, partly because *re-* is still productive (*re-electrification*) and partly because of the possible analogies with *deceive*, etc., as shown above. On the other hand the 'stem' *-ceive* is no longer usable in any productive way: its status is rather like *logan-* and *rasp-* mentioned above. It is probably best to treat items like *receive* (whose internal structure relates to etymological considerations which are no longer productive) and items like *flash* (whose internal structure relates to phonaesthetic considerations) as simple, underived lexemes.

Our conclusion then is this: it is useful to distinguish between inflectional and derivational morphology. Inflectional morphology deals with the distribution of categories introduced by the grammar, and is general and productive. Derivational morphology deals with the production of new lexemes, is less productive and often arbitrary in application: as such it belongs with the lexicon rather than the grammar. It can also be extended to make generalizations about the internal structure of some lexemes that otherwise one would wish to treat as units (cf. the discussion of phonaesthesia and etymology).

**Technical terms**

back formation
class changing
class maintaining
composition
compound word
derivational morphology
etymeme

lexical formative
lexical morphology
lexical stem
onomatopoeia
phonaestheme
productivity
recategorization

**Exercises**

*1*

The relationship between *kind* and *unkind* (and other similar pairs of words like *helpful:unhelpful*, etc.) can be described by the lexical rule *un-* + Adj ⇒ Adj; prefixing the lexical formative *un-* to an Adj(ective) stem yields another Adj. This is a 'class-maintaining' rule in that the base form and the derived form both belong to the same class, in this case Adj. Consider these words:

| | | | |
|---|---|---|---|
| class | purify | simplification | equality |
| legality | glorification | equalize | simple |
| classify | legalize | popular | centrality |
| glory | beautify | classification | centralize |
| sterilization | beauty | popularity | sterile |
| purity | popularize | legal | pure |
| legalization | central | equal | glorify |

Analyse these words into morphs. Devise lexical rules to account for the derivational relationships between the various words. Which of the rules are class changing and which are class maintaining? How productive are the rules? Make a note of any orthographic regularities in the derivational processes. Can you assign any general 'meaning' to the various lexical formatives you identify (as, for example, *un-* in the example at the top of the exercise is 'negative').

*2   Nationality nouns and adjectives*

A number of different morphological paradigms in English relate country names (e.g. *England, China*); the names given to nationals of that country (e.g. *Englishman*, *Chinese*); the adjective applied to that country (e.g. *English*, *Chinese*); and the language spoken in the country (e.g. *English*, *Chinese*). There are other grammatical differences between paradigms: sometimes, for instance, the name given to nationals has a distinct plural form (*one Englishman*; *two Englishmen*) and sometimes it doesn't (*one Chinese*; *two Chinese*). What are the relevant forms relating to the following countries?

England, Wales, Scotland, Ireland, America, Poland, Russia, France, Hungary, Switzerland, Thailand, Portugal, Denmark, Turkey, India, the Netherlands, Brazil.

# 16 Form classes and grammatical categories

Previous chapters discussed the principles by which form classes are established. The discussion assumed that the application of the principles was relatively straightforward and would yield a determinate set of classes. In this chapter we re-open the question.

Earlier chapters identified two different types of morpheme : lexical morphemes or lexemes, and grammatical morphemes. Lexical morphemes were grouped together into classes, called lexical categories, to which we assigned names like Noun, Verb, Adjective, etc. We saw that in principle such classes are 'open', in that new items can be added to them. So, for example, *sputnik* has been added to the lexical category of Noun in English. Grammatical morphemes too were grouped together into classes, called grammatical categories, to which we gave names like Tense, Number, etc. Each of these categories has a finite number of terms; they are 'closed' in that new items cannot arbitrarily be added to them. So, for example, the English category of Number has the two terms singular and plural; it is difficult to see how a new term, say 'dual', could be added since it would have extensive repercussions for the whole grammar of the language.

In discussion hitherto we have supposed that the distribution of a grammatical category, like number, and of the terms of the category, like singular and plural, is totally definable within the grammar. This is shown by the fact that our constituent structure rules develop structures which include such items as singular and plural. By contrast, whereas the grammar can define the distribution of some lexical category as a whole, it is unable to define the distribution of individual members of the category. So, for example, we can use the grammar to define the distribution of the class Verb, but we cannot in the grammar define the total distribution of some particular verb – this would require, amongst other things, a statement about the selection restrictions for the verb in question, and we have not included such information in the grammar.

A further distinction between lexical and grammatical categories is this: lexical categories are realized either as free forms (e.g. *dog*, *walk*) or as the stems of complex forms (e.g. *dog-s*, *walk-ing*). Grammatical categories, on the other hand, are very often realized as bound forms (e.g. *-s*, *-ing*, *-ed*) though they may on occasion be realized as individual words (e.g. the auxiliary verbs). These facts are reflected in oppositions commonly found in grammars between lexical (or 'full') words and grammatical (or 'form') words – lexical words are typically those that contain a lexical stem, and grammatical words are those that realize grammatical categories alone. The distinction is quite useful but not entirely clear-cut, and is not always easy to draw. The fact that grammatical categories are often realized as bound morphs leads, in many languages, to a typical association between a lexical category and a grammatical category or categories. So, for example, in English the category of Number is realized on the Noun and the category of Tense is realized on the Verb – an important point to which we return.

Considerations of this sort lie behind the establishment of a system of 'parts of speech' for a language. Discussions of parts of speech often distinguish between the 'major' (Noun, Verb, Adjective, Adverb) and the 'minor' (Article, Preposition, Conjunction, etc.). The major parts of speech are, or have stems which are, lexical categories. In descriptions of particular languages linguists have usually (but not invariably) been able to identify classes to which they assign the names of the major parts of speech. The minor parts of speech often realize grammatical categories, and descriptions of different languages vary as to the number of minor categories identified and the names given to them. For example English is usually described as having a category Article, but in many languages, Latin for instance, no such category is identified.[1]

---

1 Such observations raise a host of interesting questions that we do not have the space to explore. For example: to what extent is there a similarity between the classes named Verb in Akan, Gaelic and English which justifies their being called by the same name? Do all languages have a syntactic class to which we can appropriately apply the name Verb? Those interested in pursuing this question are directed to Lyons (1968, chapter 7) and the references there. An interesting review of word classes in a variety of languages is *Lingua*, vol. 17, 1967.

In traditional grammars, which do not recognize the morpheme as a relevant linguistic unit, parts of speech are classes of words (the traditional word corresponding to the orthographic unit). In some more recent treatments, parts of speech are regarded as classes of stems – a classification that works best with the major parts of speech, with a lexical stem, but which also works with other stems realizing only grammatical categories. The two approaches are obviously somewhat different, but not necessarily in conflict. Thus Hockett (1958, 221) defines a part of speech as:

A form class of stems which show some similar behaviour in inflection, in syntax, or both. The part of speech system of a language is the classification of all its stems on the basis of similarities and differences of inflectional or syntactical behaviour.

Compare this definition with the definitions given for some of the parts of speech in classical Greek by Dionysius Thrax, a Greek grammarian of the first century BC – he is often regarded as the forerunner of the western tradition of grammatical description (see Robins 1967, 33):

The noun is a part of speech inflected for case, signifying a person or thing.
The verb is a part of speech without case inflection, but inflected for tense, person and number, signifying an activity or process performed or undergone.
The preposition is a part of speech placed before other words in composition and in syntax.

Both Hockett and Thrax mention two types of criteria: inflectional and syntactic. As we have seen, inflection involves the internal structure of a word form, perhaps by affixation of a bound morph, etc. In the case of the major parts of speech inflection typically involves the affixation, etc. of bound morphs realizing grammatical categories to a lexical stem – as in Thrax' definition of the Noun and Verb in Greek. Syntactic criteria are distributional criteria, reflecting the external distribution of a form. It was these two criteria that we used to establish form classes on pages 34–5. Nowadays syntactic criteria are usually held to be primary: in those languages that do not inflect at all they are the only criteria available; in the case of languages in which some but not all parts of speech inflect, they are the only possible criteria for the non-inflecting parts of speech – as in Thrax' definition of the Preposition in Greek. When languages do inflect, however, inflections will obviously be an important criterion.

Thrax' definitions also include a semantic criterion lacking in Hockett's – (... 'signifying a person or thing' ..., etc.). We have already observed that we cannot rely on notional definitions (see pages 60–6). A moment's thought uncovers many forms that are syntactically nouns but do not 'signify a person or thing' – ACTION, ACTIVITY, MOVEMENT, etc. Indeed nouns like this 'signify an activity', supposedly the criterion for verbs. We do not take semantic criteria as criterial in establishing form classes. It is a different matter when we come to naming a class; since it is indeed the case, in for example English, that the formally defined class of Noun includes many items that do 'signify a person or thing', it seems sensible to retain the traditional name for this class rather than inventing a new arbitrary name. The question of naming (which may as well relate to some central semantic feature, and will yield an easily remembered name) is a different matter from the formal establishment of a class (which ignores such criteria).[2]

To exemplify inflectional and syntactic criteria, consider how we might identify the class Noun in English. English is not particularly rich in inflections and the only inflectional criterion we can apply is that members of this class co-occur with the plural morph -*s* (or inflect for number by fusion *man :men*, etc.). The inflectional criterion that they co-occur with the genitive morph -*s* is only marginally useful in English since this item might more profitably be considered to be an affix to the NP as a whole rather than to the noun specifically (*the woman next door's cat* = *the cat of the woman next door*).[3] Distributional criteria reflect the ability of the noun to operate as head of the NP, and hence to co-occur with articles, numerals, etc. within the NP. Then, as NPs they have a distribution as subject, object etc. of the verb.

2 At one time it was fashionable to discard even the names Noun, Verb, etc. since it was thought that these might smuggle in undesirable semantic considerations. Thus Fries (1957) conducts a rigorous distributional analysis of English and labels the classes he establishes with numbers and letters. It is no surprise to discover that these classes, although given arbitrary labels, turn out to be the familiar classes of Noun, Verb and so on. It is worth consulting Fries to see how far such an analysis can be pursued.

3 Various derivational affixes are also limited to noun forms – like the -*ness* in *goodness*, *helplessness*, etc. But since -*ness*, and others like it, is a lexical formative and not an inflectional affix, we do not consider such items further here.

If we apply these criteria to a set of items we find a class, including MAN, BOY, DOG, CAT, etc., that will meet them all. We call these the 'central members' of the class. Other forms meet some but not all of the criteria. Some are 'defective' with respect to the inflectional criteria: abstract nouns (SINCERITY, WARMTH, BEAUTY) and proper nouns (JOHN, FIDO) do not occur in the plural; a few nouns occur only in the plural (SCISSORS, TROUSERS, SUDS, etc.). Others are 'defective' with respect to some of the distributional criteria: proper nouns do not typically occur with articles, and so on. However defective their morphology may be, and however restricted their co-occurrence possibilities with the NP are, all the items we have mentioned occur as the head noun of an NP, and hence as subject, object, etc. of the verb. These latter are perhaps the most important criteria – note that they are syntactic. There are, however, a few items that we would probably wish to identify as nouns that barely meet even this minimal criterion: they are items like HEADWAY, TABS (*They kept tabs on him*) that occur only, or mainly, in idioms.

The preceding paragraph illustrates the principle used to establish form classes – a given set of criteria identifies a particular class. It also shows up a problem – particular items meet these criteria to a greater or lesser extent. We can establish a class of 'central members' that meet all or most of the criteria. There remain various sub-classes that meet the criteria to a greater or lesser extent, or, on the margins, hardly at all! To some extent we can turn this fact to our advantage since it allows us to identify sub-classes of the major category – in a previous chapter, for instance, we established the class of Proper Nouns in terms of the fact that they do not co-occur with the definite article. It does, however, have a drawback: the categories have no 'hard, definable edges'. Let us give a non-linguistic example to define the problem. Individuals may be assumed to have criteria by which they assign a particular plant to the category 'tree' or 'bush'. There seem to be central members of these classes: we speak of *pine* or *beech trees*, not *bushes*, and similarly of *rhododendron* or *lavender bushes* not *trees*. But what of *holly* or *hawthorn*? There is a comparable sort of indeterminancy between form classes.

We will consider this question by looking at the distinction between adjectives and nouns, and then at the distinction between adjectives and verbs in English.

We have already outlined criteria for the class Noun. Adjectives are usually defined in terms of four criteria, one inflectional and the other three syntactic. The syntactic criteria are: **i** that adjectives occur attributively as modifiers of the noun in NP (*a poor man*); **ii** that they occur predicatively after the copula (*the man is poor*); and **iii** that they can themselves be modified by intensifying expressions (*very poor, rather poor*). The inflectional criterion is **iv**: they occur in comparative and superlative forms (*poor:poorer:poorest*). On the evidence POOR is a central member in that it satisfies all four criteria. Less central members include adjectives: that do not occur attributively (*\*an afloat boat*, *\*an ablaze building*); that do not occur predicatively (*\*The difficulty is same*, *\*The reason is principal*); that cannot be modified by intensifying expressions (*\*rather afloat*, *\*very major*); and that do not compare (*\*more major*, *\*most major*). These restrictions need not in themselves worry us.

The criteria for adjectives and nouns obviously do not overlap. Now we come to the problem. We identified POOR as centrally an adjective. Yet we find that it occurs in most of the environments taken to be criteria for nouns: it co-occurs with articles (*the poor, those poor*, etc.), and it can be subject or object of a verb (*The poor are always with us*; *He pities the poor*, etc.). There are, to be sure, restrictions – it does not for instance occur in the plural (*\*The poors*). But the 'adjective' POOR seems to occur in more of the typical noun environments than a peripheral 'noun' like TABS! The converse is also true. CONCRETE, which appears to be a noun, occurs in some of the adjective environments: *a concrete floor, the floor is concrete*. It does not meet all the criteria, however – it does not compare (*\*more concrete*, *\*most concrete*) and can hardly occur with modifiers (*\*rather concrete*). Here we find the 'noun' CONCRETE occurring in more of the typical adjective environments than a peripheral 'adjective' like AFLOAT. How are we to tackle this problem?

A number of possible solutions have been mooted. We discuss four, and exemplify them with POOR.

The first is to say that we have two distinct, though homophonous, items: POOR(1) is an adjective and POOR(2) is a noun. One drawback to this solution is that POOR(2) still retains some adjective-like properties – it can be intensified (*He only pities the very poor*, cf. *\*He only pities the very man*) and it can, just, be compared (*He only pities the poorest*, cf. *\*He only pities the most man*). Nouns cannot be intensified or compared.

A second solution is to say that POOR is 'basically' an adjective, but can be 'recategorized' as a noun in certain types of structure. A drawback of this solution is that we must then say that some adjectives can recategorize easily (e.g. POOR, BEAUTIFUL. GOOD), that others do not recategorize at all (e.g. MAJOR. ABLAZE), and that yet others recategorize in some circumstances (e.g. BLACK, PINK). This seems to involve adding a statement in the lexicon for each adjective to indicate the ease with which it can be recategorized.

A third solution is to assert that POOR is an adjective, but that in certain structures additional material is 'understood'; with this solution *the poor* might derive by a transformational deletion rule from a structure like *those who are poor* or *those people who are poor*. This solution is attractive in that it sets out a semantic reading of the usage of POOR concerned, but it has problems if we extend the principle widely: *I want the black* might be related to *I want the black dress, I want the black ball* (in snooker), *I want the black man*, etc.: the 'understood' items depend on the context of utterance.

A final solution is to say that in *the poor are always with us* POOR functions as the head of an NP, and to relax our rules on the structure of NPs to allow adjectives in certain circumstances to take on this syntactic function. This solution involves distinguishing the syntactic function of an item (as head of an NP, etc.) from its syntactic class (as adjective, etc.). This final solution seems attractive in the case of items like CONCRETE, noted above, where, in a structure like *a concrete floor*, it functions as the modifier of a noun head. Many items we wish to class as nouns can occur as modifiers (*a picnic basket, a bus station, iron railings*, etc.); it does not seem sensible in these cases to identify either two items (PICNIC(1) an adjective, and PICNIC(2) a noun) or to say that PICNIC has been recategorized.[4] This solution is also attractive in the case of structures like *the down line* (a preposition modifier), *the very man* (an adverbial modifier). The discussion seems to suggest that

---

4 This solution is not, however, open to the sort of grammar that we have been considering so far: we have no satisfactory way of identifying grammatical 'functions' like modifier. The grammar is set up to account for the distribution of categories. We return to this problem on pages 254–60.

there is no unique satisfactory solution. Some instances are best handled in one way, others in another.

We now turn to consider the relationship between adjectives and verbs. We have already seen (pages 60–2) that the distinction drawn in English between adjectives and verbs is not drawn in the same way, if at all, in some languages: in these languages items that are syntactically verbs translate into English adjectives. What is the position in English? The inflectional criterion for a class Verb in English is that the category of tense and the 'aspectual' categories of progressive and perfect may be realized on verb stems. The situation is complicated by the fact that in English all these categories cannot be realized simultaneously on the verb stem, instead auxiliary verbs are introduced to carry them (see discussion on pages 107ff.).[5] Syntactic criteria for verbs would include their distribution within the VP, their 'strict subcategorization' possibilities, and so on. We should also note that verbs can be subcategorized in terms of inherent features (rather in the manner in which we subcategorized nouns by features like [±animate], etc. on pages 85ff.). The feature most usually discussed in this connection is [±state] (which we discuss in more detail in pages 288–92). For now we note that some verbs do not readily co-occur with the progressive auxiliary *He is knowing Chinese*, *He is seeming intelligent*, or in the imperative (as a command) *Know Chinese*, *Seem intelligent*. These, usually known as 'stative' verbs, can be characterized as [+state]. Other verbs that do occur with the progressive and in the imperative are known as 'active' or 'action' verbs; they can be characterized as [−state]: *He is turning off the light*, *Turn off the light*, etc.

At first glance the criteria for verbs seem to be distinct from those for adjectives. A few items can be used either as adjectives or verbs (*the grass is yellow*, *The grass is yellowing*), and there are a number of systematic derivational relationships between adjectives and verbs (RIPE: RIPEN, CLEAR: CLARIFY, etc.). On the other hand the two classes do not overlap inflectionally. The category of tense for example can be marked on verb stems (*He walks, He walked*) but not on adjective stems (*\*He poors*,

---

5 The situation is different in other languages where the verb stem can carry both tense and aspect categories – see for example the brief exemplification of Akan on page 60. Such languages often do not have a category of auxiliary verb; Akan doesn't.

*He poored*). But then we come to auxiliary verbs. Suppose we say that the verb BE is introduced as a 'dummy verb' with adjectives to carry the tense distinction (this sort of analysis seemed appropriate to account for the occurrence of the 'dummy verb' DO in negative and interrogative constructions on pages 116–17), giving *He walksn't* but *He doesn't walk*; *Walks he?* but *Does he walk?* Perhaps, by analogy, BE is a 'dummy verb' for adjectives – *He poors* but *He is poor*, *He poored* but *He was poor*. If we adopt this analysis, we can treat adjectives in English as another subclass of verb, distinguished by the fact that they require the introduction of the dummy BE!

Such a proposal is not entirely fanciful (and indeed is adopted by some linguists). If we adopt it, how do the other distinguishing criteria for verbs work out? To begin with, adjectives, like verbs, have a distribution within VP – both are 'predicators'. We can use much the same kinds of strict subcategorization frames for adjectives as we can for verbs. Some verbs take sentential complements (*I believe that the world is flat*), others (RUN, PAINT) do not. Similarly some adjectives take sentential complements (*It is odd that the world is flat*), and others (RED, INTELLIGENT) do not. Some verbs are transitive and others are not. Adjectives can be considered in a similar light if we note that non-subject NPs in this case require prepositions: *I like reading*: *Reading is easy for me*; *I delight in syntactic analysis*: *Syntactic analysis is delightful to me*; *I can't understand the argument*: *The argument is incomprehensible to me*, and so on. A further similarity involves the characterization [±state]. Just as we have stative and action verbs, so we have stative and action adjectives: RED and POOR are [+state] (*I am being poor*, *Be poor*); CAREFUL and CLEVER may be [−state] (*I am being careful*, *Be careful*). Some verbal forms occur attributively like adjectives – *singing bird*, *roaring fire*. We could derive NPs like these by exactly the same rules as we used for attributive adjectives on pages 142–3.

We note that verbs and adjectives are related; earlier we showed that adjectives and nouns were related. Does this mean that nouns and verbs are also related? Well, we could extend the classification [±state] somewhat. Nouns like PERSON and VIRGIN seem to be [+state] (*She is being a virgin*, *Be a virgin*) in contrast to HERO (*He's being a hero*, *Be a hero*). Similarly we note that some nouns take sentential complements, like

RUMOUR, INSINUATION (*Have you heard the rumour that the world is flat?*), and some nouns do not, like CAT and BOY.

The position reached in the last paragraph does not seem very helpful. If we group all these items into one large class, called, say, 'contentives', then we would still need to distinguish between those contentives that typically introduce BE to carry tense (the former class of adjectives), those that permit tense to be shown on the lexical stem (the former class of verbs) and those that may occur with articles (the former class of nouns)! For English at least it seems more sensible to retain the original classes and recognize that the classification of stems is not wholly without problems.

In any given sentence it is usually clear whether a particular lexical stem is being 'used as' a noun or adjective or verb. We were after all able to set up three separate and non-overlapping criteria for these classes. The typical problem is whether we are able to assign a particular stem to one or other class independent of its use in a sentence, and this is not always straightforward. A speaker, by using a given lexical stem in more than one class, can make subtle distinctions of meaning; English may be unusually liberal in the latitude it allows to individual stems to occur in different classes. Other languages do not seem to allow quite such freedom!

We now turn to a different though related problem: the relationship between sub-classes of a lexical category and the number and type of grammatical categories that we may wish to establish in a language. As a preliminary, we distinguish between 'overt' and 'covert' categories. Some categories are overt in that at least one term of the category is identified by a formal marker of some sort: in the English category of tense, the term past is overtly marked by the morph -*ed*. Similarly, the term plural in the category of number is overtly marked by the morph -*s* affixed to noun stems. Even though the singular term is not also overtly marked we say that the category is overt. Such categories have other syntactic implications. Thus, for example, there are co-occurrence restrictions between nouns and numerals that can, at least in part, be related to the singular–plural distinction. The numeral *one* cannot co-occur with plural nouns, and numerals other than *one* cannot co-occur with singular nouns. Some verbs require non-singular subjects or objects (so we can have *he gathered the men into a group* but not *\*he gathered the man into a group*), etc. The category of number of English controls verb concord and, to a limited extent, concord within the NP. We saw on pages 186ff. that co-occurrence restrictions and facts like concord were important in establishing the category of number. Other categories may be 'covert', in that no term in the category can be identified with a formal marker: on the other hand co-occurrence restrictions or other grammatical phenomena enable us to establish the existence of the category. Thus the French category of gender is a covert category: nouns, which are assigned to gender classes, are not themselves usually marked for gender, but the gender is clear from co-occurrence with, for example, article forms. There is no overt marker of gender in a noun like *chaise* but it must co-occur with the article *la* rather than *le*: although the category of gender is inherent in the noun, the actual formal marking of gender occurs not on the noun but on the article which it is in construction with. Covert categories are no less important in a description than overt categories.

This particular distinction also brings us into direct confrontation with problems concerned with the relation between 'notional' and 'formal' categories. This can be illustrated by considering the category of number in English. At first sight it seems a fairly straightforward matter. The grammatical category of number is an overt category with two terms, singular and plural, shown by the alternation between pairs of forms like *cat*: *cats*. The grammatical category correlates, more or less, with a notional category which we may suppose also has two terms, 'oneness' and 'more-than-oneness' – we use *cat* to refer to a single 'cat', and *cats* to refer to more than one 'cat'. So far as it goes this is correct, and the names given to the grammatical category reflect these semantic facts. Note that the particular distinction drawn in English is not universal; we have already noted that some languages, classical Greek and Arabic for example, have a three-term number category, with an additional term, 'dual', used to refer to things that typically go in pairs (arms, legs). English has no grammatical category of dual. English can and does have the means to refer to pairs of items – for example the lexical items *both*, *neither* – but the distinction is not 'grammaticalized', realized as a formal system in the grammar, but is rather 'lexicalized'.

We return to the question of number in English. It can be

argued that, prior to any singular:plural distinction, a mass:count distinction is needed, the number distinction of singular:plural only applying to count nouns. Consider the following. Count nouns in general are used to refer to discrete objects that can be counted – thus *two chairs*, *twenty cigarettes*, *a hundred pipers*, and so on. Mass nouns, on the other hand, are characteristically used to refer to items perceived not in terms of individual members, but in some mass terms: items like *water*, *sand*, *butter*, *ink*, etc. The count:mass distinction is covert, in that nouns in English are not marked in any way to show their membership of either sub-class. The distinction can, however, be established on the basis of the co-occurrence relationships of the two classes of noun (see discussion in pages 90–1). Mass nouns do not co-occur with numerals (*\*one sand*, *\*two waters*, etc.) nor in the plural (*\*butters*, *\*inks* etc.); they do not co-occur with the indefinite article (*\*an ink*, *\*a water*), but do occur with the determiner *some* (pronounced /sm/) (*some butter*, *some ink*). Count nouns are the opposite: they occur with numerals (*one boy*); in the plural form (*boys*); with the indefinite article (*a boy*); but not, in the singular, with /sm/ (*\*sm boy*). We also observe that, for the purposes of concord, both subject–verb concord and concord within the NP, mass nouns operate like singular count nouns (*This butter is . . .*; *\*These butter are . . .*). There are, of course, idiosyncracies: a few mass nouns are plural in form and take plural concord (*clothes*, *guts*, *suds*, etc.); a few are not overtly plural but take plural concord (*gentry*, *cattle*, *clergy*, etc.); and so on. These idiosyncracies apart, they offer no particular problems.

The count:mass distinction may be held to be a reflex of a notional distinction which we call a distinction between 'individuated' and 'non-individuated' referents.

The descriptive problem begins to arise when we find nouns that we might wish to regard as 'basically' mass nouns occurring with the syntax of count nouns:

1 I always have a coffee at this time of the morning
2 Two milks, please
3 I don't like either of these two wines

The converse also occurs:

4 The scrum was not producing enough ball for the backs
5 He is collecting worm for his fishing
6 This room smells of cat

As with our discussion of POOR (pages 236–7), we can adopt one of a number of solutions, each seeming attractive for some items and less attractive for others. We can suppose that two items are involved – COFFEE(1), the mass noun, and COFFEE(2), the count noun, and so on. Or we can suppose that COFFEE is basically a mass noun, and has been recategorized in **1**. Alternatively, we can suppose that some relevant quantifying expression has been elided – *I always have* [*a cup of*] *coffee* . . . .

The first solution seems attractive when the phenomenon is well established in usage, and this fact is often reflected in dictionaries. So for example LAMB is given two senses in the dictionary, LAMB(1) the 'animal' and LAMB(2) the 'meat of the animal', reflected in sentences like:

**7** I would like a lamb
**8** I would like lamb

This solution is reinforced by the fact that in some cases the animal and its meat receive two different lexical realizations PIG : PORK; COW : BEEF, etc. A similar solution is open to items like BEAVER(1), the 'animal' and BEAVER(2) the 'skin of the animal'; OAK(1) the 'tree' and OAK(2) the 'wood of the tree'. Such usages seem well established. There are, however, two points to be made. Firstly, the type of understood categorization depends to a large extent on context – in a draper's shop **8** would typically refer to the 'skin' rather than the 'meat' of the animal (and the converse is a restaurant). Secondly, the extent to which the process is established in usage (if dictionaries are any guide) is variable. Thus we might not expect to find POTATO(1) the 'vegetable' (*Give me a potato*) and POTATO(2) (*Would you like some* (*=sm*) *potato?*), and similarly APPLE, BANANA, etc.

The second solution seems attractive for examples like **4–6**. Usages like this do not seem to be established in the language – though **4** is becoming established in television commentary on rugby football, in Britain at least – and are clearly heavily context-dependent for their interpretation.

The third solution seems attractive in cases like **1–3**, though it is not without problems. In a case like *two milks* we need to account for the resiting of the plural marker (compare *two pints of milk*), but we can doubtless get round this. More difficult is that the precise quantifying expression relies once again on context: **2** relates to *two* [*pints of*] *milk* in a note to the milkman, but to *two* [*cups/glasses* etc. *of*] *milk* in a cafe.

The count:mass distinction appears to rest on a perceptual distinction, at least to some degree. Some things are characteristically perceived as non-individuated (like 'sand' and 'water'), but they may be individuated in quanta (*a bucket of water*, *a heap of sand*) and then expressed like count nouns (*two waters*). Conversely, some things are typically perceived as individuated (like 'ball' and 'cat'), but may, or some of their attributes may, be perceived as non-individuated, and then be expressed as mass nouns (cf. **4–6**).

A similar problem arises with the class of 'collective' nouns (COMMITTEE, GOVERNMENT, HERD, etc.). These occur with either singular or plural concord:

**9**   The committee has agreed to the appointment
**10**   The committee have agreed to take no further action

The usual account of such sentences is that the number choice depends on whether the collective is thought of as acting as a single body (*the committee has* . . .) or as a collection of individuals (*the committee have* . . .). With such nouns, even though they take plural concord on the verb, concord within the NP remains in the singular (*this committee have* . . .)! As in the count:mass distinction, the assignment of number appears to rest on a perceived or imputed semantic perception.

To account for this, we might suppose that in some community some 'typical' perception such as 'individuated:non-individuated' and 'oneness:more-than-oneness' is 'grammaticized' into a formal grammatical category – count:mass, singular:plural. The grammatical category is reflected in a range of syntactic behaviour; once established as a grammatical category, it is open to exploitation for semantic effect. (Not all communities grammaticize the same 'typical' percepts.)

An interesting way of looking at this problem is proposed by Jespersen (1929, 46). He suggests that we can regard language as involving three inter-related levels of description: a level of forms (the actually occurring morphological markings); a level of grammar (with formally established categories like count:mass, singular:plural, etc.); and a level of meaning (with notional categories like individuated:non-individuated; oneness:more-than-oneness etc. The grammatical level faces both ways: towards the level of form and towards the level of meaning as in Figure 94.

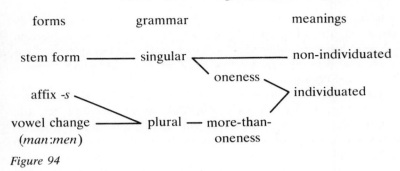

*Figure 94*

A perceptual characterization is reflected in a particular grammatical choice, which is realized as a particular form. This approach allows us both to maintain the principle of a grammar established on formal principles (the formal opposition of number, etc.) and to understand how this formal system is related to, and can on occasion be manipulated by, the semantics.

We can incorporate it into our previous description in the following manner. Recall that we suggested (pages 86–9) that nouns should be characterized in the lexicon in terms of a set of syntactic features, [±count], etc. We also saw that a characterization, say [+count], had consequences for co-occurrence with articles, etc. Suppose now we say that whereas a particular lexical item may be characterized as 'typically' [+count] or [−count], this characterization may be altered by a semantic consideration. However, once they have been altered, the grammatical consequences are predicted by the grammar. We can also accommodate within such an account those irregularities we have noted during the discussion – SUDS for example can be characterized as [−count], [+pl].

A further advantage is that this way allows us to accommodate both the situation described above for [±count] nouns in English, where a semantic characterization can influence a grammatical choice, and the sort of situation found with French gender, where the grammatical characterization is relatively uninfluenced by semantic considerations. In different languages different categories are influenced to different degrees by semantic considerations. In French, and other European languages, nouns cannot be switched from gender class to gender class for communicative effect (one might think, for instance, that French would allow *une homme* as a characterization of an effeminate man –

but this sort of thing is not permissible). Many languages do permit it: so in Lugisu, a Bantu language from Uganda, we find *mu-twe* 'head' 'recategorized' as a diminuitive *ka-twe* 'pin head', or as an augmentative *gu-twe* 'big head' by changing gender class – the effect is derogatory.

Let us now turn to another grammatical category in English, that of tense. How should our description account for the relationship between notions of time and the formal opposition between 'past' and 'non-past' established and discussed on page 109? The category is an overt two term category, called tense, because it often corresponds to notions of time, but the correspondence is far from direct. There is a frequent correspondence between past time and past tense (*I was in London last week, We went to America last summer,* etc.) but there are circumstances when a past tense form is used, with no implication of past time. If the main verb in reported speech is in the past tense, the verb in the reported speech may also be in the past tense, irrespective of the time reference. If my daughter says to me at breakfast one morning '*I am going to the pictures this evening*' (using a non-past tense verb form), I can report this to my wife at lunch time with the words '*Jane said she was going to the pictures this evening*' (using a past tense verb form). Past tense is also often used for 'unreal conditionals' – as in *If my daughter were to go the pictures . . ., If only I understood what it was all about . . ., I wish I knew . . .*, and so on. In yet other circumstances the distinction between the past and non-past tense does not reflect any time distinction at all, as in: *I wonder/wondered if you would like a cup of coffee; I think/thought you would be interested to know that . . .*; etc. The most striking cases of non-correspondence occur with the modal auxiliary verbs, where very frequently the use of a morphological past tense form bears no relation at all to past time: *I might go if you asked me; I could stop smoking if I tried; I wouldn't have the slightest idea*; etc.[6]

---

6 There are some cases where past tense and past time do correspond: *I can speak French quite well now: I could speak German when I was younger*, but this is not the regular pattern for modal verbs. There is an argument that some so-called past tense forms among modal verbs are better thought of as simply separate items. An example is *should* when used in the sense of 'duty', e.g. *You should always give up your seat on the bus to an old lady.* Replacing *should* by *shall* produces a sentence of doubtful acceptability! The interested reader is referred for further discussion to Leech (1971) and Palmer (1971).

Next consider sentences with a non-past verb form. They can sometimes be found with a 'present' time reference: *Dalglish shoots and it's a goal*, but, as we have already observed, this is not the usual way to refer to actions taking place at the time of utterance. More frequently the simple non-past verb form is used in a 'timeless' sense – *Honesty is the best policy, War solves no problems*; to refer to 'habits' – *I cycle to work every morning, I always get drunk at Hogmanay*; to refer to 'states' – *I belong to Glasgow, I speak Chinese*; and so on. Non-past verb forms may also be used to refer to future events – *I leave for Paris in the morning*; and indeed to past events (the so-called 'historic present') – *Earlier this morning I come into the kitchen and what do I find?*; and past states of affairs – *Shakespeare draws his characters from real life*. The correspondence between 'present time' and the non-past form of the verb is even less straightforward than the correspondence between 'past time' and the past form of the verb.

What, then, do we make of characterizations like 'timeless', 'habit', 'state' and so on, characterizations frequently met with in grammars. There are, to be sure, occasions when the correspondence between some such category and a term in the category of tense is reasonably direct: thus 'timeless' is typically realized by a non-past verb form (*God was good*; *Christmas was on 25 December*; *Cocks crowed at dawn* seem anomalous if they are to be understood as statements of 'general truth' which hold regardless of time!) Similarly 'past instantaneous actions' are usually realized by a simple past verb form (*I bought a coat this afternoon*; *I gave my wife a diamond ring for Christmas*). But usually the relation is less direct. 'present habits' usually correlate with a non-past verb form, but past habits frequently occur, not with a simple past form, but with a form of USED TO (*I cycle to work every morning*; *I used to cycle to work every morning*). Similarly, as we have observed before, 'present instantaneous' actions are often realized by the progressive rather than the simple non-past verb form (*I am typing this sentence now*). The relationship between notions like 'habit', etc. and some formal overt grammatical category is often indirect, but such notions can play an important part in controlling other features of the sentence. Thus, for example, 'timeless' statements usually require a noun of general reference as subject, and are restricted as to the type of adverbial modifiers they permit: *Cocks crow at dawn* can be held to be a timeless statement, but *My favourite red rooster crows at dawn most mornings* cannot. Similarly 'past habits' impose restrictions on adverbial expressions – one can hardly say *\*I used to cycle to work this morning!*

Notions like 'timeless', 'habit', etc. seem to have relevance for more than the single category of tense. Grammatical features that can be correlated with such notions extend throughout the sentence and may be relevant for grammatical selection at various places. A valuable discussion of some of these notions is Crystal (1966) to which the reader is referred (see also Leech (1971)).

The difficulty may be summarized thus: categories like 'timeless' 'habit' 'unreal condition', etc. have syntactic implications in relation to such matters as co-occurrence restrictions relating to adverbs etc.; on the other hand there is no single overt category to which they can be tied in any straightforward way. There is a further problem with respect to the notional categories – it is not clear how many such categories we need to postulate, or what the distinctions are between them. For example, we have suggested a category of 'state' – but this is clearly not a unitary category at all, there are all sorts of states. We might recognize: inherent states (*I am a man*); resultant states (*My coffee is cold* (*now, but it was hot ten minutes ago*)); transitory states (*It is fine now* (*but will be raining again in ten minutes*)); and so on. It is far from clear that reliable distinctions can be drawn clearly between them.

This is at least true for English where such categories are not relatable to a formal distinction in the grammar. In terms of our former discussion, they are not 'grammaticalized'. The situation is different in some other languages. In Finnish the distinction between 'transitory' and 'inherent' states is reflected in a difference in the case form adopted by the noun. In Akan the distinction between 'states' and 'actions' is reflected in the existence of a special 'stative' verb form, open only to verbs that describe states; the distinction between 'inherent' and 'resultant' states is typically marked by different aspect markers on the verb.

As far as English is concerned, it does not seem profitable to set up categories like 'timeless' as grammatical categories, on a par with the grammatical category of tense – though attempts have been made. It would seem more appropriate to account for such distinctions in terms of a model of description like that hinted at on page 245, but we shall not pursue this further here.

**Technical terms**

closed category
collective noun
count noun
covert category
form word
full word
grammatical category
grammatical word

lexical category
lexical word
mass noun
open category
overt category
part of speech
recategorization

**Exercises**

In the grammatical analysis of languages words are assigned to *word classes* on the formal basis of *syntactic behaviour,* supplemented and reinforced by differences of *morphological paradigms*, so that every word in a language is a member of a word class. Word class analysis has long been familiar in Europe under the title 'parts of speech', and since medieval times grammarians have operated with nine word classes or parts of speech: noun, verb, pronoun, adjective, adverb, preposition, conjunction, article and interjection. (R. H. Robins, *General Linguistics*, Longmans, 1964)

*1*

Can you think of some of the principal syntactic environments in English in which you would find members of the classes usually named noun, verb and adjective?

*2*

Can you describe some of the principal morphological characteristics of these word classes?

*3*

To what word classes (in the list given by Robins above) would you assign the words in the following and why?

'Twas brillig, and the slithy toves                    (1)
  Did gyre and gimble in the wabe;
All mimsy were the borogroves,
  And the mome raths outgrabe.

"Beware the Jabberwock, my son!                                    (5)
  The jaws that bite, the claws that catch!
Beware the Jubjub bird, and shun
  The frumious Bandersnatch!"

He took his vorpal sword in hand:
  Long time the manxome foe he sought –                            (10)
So rested he by the Tumtum tree,
  And stood awhile in thought.

And as in uffish thought he stood,
  The Jabberwock, with eyes of flame,
Came whiffling through the tulgey wood,                            (15)
  And burbled as it came.

### 4

You will find that the membership of some classes is entirely
English, while that of other classes is partly English and partly
invented. Which classes are open to invented words and which
are not? Why do you think some classes have no invented words?

# Part three

# **Functional relations**

# 17 Syntagmatic and paradigmatic relations in syntax

Part one looked at the constituent structure of simple sentences. This part widens the discussion by looking at other aspects of the structure of sentences that have been traditionally the concern of grammarians. This chapter examines some of the different types of relationships that constituents bear to each other, considers how these relations are marked in the grammars of different languages, and whether all such relationships can be satisfactorily described in the type of constituent structure grammars we have been looking at. Chapter 18 examines notions like 'agent' and 'patient' as they might be applied to a sentence like *The policeman ('agent') arrested the burglar ('patient')*, and sees how the relevant notions might be captured in a grammar. Chapter 19 examines the terms 'subject' and 'object'. Chapter 20 is concerned with some questions of word order as they apply to connected text.

This chapter is concerned with those grammatical relations that have been discussed in the linguistic literature under the general title of 'syntagmatic' and 'paradigmatic' relationships.[1]

In straightforward terms, paradigmatic relationships are those contracted between items that are mutually substitutable in some context. Form classes are paradigmatic classes. So, in the English NP, we have a paradigmatic class of determiners including *a, the, some*, etc., and a paradigmatic class of nouns, including *man, boy, house*, etc.

Syntagmatic relations are those contracted between forms or form classes within some structure. These may include relations

---

1 Other terms that relate to the same area are structure and system (cf. Abercrombie 1967), chain and choice (cf. Halliday 1963). These relationships are very general, and can be applied at all levels of linguistic description: they apply equally to phonological and semantic descriptions as they do to syntactic ones. We shall, however, only concern ourselves with such relationships in the grammar.

of order (thus in the English NP the determiner must precede the noun: *the man* not \**man the*) or relations of dependency (thus the English NP contains a 'head' usually a noun, and may optionally contain an adjective 'modifier': we find *big men* and *men* as NPs, but not simply *big*: the adjective is dependent on the noun within the NP).

These relationships are interdependent. The most general statement of an environment (a syntagmatic description) characterizes some form class (a paradigmatic description) in the widest terms. A closer specification of the environment specifies a sub-class of the major class and so on. In the most general terms the distribution of the classes determiner and noun is defined by a rule NP → Det + N. But the sub-class of mass nouns only co-occurs with a sub-class of determiners – so we have *the butter* but not \**a butter*. Our principal concern is with various kinds of syntagmatic relationship.

## Syntagmatic relations of dependency and exclusion

We will examine four types of relation – mutual or bi-lateral dependency; unilateral dependency; co-ordinate dependency and mutual exclusion – but will not discuss them in detail since they are extensively covered in introductory textbooks. There are two fundamental things to recognize about such relationships: first, that they are abstract relationships between sentence constituents, and second, that they are functional relationships indicating the syntactic and semantic function of constituents in their relationships with other constituents. Obviously a language needs to find ways of marking a particular relationship, and different languages select different ways of marking: the relationships themselves, however, are in principle independent of any particular aspect of word or sentence form. Two examples illustrate the point. The unilaterally dependent relation modifier : head can be exemplified by constructions involving adjectives and nouns. The relationship is typically realized in English in the order Adj + N (*the red book*), but in French in the reverse order, N + Adj (*le livre rouge*), without affecting the dependency. The unilaterally dependent relation possessor: possessed (which is itself a type of modifier : head construction with the possessed as the head) can be realized in English by two constructions – *the son of the king* and *the king's son*. The dependency relation is the same in both constructions, but the word order is different and each construction requires different 'markers' (*of* and *-s*) to show the relationship.

The fact that these relationships are functional means that we need to find names to label the type of relationship involved – as modifier : head, possessor : possessed, etc. Sometimes these relationships are definable in terms of constituent structure configurations, but this is not always the case, as we shall see. This is not surprising if we consider that constituent structure grammars operate on categories like NP, V, etc, which are distributionally and not functionally defined. For example, in English, both subject and object (functional descriptions), are realized by NPs (a categorial class). In English we can use constituent structure configurations up to a point to define the functional relation of the relevant NPs – as we did in footnote 2 on page 52, where we defined 'subject' as the NP dominated by S, and 'object' as the NP dominated by VP. The discussion on pages 261–84 will use languages where this definition is less easily workable, but where the functional relationships of dependency hold as in English. In our initial discussion of the relationships mentioned at the beginning of the chapter we will, however, use examples where the relations can be related to distributional characteristics.

Constructions involving bi-lateral or mutual dependency are called exocentric constructions. The definition of an exocentric construction is usually given in distributional terms: the distribution of either constituent in such a construction is different from the distribution of the construction as a whole. Constituent structure rules introducing mutually dependent constituents are usually of the form $X \rightarrow Y + Z$, e.g. $PP \rightarrow Prep + NP$. In a prepositional phrase the distribution of a PP as a whole is different from the distribution of either a preposition or of an NP: the two constituents of a PP. Many of the major syntactic relationships in all languages are mutually dependent. If we make the fundamental syntactic construction of English sentences NP + VP, we assert that all full sentences in English are of this construction type. In English most VP constructions are also bi-laterally dependent: these include the transitive verb and its object (V + NP); the copula and its complement (V + Pred); locative verbs and their locative complements (V + PP); and so on. Hockett (1958) contains a taxonomy of many different kinds of such construction. All the constructions noted are bi-laterally dependent, but it is clear that they are not all of the same kind. This is reflected in the different functional labels given above; part of the reason why a set of functional labels like this were developed is precisely to differentiate between different types of dependency. The importance of this can be appreciated by noting that the three sentences *John beat the dog*, *Fido is a dog* and *John went home* can at some level of structure all be described as strings of the form $NP + V + NP$: but the functional relationship between the second NP and the verb is different in each case – they are respectively transitive verb + object; copula + complement; and locative verb + locative complement. It will be recalled from pages 50–1 that we introduced the category Pred precisely in order to be able to distinguish between NPs introduced as objects of transitive verbs and NPs introduced as complements.

In many bilaterally dependent constructions, one constituent requires the other constituent to assume a particular grammatical form. In English, in prepositional phrases where the NP is realized as a pronoun, the pronoun must be in the 'oblique form' – we find *to him*; *to her*, etc., but not *\*to he*; *\*to she*, etc. This relationship is known as government; in this case, we say that the preposition is the governor, and governs the NP with which it is in construction. In many languages with morphological case systems, like Latin, German or Old English, the relationship between a verb and its object(s), or between a preposition and the NP with which it is in construction is marked by the fact that the NP in question must occur in a particular case; in these instances the verb, or preposition, is said to govern the NP in some particular case. Thus, in Latin, prepositions like *ad* 'to, towards', *intra* 'within', etc. governs the NPs with which they are in construction in the accusative, while prepositions like *ab* 'from', *sine* 'without' govern an NP in the ablative. Some prepositions may govern an NP in either the accusative or ablative; this typically correlates with a systematic difference in meaning: *in* + Acc. 'into, towards'; *in* + Ablative, 'in, among'; *sub* + Acc, 'up to', *sub* + Ablative, 'under'. When such prepositions govern the accusative there is a general sense of 'directional movement'; when they govern the ablative there is a general sense of 'position'. Further examples can be found in any Latin grammar. We have noted that not all bi-laterally dependent constructions in English are the same: for the examples we discussed we might say that transitive verbs govern a direct object, and that copula verbs govern a complement, adjectival or nominal. In English there are few markers of this relationship, but in a language like Latin the object of the transitive verb is usually governed in the accusative (i.e. objects are marked by the accusative case), and complements are in the nominative; they agree with the subject in case and number, and in gender too if the complement is an adjective.

In unilaterally dependent constructions, one constituent is typically obligatory and the other, the dependent constituent, is typically optional. These are called endocentric constructions; and a distributional definition states that the distribution of the construction as a whole is parallel to that of the obligatory constituent. The obligatory constituent is called the head of the construction and the optional constituent the modifier of the head. Constituent structure rules introducing unilaterally dependent constructions typically take the form $X \rightarrow (Y+) Z$, e.g. $NP \rightarrow (Det+) N$. In English NPs the distribution of unmodified nouns is parallel to that of nouns modified by determiners: the determiner is thus the modifier and the noun the head of the construction. In English, unilaterally dependent constructions occur in a variety of different orders; the modifier may precede, follow or be discontinuous about the head (in small capitals in the following examples): *a red* CAR. PEOPLE *that live in glass houses. the earliest* TIME *possible*. Such constructions in English include: Adj + N ((*big*)*man*); Intensifier + Adj ((*very*) *important*); subordinate clauses of various kinds (*I feel tired* (*when I get up*)), (*He closed the window* (*in order to keep out the rain*)); and constructions involving sentence adverbs (see pages 261–4).

It is frequentiy the case in unilaterally dependent constructions that modifiers must agree, or concord, with the head with respect to some particular grammatical category (concord is discussed in more detail on pages 278–84). Thus in English NPs demonstratives (*this* : *these*; *that* : *those*) concord in number with the head noun: *this man*, *these men*, and not *\*these man*, *\*this men*. In many European languages articles and adjectives must concord in number and gender with the head noun: so in German we find *ein junger Mann* 'a young man'; *eine junge*

*Frau* 'a young woman'; *ein junges Mädchen* 'a young girl'. In such cases the head noun controls the form of the modifiers – and we say that the head is the controller of the concord.

In constructions of co-ordinate dependency neither constituent depends syntactically on the other: in distributional terms each constituent has the same distribution as the construction as a whole. A constituent structure rule we used to indicate co-ordinate dependency is Adj → Adj* (see page 79). This introduces strings of adjectives like *a* LITTLE OLD *lady* with the interpretation 'a lady who is both little and old'. Many co-ordinate constructions include a marker of co-ordination like *and* or *or* (*My husband* AND *I*), (*you* OR *your wife*). Not all co-ordinate constructions show such a marker, as we have noted with co-ordinate modifying adjectives above. Another case of co-ordinate dependency with no marker is appositive structures: *President Kennedy*; *Professor Miller*; *Mr Bun, the baker*; *Our father, which art in Heaven*. These examples show that the distributional definition for co-ordinate constructions is less convincing than with the other types of construction we have mentioned.

Relations of exclusion are important insofar as they are useful in defining particular grammatical categories. Thus, for example, verbs of state in English do not in general occur with progressive auxiliary verbs, and this is one of their defining characteristics. We find no sentences like *\*I am knowing Chinese*; *\*Bill is seeming ill*. Proper nouns in English do not typically co-occur with the definite article (*\*the Susan*), except when they co-occur with a relative clause (*the Susan I used to go out with twenty years ago*). Mass nouns do not co-occur with plural expressions (*\*these butter*, *\*Rice are grown in India*).

The discussion has made clear the importance of dependency relations. Such relations lay behind the classification of verbs on pages 50–60: the strict subcategorization frames we established were statements of different types of bi-lateral dependency. Similarly, unilateral dependency relations lay behind our discussion of modifier head relations among NP constituents (pages 75–9) and in the discussion of adverbs (pages 69–75). These relations can be captured up to a point in constituent structure grammars, as our discussion of different rule types for different dependency relations has indicated in the foregoing discussion, and as our discussion of the 'scope' of modification on pages 69–85 showed. But this is not always entirely successful. We give three examples. First: our discussion of STAND on pages 53–4 showed that such verbs can occur either with or without an object NP (*The lamp stood on the table*; *He stood the lamp on the table*). We captured this by expanding the VP by a rule VP → V (NP) PP. But note that the 'optional' object NP stands in a relation of bi-lateral dependency to the verb, and is not in any sense a 'modifier'. Second: as discussed above, we introduced the node Pred on page 51 precisely in order to distinguish between NPs which are complements of copula verbs and NPs which are the direct objects of transitive verbs. Here additional structure was necessary to capture a dependency relationship. Even supposing that we were able to capture all the relevant dependency relations by postulating additional structure, or other additional machinery (perhaps transformations), we might ask whether such a complication of the grammar is the best way to capture these relations. Third: in our discussion of different adverb types (pages 69–75) we in fact smuggled in functional labels by differentiating between adverbs of time, adverbs of place, etc. Such labels are not, strictly speaking, categorial labels. The same applies to some extent to the category Pred noted above.

We need not be surprised that dependency relations cannot always be captured in a straightforward fashion in constituent structure grammars: constituent structure grammars are constructed in terms of formally established categories and the constructions they form, whereas dependency relations are, as the name suggests, relations. Furthermore, even if we can adequately represent these relations in constituent structure terms, we need additional interpretative machinery to interpret the relations from constituent structure trees, or constituent structure rules or both.

In early constituent structure grammars (Bloomfield 1933, Nida 1960) information about dependency was shown in one of two ways. Sometimes trees were marked to indicate the type of dependency involved, illustrated in Figure 95.[2] Alternatively, a statement of the types of relationship involved was appended to a

2 It was fashionable at the time for trees to be rooted in the ground rather than for them to depend from an S node, as is more fashionable today: either way the information is the same.

particular tree. Such statements of dependency relations are lost in some more recent descriptive approaches, as they are to a large extent in earlier transformational grammars.

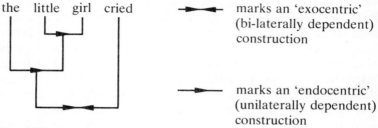

*Figure 95*

There are approaches to description in which dependency relations are more central, but to discuss them here would take us too far out of our way. The interested reader is referred to the brief discussion of 'Categorial Grammar' in Lyons (1968, 227–31).

At the beginning of this section we noted that different languages employ different formal means of marking dependency relations – word order, the use of 'markers', case inflections, etc. In the sections that follow we discuss some of these.

### Word order and grammatical markers

All languages use word order to a greater or lesser extent as a marker of various functional relationships, but different languages impose different ordering restrictions and within any one language some ordering restrictions are strict and others admit of a greater or lesser degree of latitude. It is usually possible to determine, for some particular area of some language that a particular order is the 'normal' or 'unmarked' order: deviations from this, where they are permitted, usually have some particular stylistic or communicative effect.

In addition, all languages use a number of forms, free or bound, as markers of particular relationships: these markers often have little or no lexical meaning – their function being entirely to mark relationships. Thus, in English, we find the -*s* used to mark the genitive relation (*John's book*; *the old man's dog*, etc.) and the *by* found in passive sentences to mark the agent (*The village was destroyed by an earthquake*).

We will consider word order and the use of markers in four constructions in English, and then look briefly at comparable constructions in three other languages: Akan, Scots Gaelic and Turkish.

## Noun phrases in English

The unmarked order for NP constituents in English is: Determiner, Numeral, Adjective, Noun. The noun is the head of the construction and the other constituents are unilaterally dependent on it. As far as determiners are concerned the ordering is strict: they can only occur initially in the NP, and no reordering is permitted at all. Numerals almost invariably precede adjectives and nouns. Old King Cole, it may be remembered, called for *his fiddlers three*, but this particular ordering seems dictated by the rhyme scheme and is not an option usually available in contemporary spoken English: I can hardly *feed my cats two*! Occasionally we find NPs like *the big four*, *the silent three of St Botolph's*, but the numeral here is perhaps best treated as a nominalization. *the big four* derives from *the four big powers*, where *powers* is elided and may be contextually recovered, just as in *your two will be quite grown up by now, I expect* the word *two* is held to refer to 'children', 'dogs', etc. as the context dictates (see discussion on pages 236–7).

In English the unmarked position for adjectives is preceding the noun. There are a few exceptions. When the head noun is an indefinite pronoun, ending in *-body*, *-one*, *-thing*, etc., then adjectives follow the noun: *somebody clever*, rather than *\*clever somebody* (a typical 'goon show' usage!). A few adjectives characteristically follow rather than precede the head noun, or regularly have a slightly different meaning from 'the same' adjective when it precedes the head noun:

1  Any *proper* university these days will have a flourishing department of linguistics
2  The school of shorthand is not part of the university *proper*, but is closely associated with it

More usually, re-ordering involves a particular stylistic effect:

Some postposed adjectives. especially those ending in *-able* or *-ible* retain the basic meaning they have (when they precede the noun) . . . but convey the implication that what they are denoting has only a temporary application. Thus, *the stars visible* refers to stars that are visible at a time specified or implied while *the visible stars* refers to a category of stars that can (at appropriate times) be seen [Quirk *et al.* 1972. 249].

In sentences like

**3**   He prefers his mistresses unmarried

*his mistresses unmarried* is not an NP containing a postposed adjective. *Unmarried* is, rather, a different constituent from the NP *his mistresses*: it may be called a complement. Note the different paraphrase relations between **3** and

**4**   He prefers his unmarried mistresses

Paraphrases like:

**5a**   He prefers his mistresses to be unmarried
**5b**   He prefers that his mistresses should be unmarried

relate to **3**, and a paraphrase like

**6**   He prefers those of his mistresses who are unmarried

relates to **4**.

In English, while adjectives precede the noun, there are also ordering restrictions on adjectives themselves. Thus, for example, we will find *a nippy little red sports car*, but hardly *\*a red little nippy sports car*. The restrictions in this case relate to sub-classes of adjectives which can to some extent be defined semantically – see the exercise on page 48. Sub-classes defined in terms of order are known as order classes. We noted (pages 73–5) that adverbs also fall into order classes, though restrictions there are less rigorous.

### Prepositional phrases in English

English prepositional phrases are bi-laterally dependent constructions. The preposition must always precede the NP, sometimes referred to as the 'object' of the preposition. A preposition can sometimes be separated from its object, as in relative clauses like

**7**   The knife which he cut the salami with

which we examined on pages 139–41), but the general pattern is for them to be closely connected and strictly ordered.[3]

### Genitive constructions in English

English has two genitive constructions, both unilaterally dependent. Genitive constructions can be used for a variety of functional relationships in English and in other languages: consider the variety of meanings that can be attached to an expression like *Myron's statue*, which may be: 'possessive' (the statue which Myron owns); 'subjective' ('the statue made by Myron'); objective' ('the statue of Myron'); and so on. We shall consider only the 'possessive' sense, both for English and the other languages we look at. One genitive construction uses the marker -*s*, as in:

**8** Charlie's book; Pharaoh's daughter

Here the NP marked by -*s* is distributionally equivalent to a possessive pronoun (*his*, *her*, *my* etc.). This NP, which we call the 'possessor' is the modifier of the 'possessed' NP, which is, distributionally, the head of the construction, and must always follow the possessor. The other structure involves a prepositional phrase with *of*:

**9** The daughter of Pharaoh; the roof of the car

This time the NP in the genitive construction is distributionally equivalent to a pronoun like *mine*, *hers*, etc., and the possessed precedes the possessor. However, it is still the possessor that is marked, here by the use of *of*. In both cases the head of the construction is the possessed noun – the obligatory noun and the one which controls number concord when such phrases are used as subjects in a sentence. To a certain extent these structures are interchangeable, as an old riddle shows:

---

3 We observed on page 140 that in this respect prepositions must be distinguished from homophonous items that are verbal particles:

| | | |
|---|---|---|
| He added up the bill | but | He ran up the hill |
| He added the bill up | | *He ran the hill up |
| He added it up | | *He ran it up |
| *He added up it | | He ran up it |

Verb + particle constructions are bi-laterally dependent.

**10**   Is the daughter of Pharaoh's son the son of Pharaoh's daughter?

but this is not always the case. Whichever construction is chosen, there is a strict ordering restriction, though the direction of the ordering is different in each case.

## Sentence constituents in English

In English the unmarked word order of sentence constituents is Subject – Verb – Object, which we abbreviate as S VO. Circumstances when this particular order can be changed are examined on pages 363–73.

The ordering relations found in English for these four constructions do not apply universally. We will examine such structures briefly in three other languages: Akan, Gaelic and Turkish.

## Noun phrases in Akan

In Akan, as in English, NP constructions are unilaterally dependent with the noun as the head of the construction. The normal order of constituents is Noun, Adjective, Determiner (the reverse of the English construction).

**11**   Gyinamoa ketewa bi
  cat   small a    *a small cat*

  Onipa  kɛseɛ no
  man   big  the   *the big man*

Even in NPs which contain a relative clause the Determiner is frequently the last NP constituent:

**12**   Onipa aa  ɔ-te  ha no   (yɛ me nua no)
  man relative he-lives here the  (is my brother)
     marker

$$_{NP}(^N \quad _S(\text{relative clause} \qquad )_S \text{ Det})_{NP}$$

*the man who lives here (is my brother)*

## Prepositional phrases in Akan

Prepositional phrases are bi-laterally dependent constructions. Akan has a distributional class of items similar in sense and function to English prepositions, but this class always follows rather than precedes the NP with which it is in construction: they are often called 'postpositions':

**13**  Ofie  no  ho
  house  the  exterior          *outside the house*

$$PP(_{NP}(\ N\quad Det)_{NP}Prep)_{PP}$$

  Ahina  no  mu
  pot  the  inside          *in the pot*

  ɔpono  no  so
  table  the  top          *on the table*

## Genitive constructions in Akan

In genitive constructions, the possessor precedes the possessed. No separate morph shows this relationship, but, in most genitive constructions, the possessed undergoes a tonal modification

**14**  Kofí  *Kofi* (personal name) [_ ⁻]    me  *my* [_]

  ponkɔ́  *horse* [_ _ ⁻]    nantwíé  *cow* [_ _ ⁻ ⁻]

  Kofí pónkɔ́  *Kofi's horse* [_ ⁻ ⁻ _ ⁻]

  Kofí nántwíé  *Kofi's cow* [_ ⁻ ⁻ _ ⁻ ⁻]

  me pónkɔ́  *my horse* [_ ⁻ _ ⁻]

As will be seen, the possessed noun acquires a high tone on its first tone-bearing unit.[4] The tonal modification is a necessary marker of the genitive construction since mere order alone does not suffice: this can be seen by considering the following examples, which contrast a genitive construction and an adnominal construction.

4 High tones are marked with an acute accent; low tones are unmarked. Tone-bearing units are: every consonant vowel sequence, and every consonant and vowel left over (*tw* is, phonologically, a single consonant: compare *sh* in English). Thus *Kofi* has two tone bearing units, and *ponkɔ* has three (*po-n-kɔ*), etc. High tones are realized at a higher pitch than low tones but in a sequence HLH the second high tone is usually at a slightly lower pitch than the first. The pitch pattern for the examples is as shown after each example, except that this 'lowering' effect is not represented.

**15**　nsá　*beer* [_ ‾]　　tumpáń　*bottle* [_ _ ‾ ‾]
　　ɛsiáḿ　*flour* [_ _ ‾ ‾]　　kotokúó　*bag* [_ _ ‾ ‾]

*genitive*
Nsá túmpáń *beer bottle* [_ ‾ ‾ _ ‾ ‾]
ɛsiáḿ kótokúó *flour bag* [_ _ ‾ ‾ ‾ _ ‾ ‾]

*adnominal*
Nsá tumpáń *bottle of beer* [_ ‾ _ _ ‾ ‾]
ɛsiáḿ kotokúó *bag of flour* [_ _ ‾ ‾ _ _ ‾ ‾]

## Sentence constituents in Akan

The unmarked order for sentence constituents is, as in English, SVO:

**16**　Kofi resua　　　Twii
　　Kofi is-learning Twii　　　*Kofi is learning Twii*

　　Kofi kumm gyata no
　　Kofi killed lion　the　　　*Kofi killed the lion*

Constituent order in Gaelic is different from both English or Akan.

## Noun phrases in Gaelic

The normal order for NP constituents is Determiner, Noun, Adjective, as we noted in Part one (pages 62–6): the noun is the head of the construction.

**17**　An iolair　　　mhór
　　the eagle　　　big　　　*the big eagle*

　　An coineanach beag
　　the rabbit　　　little　　*the little rabbit*

　　Am fear　　　　beag
　　the man　　　　little　　*the small man*

　　A' chaileag　　mhór
　　the woman　　　big　　　*the big woman*[5]

---

5 The variant forms of the article depend on the initial consonant or vowel of the noun stem they precede.

*Prepositional phrases in Gaelic*

Within the prepositional phrase the preposition precedes its NP object:

18  Anns    an  sporran
    in      the  purse           *in the purse*

$_{PP}$(Prep  $_{NP}$(Det  N)$_{NP}$)$_{PP}$

    Aig    a'    chladach
    at     the   shore           *at the shore*

    Air    a'    chreig
    on     the   rock            *on the rock*

*Genitive constructions in Gaelic*

In genitive constructions, the possessed precedes the possessor. The possessor is marked by appearing in the genitive case. Rules for the formation of cases in Gaelic are extremely complicated (the reader is referred to a Gaelic grammar, e.g. Mackinnon 1971) but the principle is clear from the examples; note that in Gaelic the article, as well as, or instead of, the noun may inflect for case:

19  an cat    *the cat*        (nominative, singular)
    a' chait  *of the cat*     (genitive, singular)
    nan cat   *of the cats*    (genitive, plural)
    an ceann  *the head*       (nominative singular)
    na cinn   *the heads*      (nominative plural)

    Ceann a'chait (head of the cat) *the cat's head*
    Cinn nan cat (heads of the cats) *the cats' heads*

(The article is not used with the possessed noun.) Possession is often expressed not with a construction of the sort illustrated above, but in constructions of the following sort:

20  Bha  peann aig Màiri
    Was  a pen at  Mary            *Mary had a pen*

    Tha cù   dubh  aig Calum, ach tha cat bàn   aig Màiri
    Is  dog black at  Calum but is  cat white at  Mary

    *Calum has a black dog, but Mary has a white cat*

These may be analysed as V + NP + PP, where the PP is expanded as Prep + NP. Structures of this sort may equally be used to express location:

> **21**  Tha Calum aig a'  chladach
>     Is   Calum at  the shore        *Calum is at the shore*

(Many languages, including English, show relations between 'locative' and 'possessive' constructions, see discussion, pages 303–9.)

### Sentence constituents in Gaelic

The unmarked word order for sentence constituents is VSO:

> **22**  Reic Seumas an car
>     Sold James   the car        *James sold the car*
>
>     Ghlas  Màiri an dorus
>     Locked Mary the door        *Mary locked the door*

and we have already seen that in structures like **20** the subject immediately follows the verb.

Typical word order patterns in Turkish differ from those we have already examined.

### Noun phrases in Turkish

The typical order of constituents in an NP in Turkish is Adjective, Determiner, Noun:

> **23**  Adj        Art   N
>
>     Büyük      bir   ev
>     big        a     house   *a big house*
>
>     Zeki       bir   kız
>     intelligent a    girl    *an intelligent girl*

### Prepositional phrases in Turkish

Turkish, like Akan, has postpositions, rather than prepositions – these, obviously follow the NP:

**24** Karakola yakın
police station near *near the police station*

$$PP^{(NP} \qquad Prep)}_{PP}$$

Sizler için
you (pl) for *for you*

Many expressions that in English translate into prepositional phrases are represented in Turkish by case suffixes, as in Latin. Prepositions in Turkish govern particular case forms: in the examples *yakın* governs the dative, and *için* the absolute, case.

## Genitive constructions in Turkish

There are a variety of genitive constructions, depending on such features as whether the possessor is definite or indefinite, whether it is a 'full NP' or pronominal, etc. (The interested reader is referred to a Turkish grammar, e.g. Lewis 1953.) In all cases the possessor precedes the possessed. If the possessor is definite, both nouns are marked for the relationship: the possessor is in the genitive case and the possessed is marked with a possessive suffix:

**25** Müdürün odası
director his-room *the director's room*
(*genitive*)

Kızların odaları
girls their-rooms *the girls' rooms*
(*gen. plur.*)

## Sentence constituents in Turkish

Word order in a Turkish sentence is usually SOV. If the subject is a personal pronoun it is usually omitted since the verb is marked for person. Thus:

**26** Ahmet otomobili aldı
Ahmet the car took *Ahmet took the car*

Mehmet biraz para istedi
Mehmet some money wanted
*Mehmet wanted some money*

The preceding discussion has exemplified four dependency relations in four different languages. The relations remain the same from language to language, but different languages mark the dependencies in different ways. In all of them word order is an important marker of the relation, but word order alone is not always sufficient. In most cases a formal marker of some kind is necessary in addition to word order: sometimes an additional word (like *of* in the English genitive construction); sometimes a morph (like -*s* in the other English genitive construction); sometimes case marking (as in Turkish and Gaelic genitive constructions); sometimes a tonal modification (as in the Akan genitive construction). Sometimes the marker is the only feature differentiating between constructions – as with the genitive and adnominal constructions in Akan.

In many of the constructions exemplified, the dependency relations can be captured in constituent structure terms. For example, prepositional phrases are formed by rules like:

27a   PP → Prep + NP (for English and Gaelic)
27b   PP → NP + Prep (for Akan and Turkish)

When the preposition governs the noun in a certain case, then this too can be captured by an interpretation of these rules.

In other examples the dependency relations are not so easily captured in constituent structure terms. We have already seen that rules like:

28a   S → NP + VP
28b   VP → V + NP

can account for the constituent structure of English sentences, and through such rules we can reasonably, though not entirely, successfully capture the relevant dependency relations: subject and predicate (28a); transitive verb and object (28b); etc. Indeed, we carried out the strict subcategorization of verbs by appealing to different predicate types – different expansions of VP. Such rules seem reasonably adequate for a SVO language like English. Similarly rules like:

29a   S → NP + VP
29b   VP → NP + V

seem satisfactory for SOV languages like Turkish. In these terms, Gaelic is more difficult, as it has VSO word order: the

copula and its complement and the transitive verb and its object
are discontinous around the subject.

In Gaelic, just as in English, verbs can be classified in terms of
their predicate type. Thus we find copula + complement:

**30**  Bha – an cù – dubh
       V    NP    Adj
       (Was – the dog – black) *The dog was black*

(The sentences are analysed into their constituents) copula +
locative complement:

**31**  Bha – Tearlach – anns an Fhraing
       V      NP         PP
       (Was-Charlie-in the France) *Charlie was in France*

intransitive verb:

**32**  Bhàsaich – Tearlach (Died-Charlie)
       V           NP       *Charlie died*

transitive verb + object:

**33**  Ghlac – Calum – breac (Caught-Calum-a trout)
       V       NP      NP    *Calum caught a trout*

The above characterizations, like those established previously for
English, rely on 'predicate' types – reflected in co-occurrence
relations between a verb and some other constituent in the
sentence (an intransitive verb in Gaelic, as in English, occurs with
one NP, the subject; a transitive verb occurs with two NPs,
subject and object; etc.). However, do we want in Gaelic to
establish a constituent VP? If we do so, then we need a
reordering rule to take the verb and place it at the beginning
of the sentence in front of the subject NP; do we really want
such a drastic structure-changing rule to be involved in the
generation of simple sentences? It seems that in Gaelic
dependency relations are not as readily interpretable from
constituent structure configurations as they may be in English.

A similar problem arises in 'free word-order' languages. Latin
is often said to be such a language since the translation
equivalents of a sentence like 'The boy loves the girl' include:

**34a**  Puer puellam amat (the boy-the girl-loves) SOV)
**34b**  Puer amat puellam (SVO)
**34c**  Amat puer puellam (VSO)

and any other permutation of the three constituents involved. (Latin is not a language in which *anything* goes with respect to word order – prepositions and their objects are strictly ordered, for instance.) The grammatical relations of subject and object are marked in Latin by case (the subject takes the nominative case and the object, for most verbs, the accusative case – as in the example) rather than order, but the relations remain as relevant as they are in English! A MO is a transitive verb, and in a relation of bi-lateral dependency with its object N P. Clearly we can decide that one of these orders is basic, either *a priori* or on some other grounds, frequency of occurrence for instance. So we might decide that the order shown in **34a** is 'basic' and postulate rules like:

**35**   $S \rightarrow NP + VP$
        $VP \rightarrow NP + V$

etc. This analysis enables us to identify in constituent structure terms which N P is the subject and which the object and makes the assignment of the appropriate case relatively straightforward, but involves postulating a transformation 'scrambling' the constituents into any of the permissible orders. But such a description may only be a convenience, and one which derives from an 'English' view of word order.[6]

The point at issue is this. Since grammatical relations of dependency etc. are crucial in the description of a language, we need to know which constituents are dependent on which other constituents, and just what type of dependency relation is involved. On the one hand such relations seem, to an extent which varies between different languages, independent of the facts of word order etc.; on the other, constituent structure is also important. Both need to be accommodated in a linguistic description. It happens that in English many dependency relations can be described in terms of constituent structure relationships. In some other languages this does not seem the case. Clearly it is possible to force a description of dependency in

---

6 There is also the problem that we can find sentences like *puellam amat* 'he loves the girl', where no separate word is identifiable as the subject. Since the Latin verb is marked for 'person' (*amo* 'I love', *amas* 'you love', *amat* 'he loves', etc.) the subject is not usually realized as a separate constituent when it is 'pronominal'. We do not consider this complication further.

constituent structure terms on any language (as by the use of rules for Gaelic and Latin like those suggested above), but is this legitimate or appropriate?

A final comment on word order is in order. There appears to be a tendency in languages for certain types of ordering restrictions to occur together. In an influential article Greenberg (1963) writes:

> Linguists are, in general, familiar with the notion that certain languages tend consistently to put modifying or limiting elements before those modified or limited, while others just as consistently do the opposite. Turkish, an example of the former type, puts adjectives before the nouns they modify, places the object of the verb before the verb, the dependent genitive before the governing noun, adverbs before adjectives which they modify, etc. Such languages, moreover, tend to have postpositions for concepts expressed by prepositions in English. A language of the opposite type is Thai [or, as we have seen in this section, Gaelic] in which adjectives follow the noun, the object follows the verb, the genitive follows the governing noun, and there are prepositions. The majority of languages, as for example English, are not well marked in this respect .... More detailed consideration of these and other phenomena of order soon reveals that some factors are closely related to each other, while others are relatively independent.

These facts about order lead Greenberg to postulate a number of universal tendencies, some of which are:

*Universal 1:* In declarative sentences with nominal subject and object, the dominant order is almost always one in which the subject precedes the object. (This means that although six orders are possible (SVO, SOV, VSO, VOS, OSV, OVS), only three orders occur frequently (SOV, VSO and SVO) and the other three are rare.

*Universal 2:* In languages with prepositions, the genitive almost always follows the governing noun, while in languages with postpositions it almost always precedes.

*Universal 3:* Languages with dominant VSO order are always prepositional.

*Universal 4:* If a language has dominant SOV order and the genitive follows the governing noun, then the adjective likewise follows the noun.

The interested reader is referred to Greenberg's book for further discussion and exemplification of these universals.

**Linkage**

Under the general heading of linkage (a term deriving from Hockett 1958) we may group together a number of grammatical constructions whose function is to show that two constituents are grammatically or referentially related. We will briefly exemplify two types of linkage, 'pronominal cross-referencing' and 'concord' or 'agreement'.

Pronominal cross-referencing can be illustrated in English with the sentence

**36**   John thinks that he is intelligent

The sentence has two possible readings: 'John thinks that he (John) is intelligent' and 'John thinks that he (someone else) is intelligent', depending on whether *John* and *he* are used to refer to the same individual, or co-refer, or refer to different individuals. We indicate reference by subscripts: if two items co-refer, then they will have the same subscript; if they do not they will have different subscripts. Thus the two readings of our sentence are:

**37**   John$_1$ thinks that he$_1$ is intelligent (he = John)
**38**   John$_1$ thinks that he$_2$ is intelligent (he ≠ John)

We suppose that a sentence like **36** is produced by the grammar and that later rules are able to identify co-referentiality. Exactly how these rules operate is complex and not yet fully understood, but the following two informal generalizations account for many, though by no means all, of the curious features of English cross-reference:

**i**   If a 'full' NP *precedes* a pronoun, then they may be co-referential.
**ii**   If a 'full' NP *commands* a pronoun, then they may be co-referential.

The relation of 'command' can be most straightforwardly illustrated with respect to 'main' and 'subordinate' or embedded sentences. An NP in the main sentence commands an NP in a subordinate sentence if the S that immediately dominates the main sentence also dominates the subordinate sentence.[7]

---

7 The notion derives from Langacker (1969), who formulates the relation more precisely. The interested reader is referred to this article for further discussion of this interesting area of English grammar.

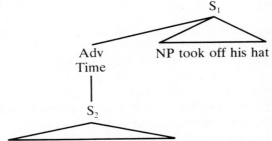

*Figure 96*  After NP came into the room

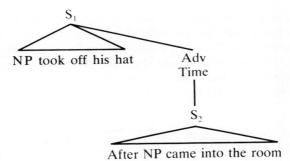

*Figure 97*  After NP came into the room

The first generalization is met in **36**: *John* precedes *he*, so they may be co-referential, as is marked in **37**. The qualification 'may' is introduced since the two do not have to be co-referential, as is shown by **38**. The second generalization is illustrated in Figures 96 and 97. In Figure 96 the NP in the subordinate sentence, S2, precedes but does not command the NP in the superordinate sentence, S1, so by generalization **i**:

**39**  After John$_1$ came into the room, he$_1$ took off his$_1$ hat

is well formed. In the same figure the NP in S1 commands, though it does not precede, the NP in S2, so by generalization **ii**:

**40**  After he$_1$ came into the room John$_1$ took off his$_1$ hat

is also well formed. In Figure 97 the NP in S1 both precedes and commands the NP in S2, so:

**41**  John$_1$ took off his$_1$ hat after he$_1$ came into the room

is well formed. But the fourth possibility:

**42** *He₁ took off his₁ hat after John₁ came into the room

is not well formed since the, NP in S2 neither precedes nor commands the NP in S1. In general 'forwards' cross-referencing, as in **39** and **41** is well formed, since the full NP precedes, and may or may not command, the pronoun, but 'backwards' cross-referencing is only possible when the pronoun is commanded by a full NP; thus **40** is well formed, but **42** is not. So to return to our original example: **36** is well formed since *John* precedes and commands *he*, but:

**43** *He₁ thinks John₁ is intelligent

is ill formed since *John* does not command *he*. (Both **42** and **43** are, of course, well formed if *he* and *John* are not understood to be co-referential.) Note that in co-ordinate structures like that illustrated in Figure 98 forward cross-referencing is possible, by generalization **i**; but since neither NP commands the other, backwards cross-referencing is not:

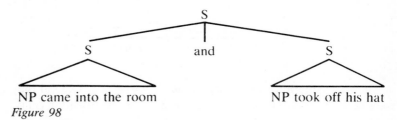

*Figure 98*

**44a** John₁ came into the room and he₁ took off his hat
**44b** *He₁ came into the room and John₁ took off his hat

Our two generalizations will account for the well-formedness or otherwise of the following:

**45a** Mary₁ married someone she₁ met at college
**45b** *She₁ married someone Mary₁ met at college

**46a** John₁ said that he₁ wanted to go
**46b** *He₁ said that John₁ wanted to go

**47a** The insinuation that John₁ was stupid angered him₁
**47b** The insinuation that he₁ was stupid angered John₁
**47c** John₁ was angered by the insinuation that he₁ was stupid
**47d** *He₁ was angered by the insinuation that John₁ was stupid.

We will not pursue the mysteries of English forward and backward pronominalization further. We must, however, make one further observation about generalization **i**, since it needs a modification to cover instances like

**48** John$_1$ injured himself$_1$
**49** John$_1$ injured him$_2$

In a simple sentence, when all the constituents are dominated by the same S, as in **48** and **49**, a full NP and a following non-reflexive pronoun cannot be co-referential (there are a few exceptions to this generalization in sentences like *John kept the book near him(self)*). In such circumstances co-referentiality depends on the presence of a reflexive pronoun, as in **48**.

The types of cross-referencing shown for English seem also to occur in many other languages. Some languages, however, can draw distinctions that English does not. Thus, several of the Kwa languages, spoken in West Africa, employ morphologically distinct pronominal forms in some constructions involving 'verbs of reported speech' to distinguish between reference to the speaker and reference to other parties. Thus in Efik, a Nigerian language, the two senses of the sentence:

**50a** Okon$_1$ agreed that he$_1$ would pay the debt
(Okon = he)
**50b** Okon$_1$ agreed that he$_2$ would pay the debt
(Okon ≠ he)

are differentiated by the use of two different pronouns.

| **51a** | Okon$_1$ | enyime | ete | imɔ$_1$ | eyekpe | isɔn | oro | |
| | Okon | agreed | that | he | would pay | debt | the | (= **50a**) |
| **51b** | Okon$_1$ | enyime | ete | enye$_2$ | eyekpe | isɔn | oro | |
| | Okon | agreed | that | he | would pay | debt | the | (= **50b**) |

The 'obviative' pronoun *imɔ* is only found in embedded sentences like **51a** where it cross-refers to the subject of a verb of reported speech.

In many languages the main verb may be marked for cross-reference to the subject. Thus in the Latin sentence:

| **52** | Puer | puellam | amat | |
| | boy | girl | he loves | *the boy loves the girl* |

the form of the verb indicates cross-reference to the subject *puer*.

In such languages, a sentence need not contain an NP subject expression. Thus

**53**   puellam amat
girl     he loves     *he loves the girl*

is well formed. In such a case we say that the verb has 'deictic reference'. This may be to an NP elsewhere in the linguistic context – in a preceding sentence perhaps – or to an individual in the non-linguistic context. In those languages in which verbs are marked in this way, intransitive verbs may, of course, form a complete single-word sentence – this is the case with many modern European languages, like Italian. (This causes problems for a constituent structure grammar of the sort we examined in Part one.)

We now turn our attention to 'concord' or 'agreement'. Two, or more, constituents are said to be 'in concord' when they are both, or all, marked for the same grammatical category. Thus in English demonstratives and the head noun are said to be in concord within the NP: *this book, these books; that book, those books*. The singular form of the demonstrative can only co-occur with the singular form of the noun, and the plural form of the demonstrative with the plural form of the noun – there are no NPs like *these book*. In such constructions one constituent is the 'controller' of the concord (in the case illustrated above it is the head noun), and the other constituents are 'in concord' with the controller: so we say that demonstratives in English concord in number with the head noun within an NP.[8] The reasons why the head noun in English is held to be the controller were explored on pages 193–6.

---

8 It is possible to take a different view. We have taken the view that number is a category of the noun in English, and that other constituents are in concord with the head noun for number. We might instead assert that number is a category of the NP as a whole, and that all relevant constituents within the NP must be marked for this category. To some extent these different views can be accommodated in different rules. Thus a rule like:

NP → Art + Noun
Noun → N + Number

shows number unambiguously as a category of the Noun. But a rule like:

NP → Art + N + Number

can imply that Number is a category of the NP as a whole.

In cases like *these books* the concord category is overtly marked on the controller (*book-s* has a plural marker). This is not always the case: sometimes the controller is not overtly marked for the category which controls the concord. Thus in French GARÇON is not overtly marked for gender, but it is 'inherently' masculine. This covert category controls concord on other NP constituents, like the article – *le garçon*, not *\*la garçon*. Similarly in German MANN and FRAU are not overtly marked as masculine and feminine respectively, yet this covert categorization controls concord on articles, adjectives etc. within the NP – *ein junger Mann, eine junge Frau.*[9]

In many languages concord is particularly to be noticed in the following constructions:

i   NP constructions: articles, adjectives and other noun modifiers often concord with the head noun: concord may be for number and/or gender and/or case, and possibly other categories as well.

ii  subject + main verb constructions: the main verb is often in concord for number with the subject; often other categories, like gender in Arabic and Hebrew, can also concord.

iii copulative constructions: the complement is often in concord with the subject, often in number and gender.

English has a limited degree of concord. Some, but not all, NP constituents show concord as we have seen. Subject–main verb concord does operate:

**54a**  My father (sing) lives (sing) in Somerset
**54b**  My parents (pl) live (pl) in Somerset

but only in a patchy way (see discussion on pages 210–11). There is number concord in copulative constructions with NP complement:

---

9 Some writers distinguish between 'concord' and 'governmental concord' depending on whether the concord category is overt (concord) or covert (governmental concord) on the controller. Thus in French, gender is an instance of governmental concord (since gender is covert), but number is a matter of simple concord (since number is overt – *les garçons*). The term governmental concord is clearly derived from the notion of government, discussed on page 256.

**55a**   This man (sing) is a fool (sing)
**55b**   These men (pl) are fools (pl)

Many languages show no concord at all, or very little. Thus in Akan we find:

**56**   Onipa kɛseɛ no (man big the)                          *the big man*

Nnipa kɛseɛ no (men big the)                          *the big men*

Onipa no rekasa (man the is-speaking)

*the man is speaking*

Nnipa no rekasa (men the are-speaking)

*the men are speaking*

Onipa no yɛ kɛseɛ (man the is big)        *the man is big*

Nnipa no yɛ kɛseɛ (men the are big)    *the men are big*

(Number is shown on the noun by the alternation in the form of the prefix – *o-nipa* (man) *n-nipa* (men).) These examples show no concord at all.

By contrast some languages show very extensive systems of concord. An example is Luganda, a Bantu language spoken in Uganda. All nouns in this language have a structure prefix + stem. The prefix shows two things: the gender class to which the noun belongs, and the number of the noun, singular or plural. Luganda, like other Bantu languages, divides nouns into a large number of gender classes: we note only three and refer to them as the *omu-aba*, *en-en* and *omu-emi* classes, since these are the forms of the singular and plural prefixes taken by the classes in question. First we illustrate concord within NP, which has the constituent order N + Adj + Demonstrative + Numeral. As you will see Adjectives, Demonstratives and Numerals concord for number and gender class with the head noun:

**57a**   Omu-kazi   omu-lungi   o-no
         woman        pretty      this    *this pretty woman*

**57b**   Aba-kazi   aba-lungi   ba-no   aba-satu
         woman        pretty      this    three

*these three pretty women*

**58a**   En-jovu    en-kadde   ey-o
         elephant      old       that    *that old elephant*

**58b** En-jovu     en-kadde ez-o    es-satu
     elephant     old     that     three
                        *those three old elephants*

**59a** Omu-ti     omu-tono gu-no
     tree     small     this     *this small tree*

**59b** Emi-ti     emi-tono gi-no e-satu
     tree     small     this     three
                        *these three small trees*

Two observations are in order: firstly, while the concord prefixes for the noun head and the adjective modifier are the 'same', different forms of concord prefix may be found on the demonstrative and numeral modifiers. Secondly, while the singular noun and adjective concord prefix is the same for the *omu-aba* and the *omu-emi* classes, the demonstrative and numeral concord prefixes are differentiated for each class. Similarly the singular and plural noun and adjective prefixes are the same for the *en-en* class, the demonstrative and numeral prefixes differ. This sort of pattern is very common in Bantu languages.

In sentence constructions there is cross-reference between the subject NP and the main verb. The verb word always carries a subject prefix, which is always the initial morph. This subject prefix not only cross-refers to the subject of the sentence, but it must also be in number and gender concord with the subject NP. In the following examples the verb has the structure subject prefix + tense marker + verb stem:

**60a** Omu-kazi     o-no a-li-fa
     woman     this     she-future-die
                        *this woman will die*

**60b** Aba-kazi ba-no ba-li-fa     *these women will die*

**61a** En-jovu     ey-o     e-ri-fa
     elephant     that it-will-die     *that elephant will die*

**61b** En-jovu ez-o zi-ri-fa     *those elephants will die*

**62a** Omu-ti     gu-no gu-li-fa
     tree     this it-will-die     *this tree will die*

**62b** Emi-ti gi-no gi-li-fa     *these trees will die*

As in Latin (see discussion of examples **52** and **53**, pages 277–8), and for the same reasons, the verb word in Luganda can form a one-word sentence. In this case we say that the pronoun prefix has deictic reference. So *erifa* (see **61a**) is appropriate if the speaker refers to a single elephant, cow or other object which nouns of the *en-en* class are used to refer to. Similarly *gulifa* (see **62a**) is appropriate if the speaker refers to a single tree or some other item which *omu-emi* class nouns are used to refer to.

We now turn to consider patterns of concord and cross-reference in transitive sentences. Basic constituent order is Subject–Verb–Object (SVO). In SVO sentences the verb carries a pronoun prefix which cross-refers to the subject and is in concord with it for number and gender class. There is no cross-reference shown in the verb to the object:

> **63a**   Omu-kazi    a-li-goba    en-koko
>           woman she-will-chase    chicken
> > *the woman will chase the chicken*

> **63b**   Aba-kazi    ba-li-goba    omu-sota
>           women they-will-chase    snake
> > *the women will chase the snake*

(-*koko* 'chicken': class *en-en*; -*sota* 'snake': class *omu-emi*.) Now consider sentences like:

> **64a**   Omu-kazi    a-li-gi-goba
>           woman she-will-it-chase
> > *the woman will chase it (sc. chicken)*

> **64b**   Aba-kazi    ba-li-gu-goba
>           woman they-will-it-chase
> > *the women will chase it (sc. snake)*

Comparing the sentences in **63** and **64**, we see that when a transitive verb has no object NP expression, the verb carries an object pronoun between the tense marker and the verb stem. This has deictic reference to some appropriate object in the context, and must be in the appropriate form for the gender class and number of the noun which is used to refer to such an object. Object pronouns do not occur within the verb word in sentences of basic SVO constituent order. Let us give some more examples:

**65a**  Omu-sota  gu-li-goba  omu-kazi
      snake  it-will-chase  woman
                    *the snake will chase the woman*

**65b**  Omu-sota  gu-li-mu-goba
      snake  it-will-her-chase
                *the snake will chase her (sc. woman)*

**66a**  En-koko  e-li-goba  omu-sota
      chicken  it-will-chase  snake
                *the chicken will chase the snake*

**66b**  En-koko  e-li-gu-goba
      chicken  it-will-it-chase
                *the chicken will chase it (sc. snake)*

In Luganda, unlike English, object pronouns in such sentences are not found as separate constituents, but are rather infixed into the verb word.

Both subject and object may be represented by pronouns within the verb word: then we get one-word sentences like:

**67a**  A-li-gi-goba
             *she (sc. woman) will chase it (sc. chicken)*

**67b**  A-li-gu-goba
             *she (sc. woman) will chase it (sc. snake)*

**67c**  Gu-li-mu-goba
             *it (sc. snake) will chase her (sc. woman)*

**67d**  Gu-li-gi-goba  *it (sc. snake) will chase it (sc. chicken)*

**67e**  E-li-gu-goba  *it (sc. chicken) will chase it (sc. snake)*

and so on.

Finally, we discuss a case where the system of concord and cross-referencing can be used for a particular communicative effect. When the order of sentence constituents is SVO we have seen there is no object pronoun within the verb word. Now note these sentences, where this basic word order is disturbed: pronoun referencing within the verb allows the speaker and his hearer to keep track, as it were, of 'who is doing what to whom'. The English translations are an attempt to indicate the emphasis etc. that these sentences carry (small capitals indicate stress in English):

**68a**   Omu-kazi a-li-goba en-koko (SVO)
*the woman will chase the chicken*

**68b**   Omu-kazi a-li-gi-goba (SV(O))
*the woman will chase it*

**68c**   Omu-kazi en-koko a-li-gi-goba (SOV)
*the woman will chase the* CHICKEN

**68d**   En-koko omu-kazi a-li-gi-goba (OSV)
*it's the|*CHICKEN *the woman will chase*

**68e**   En-koko a-li-gi-goba omu-kazi (OVS)
*it's the* CHICKEN *that will be chased by the woman*

**Technical terms**

| | |
|---|---|
| agreement | exocentric |
| bi-lateral dependency | government |
| command | linkage |
| concord | marker |
| controller (of concord) | mutual dependency |
| co-ordinate dependency | mutual exclusion |
| co-reference | paradigmatic |
| cross reference | pronominal cross-reference |
| deictic reference | reflexive |
| dependency | syntagmatic |
| endocentric | unilateral dependency |

**Exercises**

These two exercises illustrate concord systems in two languages, Luganda and Gaelic. Both build on previous exercises: Luganda on pages 215–17 and Gaelic on pages 67–8.

*1 Luganda*

All the strings in any one group of sentences have the same structure, indicated at the head of the groups. All the strings are morphologically analysed. The numbers 1,2,3 correspond to classes 1,2,3 in the previous exercises; sg = singular and pl = plural. As before the noun word can be analysed as consisting of prefix + stem, the form of the prefix depending on the class of the stem. Adjectives, Demonstratives etc. all bear a prefix concording with that on the noun stem. The verb also, where appropriate, has a prefix concording with the subject noun. Fill in the matrix provided.

| *A & B* | $NP(N + Adj + Dem_1 (+Num))$ | |
|---|---|---|
| *A1sg* | omu-kazi omu-lungi o-no | (this pretty woman) |
| *A2sg* | en-te en-nungi e-no | (this nice cow) |
| *A3sg* | omu-ggo omu-lungi gu-no | (this nice stick) |
| *B1pl* | aba-kazi aba-lungi ba-no aba-satu | These three pretty women) |
| *B2pl* | en-te en-nungi zi-no es-satu | (these three nice cows) |
| *B3pl* | emi-ggo emi-rungi gi-no e-satu | (these three nice sticks) |

| *C & D* | $NP(N + Adj + Dem_2) + Vb$ | |
|---|---|---|
| *C1sg* | omu-sajja omu-kadde oy-o a-li-fa | (that old man will die) |
| *C2sg* | en-jovu en-kadde ey-o e-ri-fa | (that old elephant will die) |
| *C3sg* | omu-ti omu-kadde ogw-o gu-li-fa | (that old tree will die) |
| *D1pl* | aba-sajja aba-kadde ab-o ba-li-fa | (those old men will die) |
| *D2pl* | en-jovu en-kadde ez-o zi-ri-fa | (those old elephants will die) |
| *D3pl* | emi-ti emi-kadde ogy-o gi-li-fa | (those old trees will die) |

| *E & F* | $NP(N + Adj + Dem_3 (+Num))$ | |
|---|---|---|
| *E1sg* | omu-sajja omu-tono o-li | (yonder small man) |
| *E2sg* | en-te en-tono e-ri | (yonder small cow) |
| *E3sg* | omu-ggo omu-tono gu-li | (yonder small stick) |
| *F1pl* | aba-sajja aba-tono ba-li aba-taano | (yonder five small men) |
| *F2pl* | en-te en-tono zi-ri et-taano | (yonder five small cows) |
| *F3pl* | emi-ggo emi-tono gi-ri e-taano | (yonder five small sticks) |

| class | noun | adjective | numeral | demonstrative 'this' | 'that' | 'yonder' |
|-------|------|-----------|---------|------------------------|--------|----------|
| *1sg* | omu- | omu- | ----- | o- | oy- | o- |
| *pl* | | | | | | |
| *2sg* | | | ----- | | | |
| *pl* | | | | | | |
| *3sg* | | | ----- | | | |
| *pl* | | | | | | |

## 2  Gaelic

Previous exercises examined N Ps of the structure $NP \rightarrow Art + N$: the following N Ps contain adjectives as well:

| | |
|---|---|
| an taigh bàn | 'the white house' |
| an ràmh gearr | 'the short oar' |
| an tunnag bhàn | 'the white duck' |
| an nàbaidh math | 'the good neighbour' |
| an duilleag mhór | 'the big page' |
| an sgadan beag | 'the little herring' |
| an ramh geàrr dubh | 'the short black oar' |
| an sgoil bheag dhona | 'the small bad school' |
| an tunnag bheag bhàn | 'the little white duck' |
| an sgadan beag math | 'the good little herring' |
| an luinneag mhath | 'the good song' |
| an là fada | 'the long day' |
| an sgoil bheag | 'the little school' |
| an nighean gheàrr | 'the short girl' |
| an duine mór | 'the big man' |
| an oidhche fhada | 'the long night' |

(a) Write a constituent structure rule that generates the N Ps in this data.

(b) How many gender classes are there in Gaelic? Assign the Nouns to your gender classes.

(c) In the data given which word class inflects for gender?

(d) You will discover that inflexion for gender (as illustrated in the data) involves changing the initial consonant of some words. This process is generally known as *lenition*. Orthographically lenition is often marked by 'adding an h' (e.g. *bàn:bhàn*). Phonologically lenition is manifested in various ways. In the data the correspondences are as follows – the orthographic forms are shown first (and in italics), the phonological realizations are shown in phonemic brackets:

| | | | | | |
|---|---|---|---|---|---|
| *b* : /b/ | *bh* : /v/ | *m* : /m/ | *mh* : /v/ | *f* : /f/ | *fh* : ∅ |
| *g* : /g/ | *gh* : /ʋ/ | *d* : /d/ | *dh* : /ʋ/ | | |

(e) Describe the rule for gender concord within the NP.

Previous Gaelic exercises examined some sentences using the 'attributive copula' verb form *bha*. Please refer to that data and your analysis. Here are four more similar sentences:

| | |
|---|---|
| bha an taigh beag | 'the house was little' |
| bha an duine math | 'the man was good' |
| bha an oidhche fada | 'the night was long' |
| bha an nighean dona | 'the girl was bad' |

(f) What is the rule for concord in these sentences between the subject noun and the adjective?

On the basis of your analysis to earlier questions, analyse the following sentences:

| | |
|---|---|
| bha an tunnag bheag bàn | 'the little duck was white' |
| bha an tunnag beag bàn | 'the duck was little and white' |
| bha an sgoil mhór dona | 'the big school was bad' |
| bha an sgoil mór dona | 'the school was big and bad' |
| bha an duine mór dubh | 'the big man was black'/ |
| | 'the man was big and black' |
| bha an taigh beag bàn | 'the little house was white'/ |
| | 'the house was little and white' |

(g) Notice that no ambiguity arises in the first two pairs of sentences, but that the last two sentences are ambiguous. How do you account for this?

(h) Draw two tree diagrams for the final sentence which will show how the ambiguity arises.

# 18 Processes and participants

This chapter is concerned with what we shall refer to as the 'propositional structure' of the sentence. By this we mean a specification of:

i   the type of 'state' or 'action' described by the sentence – this we call the 'process' of the sentence, and it is largely associated with the verb.

ii  the 'participant roles' involved in the state or action – these are typically associated with NPs in construction with the verb, and describe their functional relation to the verb.

A description of the process and participants forms the 'propositional nucleus', which it is convenient to describe as 'one place' (e.g. *John ran*), 'two place' (*John sharpened the knife*), 'three place' (*John gave a book to Mary*), etc., depending on the number of participants we identify. From time to time it is useful to refer to 'circumstantial' roles associated with the propositional nucleus: these are typically adverbial expressions of time, place, manner, etc., which we have already observed to be optional constituents of a constituent structure description, and are, in general, optional also to the propositional structure, for much the same reasons. *John sharpened the knife in the woodshed last night* involves a two-place propositional nucleus with circumstantial constituents of place and time. Our major concern is the propositional nucleus. The sorts of processes and participants we identify are probably common to all languages, though their sentential realizations differ from language to language, and our discussion focuses on English.

Let us begin by considering the sentences:

1   John sharpened the knife
2   The knife was sharp

In simple constituent structure terms, discussed earlier, these sentences are dissimilar: **1** is a transitive and **2** a copular sentence. In propositional terms they are more closely related: **1** describes an action ('sharpening a knife') that brings about the state of affairs ('the knife being sharp') described in **2**. The link is reflected in the lexical relations between the sentences. The NP *the knife* that is the object of the action sentence is the subject of the state sentence; furthermore the verb SHARPEN in **1** is morphologically related to the adjective SHARP in **2**.

The distinction between sentences describing actions and those describing states is a fundamental one that we will find in other pairs of sentences we will examine.[1]

We need to recognize different types of [action] and [state], so we must add a further specification to each characterization. We say that **1** expresses a [directed], [causative], [action]. It is [directed] because it involves the action of an [agent] (*John*) on a [patient] (*the knife*): the [agent] is the participant responsible for performing the action, the 'doer'; the [patient] is the participant which, to use traditional terminology, 'receives or suffers the action of the verb'. Not all two-place [action] propositions involve the [directed, action] of an [agent] on a [patient]:

**3** John played tiddly winks
**4** John ran a mile

In these cases, the [agent] cannot be seen as 'doing anything' to the other participant. In **1** the [action] is [causative] because the action of 'sharpening the knife' causes the state of affairs where the 'knife is sharp' as may be seen from the somewhat stilted paraphrases:

**5a** John made the knife sharp
**5b** John caused the knife to be sharp

Not all two-place propositions are [causative]: those in **3**, **4** are clearly not, and no paraphrase like **5** is open to them. Nor are all [directed action] propositions [causative]:

1 To avoid confusion we call sentences like **1** [action] sentences, rather than 'active' sentences, reserving the form 'active' for the opposition 'active: passive'. Thus we may say the **1** is an [action] sentence in the 'active' form. The corresponding 'passive' form of this [action] sentence is *The knife was sharpened by John*. We enclose characterizations of processes and participants in square brackets, to indicate that these are syntactico-semantic 'features' of the relevant propositions ('syntactico-semantic', since they have both semantic and syntactic implications).

**6a** John beat the dog
**6b** John built a house

The [state] proposition in **2** can be further specified as [descriptive]: the knife is described as having the [attribute] 'sharpness'. This contrasts with other [state] specifications examined later – a [possessive, state] **7** and [locative, state] **8**:

**7** John has a knife
**8** John is in bed

Turning now to the participants involved, note first that both sentences contain the NP *the knife*. Since this participant is common to both propositions we call it a [neutral] participant (other reasons for choosing this characterization will emerge). We have already seen a further characterization of the [neutral] participant in **1** as a [patient], and we can characterize the object of **6a** also as [neutral, patient]. The characterization as [patient] is clearly not appropriate to the object of BUILD in **6b** – this we characterize as [neutral, result], since the house can be seen to be the result of the building (in a way that *the dog* in **6a** can hardly be described as the result of the beating). The participants *tiddly winks* and *a mile* in **3** and **4** cannot appropriately be specified as either [patient] or [result]; we characterize them as [range], thus further characterizing the type of process by further specifying it, limiting it in some way, expressing a measure, etc. (This participant type could be further subclassified, since it covers a number of different semantic notions.) None of the [range] participants of this description can be considered in any way the 'object' of the verb concerned – whereas [patient] and [result] participants can be classified appropriately in this way. Some verbs that can be characterized in these terms are shown in Figure 99. (Note that both [patient] and [result] participants can expect to become the subjects of passive sentences, but this is in general impossible or infelicitous for [range] participants.)

The remaining participant in **1**, (*John*), we have already specified as [agent], and we offer no further sub-classification of [agent] in this chapter (but see footnotes 8 and 13 below). We specify the participant realized by *John* in sentences **3–6** also as [agent]. Such a characterization is clearly inappropriate for **7–8**, and we return to discuss these sentences later. Turning now to **2**, we have already characterized *the knife* as a [neutral] participant,

*Verbs involving* [range] *participants* (see **11**)

| agent | action | range |
|-------|--------|-------|
| John | is playing | tiddly winks |
| Mary | sang | a song |
| Harold | ran | a mile |

*Verbs involving* [range] *participants, but not* [agent] *subjects*

| neutral | state | range |
|---------|-------|-------|
| John | weighs | twelve stone |
| This | cost | £100 |
| Her bust | measures | 42 inches |

*Non-*[causative] *verbs with* [neutral, patient] *participants* (see **12**)

| agent | action directed | neutral patient |
|-------|-----------------|-----------------|
| John | beat | his wife |
| The cat | chased | the dog |
| The vandal | slashed | the priceless painting |
| The cat | has scratched | me |
| I | painted | the sitting room |

*Verbs involving* [result] *participants* (see **13**)

| agent | action | neutral result |
|-------|--------|----------------|
| Wren | built | St Paul's Cathedral |
| Peter | is digging | a hole |
| John | burnt | a hole (in the carpet with his cigar) |
| Velasquez | painted | the Rokeby Venus |

Note that some verbs can take either a [result] or a [patient] participant:

| | |
|---|---|
| Velasquez painted the Rokeby Venus | [result] |
| I painted the sitting room | [patient] |
| John burnt a hole in the carpet | [result] |
| John burnt his old love letters | [patient] |

*Figure 99*

and no further characterization seems necessary; we have noted that we can describe *sharp* in **2** as an [*attribute*].

These observations are summarized in **9–13**: we refer to such characterizations as propositional structures.

| | | | | |
|---|---|---|---|---|
| **9** | agent | action directed causative descriptive | neutral patient | (=**1**) |
| **10** | neutral | state descriptive | attribute | (=**2**) |
| **11** | agent | action | range | (=**3, 4**) |
| **12** | agent | action directed | neutral patient | (=**6a**) |
| **13** | agent | action directed | neutral result | (=**6b**) |

(Propositional structures for **7–8** are discussed later.)

We will represent propositional structure, as here, in a form which corresponds to the order of constituents in an active declarative sentence. They should however be regarded as abstract representations of the propositional relations within sentences and will consequently correspond to a variety of actual sentences, where the form depends on considerations other than simple propositional structure. Thus **9** is the propositional structure appropriate for both:

**14**   John sharpened the knife
    The knife was sharpened by John

The relationship between propositional and constituent structures is discussed briefly at the end of this chapter.

So far our characterization has been entirely in semantic terms, but the footnote on page 289 said that features like [action] are syntactic-semantic, and we now enquire whether there are syntactic correlates to these features. We will see that there are no absolute one-to-one correlations, but a number of generalizations can be usefully made.

The [state] : [action] distinction is reflected in the following (we exemplify using the propositional structures **9** and **10**: the reader is invited to verify the observations with respect to other examples given here and later). The verb in [state] sentences cannot occur in progressive form: (but see **110**, page 311, for an exception to this)

**15a** John is sharpening the knife
**15b** *The knife is being sharp

Only [action] propositions containing an [agent] can be put in correspondence with imperative sentences:

**16a** Sharpen the knife
**16b** *Be sharp!

Only [action] propositions are typically associated with [instrument] **17** and [benefactive] **18** roles:

**17a** John is sharpening the knife with a whetstone
**17b** *The knife is sharp with a whetstone

(The [instrument] role is realized by *with a whetstone*: note that [instrument] roles are frequently identifiable by the use of the preposition *with* – we note the frequent association of roles with particular prepositions.)

**18a** John is sharpening the knife for his mother
**18b** *The knife is sharp for his mother

(The [benefactive] role is realized by *for his mother* – she is the participant who 'benefits' from the action: it can frequently be identified by the preposition *for*. [State] propositions cannot usually be associated with circumstantial roles of manner, place and intention:

**19a** John is sharpening the knife carefully
**19b** *The knife is sharp carefully                                     (manner)

**20a** John is sharpening the knife in the woodshed
**20b** *The knife is sharp in the woodshed                         (place)

**21a** John is sharpening the knife intentionally
**21b** *The knife is sharp intentionally                               (intention)

Circumstantial roles of manner and intention seem characteristically tied to the occurrence of [agent], as *John was careful in sharpening the knife. John acted intentionally in sharpening the knife.* One might attest **21b**, but only if it has the sense 'it was someone's intention (agentive) that the knife should be sharp': this sentence can hardly be construed with the sense 'the knife had the intention of being sharp'. Place participants, on the other hand, appear tied to the proposition as a whole: *Where John sharpened the knife was in the woodshed. *Where the knife was sharp was in the woodshed* is nonsense – it implies that it wasn't sharp elsewhere!

Let us now turn to some distinctions that can be drawn between the various types of [action] proposition. They can typically be questioned by:

>    **22**   What happened?

Thus:

>    **23a**   What happened?
>    **23b**   John sharpened the knife
>    **23c**   John ran a race

etc. This is not possible for [state] propositions. [Action] propositions with [agent] can typically be questioned by:

>    **24**   What did [agent] do?

Thus:

>    **25a**   What did John do?
>    **25b**   He sharpened the knife
>    **25c**   He built a house

etc. We have not yet encountered [action] sentences without [agent], but this generalization can be tested when we do. [Action] propositions with [agent] and [patient] can typically be questioned with:

>    **26**   What did [agent] do to [patient]?

Thus:

>    **27a**   What did John do to the knife?
>    **27b**   He sharpened it
>    **28a**   What did John do to the dog?
>    **28b**   He beat it

but hardly:

>    **29a**   What did John do to the house?
>    **29b**   He built it

etc. Similarly we find the question:

**30a** What happened to [patient]?

as in:

**31a** What happened to the dog?
**31b** John beat it

but not:

**32a** What happened to the race?
**32b** John ran it

Note also that [action] sentences with [agent] and [patient] or [result] correspond to passive sentences:

**33** The dog was beaten by John
The house was built by John

but less felicitously:

**34** Tiddlywinks was played by John

Further observe that the preposition *by* marks [agent] participants (as *with* marks [instrument] and *for* [benefactive]).

Propositional structures with [state] do not lend themselves to question-and-answer sequences like those illustrated above: a proposition like **10** can only typically be questioned by questions like:

**35** What was the knife like?
**36** Can you describe the knife?

Another propositional structure seems to be, as it were, intermediate between the structures of **9** and **10**. The relationship between these two structures and our new structure can be illustrated in the three sentences:

**37** The shirt is torn                             (= **10**)
**38** The shirt is tearing
**39** John is tearing the shirt                    (= **9**)

We characterize **38** as

**40**           neutral          action
                 patient          inchoative
                                  descriptive

The subject participant we characterize as [neutral, patient] since it is affected by the action of the verb, just as the object participant is in **39**. The characterization [inchoative] in **40** is the traditional term for 'change-of-state' verbs: the sentence **38** describes a shirt changing from a state where the shirt is not torn to one where it is torn. These characterizations can be checked by using the tests outlined in **15** onwards.

A very large number of sentences in English can be related to each other in the manner shown in 37–39: [state], [inchoative, action] and [causative, directed, action]. Some lexical items that are related in this way are shown in Figure 100, and the reader is invited to check this by constructing appropriate sentences. In Figure 100 the three columns are to be understood as relating, respectively, to the characterizations in **10**, **40** and **9**.

|   | *state* *descriptive* (= **10**) | *action* *inchoative* *descriptive* (= **40**) | *action* *directed* *causative* *descriptive* (= **9**) |
|---|---|---|---|
| a | RIPE | RIPEN | RIPEN |
|   | WIDE | WIDEN | WIDEN |
| b | YELLOW | YELLOW | YELLOW |
|   | COOL | COOL | COOL |
| c | TORN | TEAR | TEAR |
|   | CLOSED | CLOSE | CLOSE |
| d | MOLTEN | MELT | MELT |
|   | ROTTEN | ROT | ROT |
| e | SHARP | — | SHARPEN |
|   | MOIST | — | MOISTEN |
| f | LARGE | — | ENLARGE |
|   | BOLD | — | EMBOLDEN |
| g | PASSIVE | — | PASSIVIZE |
|   | BEAUTIFUL | — | BEAUTIFY |
| h | DEAD | DIE | KILL |
|   | HIGH | RISE | RAISE |
| i | — | VANISH | — |

*Figure 100*

A number of observations can be made about the sets of items shown in Figure 100. The relationship typically involves a form that is syntactically an adjective (left-hand column), a form that is an intransitive verb (central column), and a transitive verb (right-hand column). Sometimes (**a, e, f, g**) there is a morphological relationship of derivation (RIPE : RIPEN, etc.), sometimes (**b**) the 'same' form is used in all three columns (YELLOW); sometimes (**c**) the 'adjectival' form is the same as the passive participle of the corresponding verb (TORN : TEAR); sometimes (**d**) the adjectival form is a former passive participle (MOLTEN : MELT);[2] sometimes (**h**) there is a suppletive relationship between adjective, and one or more of the verb forms (DEAD : DIE : KILL). There are also cases where there is a causative form, but no corresponding inchoative (SHARP : SHARPEN).[3]

Some other asymmetries are shown in Figure 100.

In some of the cases involving asymmetries an alternative expression, as it were, 'fills the gap'. Thus, for example, corresponding to:

**41a** The gap is narrow
**41b** The gap is narrowing
**41c** John is narrowing the gap

we find:

**42a** The gap is large
**42b** The gap is getting larger/the gap is becoming larger
**42c** John is enlarging the gap

but there is no sentence:

**43** *The gap is enlarging

Sentences like **42b** can also be constructed corresponding to, and paraphrasing, **41b**:

---

2 This fact may lead one to question the analysis of the passive adopted so far. Note that the 'short' passive form, where the agent is deleted (*The shirt was torn (by John)*) is identical to the adjective form. It is usually held that the adjectival and passive forms can be distinguished by the possibility of inserting an adjective modifier in the one but not the other: thus, *the shirt was rather torn* but *\*the shirt was rather torn by John*.

3 The sentence *The knife is sharpening* is not typically found in the inchoative sense 'The knife is becoming sharper'. Note that we can find sentences like *The knife sharpens easily*. Jespersen (1927) describes such sentences as 'medio-passives', intermediate between an active and a passive use. They are typically understood in a sense like 'I find it easy to sharpen this knife': i.e. a sense involving an understood [agent]. Such sentences usually require an adverbial expression. We will not consider them further here.

**44**    The gap is getting narrow
       The gap is becoming narrow

What is the relationship between **41b** and the paraphrases in **44**? We postulate a propositional structure as in **45** for such sentences:[4]

**45**    *neutral*      *action*         *attribute*
         *patient*      *inchoative*
                       *descriptive*

We may compare **45** with the characterization already given for [state] sentences, like **41a**:

**46**    *neutral*      *state*          *attribute*
                       *descriptive*

and [inchoative] sentences like (**41b**)

**47**    *neutral*      *action*
         *patient*      *inchoative*
                       *descriptive*

These propositional structures are related in interesting ways. The structure in **46** is that realized by a [state] copulative sentence, which we have seen typically involves the copular verb BE, though other copular verbs like SEEM are equally appropriate in such structures. The structure in **45** is also that of a copular sentence, but this time involves an [action, inchoative] copular verb, BECOME, GET, and we may add TURN (see pages 50–1 for a discussion of copular sentences). The structures in **45** and **47** both involve an [action, inchoative, descriptive] process, but in **45** we find a copular verb (BECOME, etc.) in construction with an adjective, whereas in **47** we find the [inchoative] verb that mor-

---

4    We may also observe that the attribute tends to denote a 'result' rather than a 'state'. This is particularly noticeable if we consider such sentences with the perfect verb form: *My tea has got cold* implies that it is now cold, but once was not cold – such sentences are sometimes said to involve a 'resultant state' (a state reached after some inchoative process), in contrast to a simple 'state', as in *the tap water is cold*, where one might suppose either that it never was hot, or that the speaker is not concerned to make this implication. The sentence *the tap water has got cold* is appropriate if the speaker refers to the 'hot' tap which is now running 'cold' as the 'hot water' is no longer 'hot', or if the water is colder than usual. This is perhaps why sentences like *the ice has got cold* are anomalous, since there is an apparent and curious implication that 'the ice' was once 'not cold'.

phologically corresponds to the adjective appropriate to **45**. This suggests that sentences like:

**48**  The apples are getting ripe

are in some sense 'analytic': the [inchoative] feature of the process is overtly 'spelled out' by the verb GET; while sentences like

**49**  The apples are ripening

are in some sense 'synthetic', the [inchoative] feature is as it were 'incorporated' into the adjective, which now becomes morphologically a verb. An idiosyncracy of the lexical structure of English is that this process is inhibited for LARGE, so we find no sentence like **43**. (It is possible to consider INCREASE in the sentence *the gap is increasing* as a suppletive, inchoative form – there is no adjective corresponding to INCREASE.)[5]

We can make similar observations with respect to the [causative] structures we have identified. Thus, for example, VANISH is only found as an intransitive [inchoative] verb:

**50**  The rabbit is vanishing

and there is no corresponding [causative] (though it would be comprehensible if it did occur):

**51**  *The magician vanished the rabbit

There are, however, the [causative] constructions:

**52**  The magician made the rabbit vanish
   The magician caused the rabbit to vanish

---

5 We may also observe that in some languages what in English is realized as a construction BE + Adj. is realized as a verb (page 60). In Akan there is no adjective corresponding to COLD in English; instead we find the verb DWO 'to be, or become, cold'. Furthermore, there is in this language a special 'stative' verb form that is appropriate for such verbs. So we find:

   nsúó nó dwò (water the be-cold (stative)) 'the water is cold'

as the [state] sentence corresponding to the English translation given. In this language an [inchoative] sense is realized, much as in English, by the progressive verb form:

   nsúó nó redwó (water the is-cooling) 'The water is getting cold'

In this respect Akan is a 'synthetic' language in a way that English is not: since both the Akan examples involve intransitive verbs.

and we have already seen (see **5**) that such sentences paraphrase causative sentences. Here again we can consider that MAKE and CAUSE function as overt markers of the causativity of the sentences involved, and that sentences like **52** or **53b**, **53c** are 'analytic', while sentences like **53a** are 'synthetic'.

**53a**   The sun ripened the apples
**53b**   The sun made the apples ripen
**53c**   The sun caused the apples to ripen

By exactly the same sort of argument we can analyse DO and HAPPEN discussed in **22** to **32**, as items that spell out the [action] nature of sentences which they paraphrase:

**54**   What the magician did was make the rabbit vanish

So an analytic sentence like

**55**   What the sun did was make the apples become ripe

which paraphrases the synthetic

**56**   The sun ripened the apples,

overtly marks the [action] (DO), [causative] (MAKE) and [inchoative] (BECOME) senses underlying **56**.

Two questions immediately present themselves: why does English have these two opposing tendencies?[6] Does this fact affect our analysis?

6 Both tendencies are very common in English, and may be attested in a much wider range of examples than we have space for. Thus, for example, there is a paraphrase relation between the complex expressions in the left-hand column below, and the corresponding single verbs in the right-hand column.

| | |
|---|---|
| fix with a nail | nail |
| feed with a spoon | spoon feed |
| hit with the hand | slap |
| poke with the finger | finger |
| make a hole | hole |
| travel by foot | walk |
| make a presentation to | present |
| give a battering to | batter |

The process shown is still extremely productive, as can be seen from sentences like:

She eyeballed the student's essays
I train to work every morning

The chief communicative value of the analytic forms appears to be that they enable a speaker to make some particular distinctions that are either neutralized in the synthetic forms, or are syntactically impossible. A distinction which is neutralized with the inchoative verbs is that between a comparative and an absolute usage. Thus:

**57** The blackberries are ripening

does not distinguish between:

**58** The blackberries are getting riper (comparative)

and:

**59** The blackberries are getting ripe (absolute)

In a sentence like:

**60** Let the blackberries ripen before you pick them

it is not clear whether the sense is:

**61** Let the blackberries get riper before you pick them

or

**62** Let the blackberries get ripe before you pick them

Cases which involve syntactic impossibilities are those where the analytic form permits one constituent to be modified, say by an adverbial expression, but where no comparable synthetic form is possible. Thus:

**63** The blackberries are getting somewhat too ripe

cannot be paraphrased by a sentence using the corresponding inchoative verb.[7]

The derivational relationships that can be established are various, and work both as a 'verbalizing' process (e.g. *fix with a nail – nail*) and as a 'nominalizing' process (e.g. *batter – give a battering to*). For an interesting and wide-ranging discussion of such examples see Liefrinck (1973).

7 This feature is even more noticeable with the analytic expressions mentioned in the previous note. There are no synthetic expressions that can correspond to 'poke with the forefinger'; 'travel by the nine o'clock train'; 'fix with a four inch rusty nail'; etc.

The problem that examples like **55** pose for the analysis adopted hitherto is that such sentences clearly involve embedding. An analysis sometimes suggested looks like:

**64**    (Sun CAUSE (apples BECOME (apples BE ripe)))

or indeed, if we wish to indicate the action nature of the sentence:

**65**    (Sun DO (sun CAUSE (apples BECOME (apples BE ripe))))

A formula of this sort quite neatly captures the relationships we have been discussing, since the successive bracketings represent the [state] proposition ((apples BE ripe)); the [inchoative] proposition ((apples BECOME (apples BE ripe))); the [causative] proposition; etc. We can then suppose that the minimum amalgamation of the various elements of the representation would involve the most analytic form – perhaps:

**66**    The sun did make the apples come to be ripe

(if this is acceptable!) – and the maximum amalgamation of the various elements results in the most synthetic form:

**67**    The sun ripened the apples

Such an analysis obviously has its attractions, and many of the structures we discuss can usefully be examined in this light: some indeed involve embedding more obviously than the structures we have been considering.[8] We will not, however, pursue such

---

8 Such analyses also raise questions. For example, how widely can the paraphrases involving BECOME, GET, MAKE, CAUSE be applied, and what restrictions are there on such paraphrases? One example will suffice. We have analysed sentences like the following as containing an [agent] participant:

**a** John split the wood
**b** The sun split the wood

However, to group together 'animate' expressions like *John*, and 'natural forces', like *the sun*, begs questions. In **a** *John* is a 'direct' agent in that he actually splits the wood – thus we can add instrumental phrases like *with an axe*; in the **b** sentence the sun seems to be an 'indirect' agent and instrumental phrases seem rather odd (unless we see the sun as 'personified'):

The sun split the wood with its great heat

Furthermore, the paraphrase with MAKE only seems to apply felicitously when we are dealing with the indirect agent:

analyses further here since our purpose is to take a more straightforward and taxonomic look at some propositional structures in English and classify verbs in terms of the propositional structures, they can enter.

We now turn to some further propositional structures, which, for reasons of space, are discussed in less detail. We begin with:

**68**   John had a book

**69a**   Mary gave John a book

**69b**   Mary gave a book to John

Again note a distinction between a [state] process **68**, and an [action] process **69**. The [state] process is further characterized as [possessive], for obvious reasons; and the [action] process as [directed] and [causative], in the senses already discussed.[9]

As to the participant roles involved, we say that in both sentences *a book* realizes a [neutral] role. In **69a** *John* realizes the participant role of [goal], the book changes hands from *Mary*, the [source] of the book, to *John*, the [goal]. We also say that Mary realizes an [agent] role, since she is the actor responsible for the transfer. This description contrasts with the description appropriate for a sentence like:

The sun made the wood split

If we have:

John made the wood split

John, it seems, must be understood as an indirect agent – he might have made it split by leaving it in the sun, forgetting to apply teak oil, etc., but we hardly understand this sentence as involving direct agency:

?John made the wood split with an axe

One reason why VANISH is not used as a transitive verb may be that it involves indirect, rather than direct agency. After all, it is 'the rabbit' which 'does the vanishing'! A possible answer is to make further subclassifications of the participant role [agent], but it is not clear how far this process would have to be taken, or even if there would be an end to it! We shall continue to recognize a single participant agent.

9 The feature [possessive] must be understood in a wide sense since, as will become clear, not all the verbs involved are 'possessive' in the ordinary language sense. However, all the verbs do fall into a semantic class which involves possession and other notions related to this. The same is true, to a greater or lesser extent, of all our characterizations.

**70**   Mary took the book from John

where John is now to be identified as [source] and Mary as both [actor] and [goal]. In **69b** the [goal] participant is identified by the preposition *to*, the typical [goal] preposition, and in **70** the [source] participant is identified by the preposition, *from*, the typical [source] preposition. What now of the participant realized by *John* in the [state] sentence **68**? This role we identify as [dative]; *John* here is neither [source] nor [goal], if these bear the connotations of movement 'to' and 'from' suggested by our previous description. [Dative] is typically found in [state] propositions, and it too, when not in subject position, may be associated with the preposition *to*, as in:

**71**   The book belongs to John

where the order of participants is [neutral]–[dative], rather than [dative]–[neutral] as in **68**.

There is one further characterization to be made. In **69** are two alternative versions of the sentence, one in which *John* and the other in which *a book* is the object of GIVE. Further, when the [goal] participant becomes the object of the verb, it loses its preposition. We account for this by supposing that the further characterization [patient] can be added to either [goal] or [neutral]. One advantage is that this enables us to say that the [patient] participant may become the subject of the corresponding passive sentence: we find both:

**72a**   John was given a book by Mary
**72b**   A book was given to John by Mary

Some support for this analysis may be gained by observing that this additional specification may be made only to [goal] or [neutral] participants: the [source] cannot become also [patient]. Thus the sentence:

**73**   Mary took John a book

can only be understood as:

**74**   Mary took a book to John

not as:

**75**   Mary took a book from John

In **73**, according to our analysis, John is [goal], and the generalizations made above hold; in **75** John is [source] and this cannot become a [patient] participant. Similarly the passive sentence:

**76**  John was taken a book by Mary

can only be understood in a sense where John is [goal] not [source]. Finally, [source] participants do not usually lose their preposition *from*.

The propositional structures we propose, then, are:[10]

**77**  *dative*   *state*        *neutral*
                   *possession*

**78**  *agent*    *action*       *neutral*        *goal*
        *source*   *directed*
                   *causative*         \ *patient* /
                   *possession*

| D St N | A/S Ac N G | A/G Ac - N/P S |
|--------|------------|----------------|
|        | ＼ P ／     |                |
| HAVE   | GIVE       | TAKE           |
| OWN    | TAKE       | BUY            |
|        | SELL       | BORROW         |
|        | LEND       | RENT           |
|        | HIRE       | HIRE           |
|        | RENT       |                |

| N St D | | |
|--------|--------|--------|
| BELONG | PRESENT |       |
|        |        | SNATCH |
|        |        | GRAB   |
|        |        | GET    |

*Figure 101*  (see footnote 11, page 306)

10 In **78** we indicate by the arrows that [patient] may be attached either to the [neutral] or to the [goal] participant.

**79**   *agent*      *action*          *neutral*    *source*
         *goal*       *directed*        *patient*
                      *causative*
                      *possessive*

Some of the verbs that can occur in these structures are set
out in Figure 101.[11] Some are in pairs (BUY : SELL;
BORROW : LEND) that contrast as to whether they have [agent,
source] or [agent : goal] subjects; some (e.g. TAKE) can occur
in either structure; and others (e.g. GRAB, PRESENT) can only
occur in one or the other structure.

This analysis can be extended to cover a number of other
verbs, but a problem is that [neutral] participants are sometimes
obligatorily marked with prepositions: so, for example:

**80**   John robbed Mary of £10

We suggest here a propositional structure of the form:

**81**   *agent*      *action*          *source*     *neutral*
         *goal*       *directed*        *patient*    (OF)
                      *causative*
                      *possessive*

Note the source participant is marked as necessarily [patient],
indicating that it must be the object of the verb (as discussed
above), and may be the subject of the corresponding passive
sentence: we have also shown the [neutral] participant as marked
by the proposition *of*. This is the only possible structure for
ROB since there is no sentence:

**82**   *John robbed £10 from Mary

This 'sense' must be expressed as:

**83a**  John stole £10 from Mary

**84**   *agent*      *action*          *neutral*    *source*
         *goal*       *directed*        *patient*
                      *causative*
                      *possessive*

11 Here and in subsequent figures, we use the following abbreviations: D(ative);
A(gent); S(ource); G(oal); P(atient); N(eutral); St(ate); Ac(tion) – other process
characterizations can to be supplied from the text.

where this time the [neutral] participant must be [patient] (it must be object of the active sentence, and may be subject of the corresponding passive sentence): we have not specified the preposition for [source], since this is the typical preposition *from*. A final instance may be illustrated with the sentences

**85**   The Chinese supplied arms to the Vietcong

**86**   The Chinese supplied the Vietcong with arms

**87**   *agent        action           neutral            goal*
          *source       directed        (WITH)              patient*
                        *causative*

Here, either the [neutral] or [goal] participant may be [patient]: as such it becomes the object of the verb in an active sentence, and appears with no preposition, or may be the subject of a passive sentence. The typical [goal] preposition, is *to* and is not therefore specified. Other verbs that can enter a propositional structure like **87** include FURNISH, ISSUE, FEED, AWARD.

We now turn from propositions related to possession to consider some locative propositions. Consider the sentences:

**88**   The lamp is on the table

**89**   John put the lamp on the table

**90**   John took the lamp off the table

We characterize these as:

**91**   *neutral        state              Lplace*
                        *locative*

**92**   *agent          action             neutral            Lgoal*
                        *directed           patient*
                        *causative*
                        *locative*

**93**   *agent          action             neutral            Lsource*
                        *directed           patient*
                        *causative*
                        *locative*

Some verbs that can enter the propositional frames shown in **91–93** are shown in Figure 102.

There are two points to make about these structures. First, note that [state, locative] verbs occur in the progressive form, even though they are [state] sentences (see remarks on **15**, page

| N | St | LP | A | Ac | N/P | LG | A | Ac | N/P | LS |
|---|----|----|----|----|-----|-----|----|----|-----|-----|
| STAND | | | | | STAND | | | | | REMOVE |
| SIT | | | | | SIT | | | | | TAKE |
| LIE | | | | | LAY | | | | | EXTRACT |
| HANG | | | | | HANG | | | | | EJECT |
| | | | | | PUT | | | | | |
| | | | | | PLACE | | | | | |
| | | | | | TAKE | | | | | |

*Figure 102*

293). We will see later (see **109**) that sentences like *John is sitting down* have two senses: one is a [state] sense (in the state of being sat down) as is required in the present examples: the other an [inchoative] sense (in the process of sitting down), which we discuss later. The other remark we may make is with respect to the specification [Lgoal] (locative goal) and [Lsource] (locative source). These specifications remind us of the close connections between [possessive] and [locative] propositions. Semantically, the relevant constituents are as much [goal] and [source] here, as they were in the [possessive] sentences, and some verbs can enter both [locative] propositional structures and [possessive] propositional structures:

> **94a**  John took the lamp from Mary
> **94b**  John took the lamp from the table

There are differences. [Source] and [goal], we have seen, are characteristically identified by the prepositions *from* and *to* respectively. [Lsource] and [Lgoal] have a wider range of prepositions open to them – we can replace *from* in **94b** by *off* (and in other sentences by *out of*, etc.) The prepositions in [locative] sentences have a more significant semantic role to play than the simple marking of propositional function. Furthermore, as we have seen, [source] and [goal] may combine with [agent] – see Figure 101 and associated discussion – but [Lgoal] and [Lsource] do not characteristically combine with [agent] in this fashion. On the other hand there are interesting inter-relationships. Here we mention only one. The typical [state, possession] verb is HAVE; one of the commonest [state, locative] verbs is BE, often referred to as a locative copula:

**95** John has a book
**96** The lamp is on the table

Now consider the sentences:

**97** The book is John's
**98** The table has a book on it.

HAVE and BE have 'changed places'. One thing peculiar about this relationship is that it appears to be related to the definiteness of the [neutral] participant. Thus in the [possessive] sentences, if the [neutral] participant is indefinite, we typically use HAVE rather than BE:

**99a** John has a book
**99b** ?A book is John's

and the same is true of the [locative] sentences:

**100a** The table has a book on it
**100b** ?A book is on the table

Indeed, many [possessive] meanings appear to be realized as apparently [locative] sentences:

**101a** Have you any matches on you?
**101b** The book is in my care
**101c** The evidence is in my possession

For now we need merely note that there is some justification for an apparently similar analysis.

Another set of [locative] sentences, that once again show a similarity to [possession] propositional structures, can be illustrated with:

**102a** John planted roses in the garden
**102b** John planted the garden with roses

**103**  *agent     action         neutral↘          Lgoal*
                  *directed       (WITH)↘        ↗*
                  *causative               patient*
                  *locative*

Like the similar [possessive] structures discussed in **86–87**, we find that either the [neutral] or the [goal] participant may become the object of the verb (or the subject of the corresponding passive sentence); hence, once more, we identify [patient] as a role associated with either participant. And, as before, if the [neutral] participant is not also [patient] then it occurs with the preposition *with*. Some other verbs that enter this structure are shown in Figure 103. (They fall roughly into semantic 'sets', and are set out in this way in Figure 103: the reader is invited to supply further examples.) A peculiarity of many, but not all, verbs that enter this propositional frame is that when [patient] is associated with [Lgoal], the sentence tends to have an implication of 'completeness': thus **102b** tends to imply that the whole garden, or the whole of the relevant parts of the garden, has been 'planted with roses'. The corresponding sentence, where [patient] is associated with the [neutral] participant, has no such implication. This implication can be confirmed by comparing the following:

**104a**   John planted a rose in the garden
**104b**   *John planted the garden with a rose

**105a**   John planted the garden all over with roses
**105b**   *John planted roses all over in the garden

This implication may account for the fact that FILL, which necessarily implies completion, can only occur in a sentence of the form **102b**:

**106a**   John filled his house with flowers
**106b**   *John filled flowers in his house

in contrast with POUR, which can only occur in a sentence of the pattern **102a**:

**107a**   John poured petrol over the floor
**107b**   *John poured the floor with petrol

It does not however explain why some verbs do not have any particular implications associated with either order:

**108a**   He marked his name on his shirt collars
**108b**   He marked his shirt collars with his name

Finally a few verbs occur in a structure like **103**, but, instead of an [Lgoal] participant, we find an [Lsource] participant:

**109a**   John stripped the bark off the tree
**109b**   John stripped the tree of its bark

Constructions like these lend themselves very interestingly to an analysis in terms of embedded predications.

A   Ac   N (with) LG   A   Ac   N(of)   LS      A   Ac   N   LG/P
            ↖P↗                  ↖P↗

| | | | |
|---|---|---|---|
| PLANT | MARK | STRIP | POUR |
| CRAM | ENGRAVE | EMPTY | PUT |
| PILE | INSCRIBE | | |
| STACK | | | A   Ac   N/P(with)   LG |
| DAUB | | | FILL |
| PAINT | | | COVER |
| SPRAY | | | |
| SMEAR | | | *Figure 103* |

Thus far we have considered [state] and [action, causative] propositions involving [possession] and [locative] verbs. We may now enquire whether there are also [inchoative] verbs in these classes. We first discuss [locative] verbs. Consider the sentence:

**110**   John is sitting down

We have already noted (page 308) that **110** is capable of a [state] interpretation and the verb is in the progressive form, even though it realizes a [state] proposition. We have also noted that **110** is capable of an [action] interpretation. The two interpretations we might represent as:

**111a**   John is (in the state of) sitting down
**111b**   John is (in the process of) sitting down

The latter interpretation may be analysed as [inchoative]. We propose a propositional structure:

**112**   *agent*        *action*          *Lplace*
       *patient*      *inchoative*
                *locative*

The only comment we make here on this frame is with respect to the characterization of the subject as both [agent] and [patient]: i.e. both the agent responsible for the action, and the patient who is affected by the action. This analysis implies that such structures are 'reflexive'.[12]

We also find sentences with a non-agentive subject expression:

**113**  The tree is falling into the river

which we analyse as:

| **114** | *neutral patient* | *action inchoative locative* | *Lgoal* |

and corresponding to this we find the [causative] sentence:

| **115** | John felled the tree | | |
| | *agent* | *action directed causative* | *neutral patient* |

These two structures lead us to a large class of locative verbs which can be called verbs of 'motion'. They can be illustrated by:

**116**  The pebble rolled to the bottom of the hill

| **117** | *neutral patient* | *action motion* | *Lgoal* |

**118**  John rolled the pebble to the bottom of the hill

| **119** | *agent* | *action causative motion* | *neutral patient* | *Lgoal* |

Once again we note a non-causative:causative relationship. In such

---

12 Reflexive structures are those where the agent of the verb carries out the action of the verb upon himself. This is overtly shown in sentences like *John hurt himself, John killed himself*, etc., where the constituent *himself* is described as a reflexive pronoun. There are a few verbs in English that permit the reflexive pronoun to be deleted, and yet sentences with these verbs are understood reflexively: *John shaved, John washed*, etc. In this latter sense we describe sentences like *John sat down* as reflexive. In English such verbs do sometimes appear as overt reflexives: thus we find *Sit yourself down, The man came into the room and sat himself comfortably in an armchair*. We may also observe that in some languages such verbs are often syntactically 'reflexive verbs' cf. French, SE RASER 'to have a shave', S'ASSEOIR 'to sit down'.

sentences there is also the possibility of not only an [Lgoal] but also an [Lsource]; and the locative participant is not obligatory.

**120a** John pushed the car from his house to his garage
**120b** John swam from Dover to Cap Gris Nez

A selection of such propositional frames and the verbs which can enter them is shown in Figure 104. We have not discussed all of the structures shown in this figure, but they are self-explanatory.

1  A  Ac $\begin{cases} \text{(LP)} \\ \text{(LG)(LS)} \end{cases}$    2  A  Ac  (LG)

       JUMP                  DESCEND
       WALK                  ENTER
       RUN                   DISAPPEAR
       SKIP
       LEAP

3  A  Ac  (LS)    4  N  Ac  LP

       DEPART             LIVE
       LEAVE             STAY
       EMERGE

5  N/P  Ac  (LG)(LS)    6  A  Ac  N/P  (LG)(LS)
                           *              *

       ROLL                   ROLL
       SLIDE                  SLIDE
       FALL                   DROP
       DROP                  PUSH
                                DRAG
                                SHOVE

*Examples*

1  John jumped on the table/onto the table/off the table
2  He descended into Hell
3  The butterfly emerged from its chrysalis
4  I live in Edinburgh
5  The apple fell from the tree onto Newton's head
6  The policeman dragged the prisoner from the cell into the dock.

*Figure 104*

Three comments may be made. Firstly, many verbs of motion may take either an [Lgoal] or an [Lsource], or both, or neither. This is represented by the linked brackets in Figure 104. It is also appropriate, for many verbs of motion, to postulate a participant [Lpath] to indicate the path followed by some other participant in the sentence, when this is clearly neither [Lsource] or [Lgoal]. Thus for example:

**121a**   The ball rolled across the room
**121b**   John went from London (LS) to Edinburgh (LG) via
            Leeds (LP)

Prepositions appropriate to [Lpath] include *across*, *through*, *via*, etc. We do not pursue this suggestion further here. This range of choice is not characteristically available for verbs of possession – as Figure 102 makes clear, and as the reader is invited to verify. Secondly, note that some verbs of motion are analysed as occurring either with an [Lgoal] or an [Lsource] or with an [Lplace] expression. The latter may be illustrated in sentences like:

**122a**   John is walking in the park
**122b**   John is jumping on the table

Both of these have an interpretation where the motion is being carried out in some place. The second sentence has another interpretation more unambiguously expressed by:

**123**   John is jumping onto the table

where the locative expression is clearly an [Lgoal].[13]

---

13   JUMP can be used both non-causatively, as in the example, or causatively as in:

John jumped the horse over the fence

This sentence, however, poses an analytic problem. *John* may quite appropriately be analysed as realizing an [agent] role. The horse may also appropriately be analysed as realizing a [patient] role (the object, etc. affected by the action). In this case, since it is the horse that does the jumping, it should perhaps also be considered an [actor]. This suggests we should distinguish between the [agent] (the instigator or initiator of the action) and the [actor] (the performer of the action). It might further be observed that for many of the verbs of motion shown in Figure 104, a description as [factor] rather than as [agent] may seem appropriate. The problem with JUMP may be more appropriately solved by considering it to realize an embedded proposition.

This leads us to a final comment on Figure 104: it is possible to sub-categorize the prepositions that occur in these sentences as to whether they relate to [Lplace], [Lgoal] or [Lsource]. Thus, typically *in*, *on*, *near*, *beside* are [Lplace] prepositions; *in(to)*, *on(to)*, *to*, *towards*, are [Lgoal] prepositions. Some prepositions, like *under*, *over*, *by*, may be either [Lplace] or [Lgoal] prepositions.

We now turn again to [possessive] processes. A few verbs may be analysed as realizing an [inchoative] process. These include those shown in:

**124a**  John has acquired a new PhD student
**124b**  John obtained a distinction (in his exam)

**125**  *dative*      *action*        *neutral*
                  *inchoative*
                  *possessive*

providing they are understood in a non-agentive sense as 'come to have', not in an agentive sense as 'actively sought and got'. In the latter sense we analyse them as occurring in a proposition with an [agent] subject. One further possessive structure is illustrated by:

**126**  John collected the books for Mary

**127**  *agent*      *action*        *neutral*       *benefactive*
                  *possessive*    *patient*

Note that in such structures the [agent] is not analysed as also being either [source] or [goal] (as the structures in Figure 101 were) and a new participant role, [benefactive], is introduced. This role appears to differ from the role [goal] introduced earlier: it may for example be paraphrased by *on behalf of*, an option not open to goal expressions.

The last set of sentences we will concern ourselves with in this chapter can be illustrated by:

**128a**  John is the chairman
**128b**  The chairman is John

**129a**  The committee elected John chairman
**129b**  The committee elected John as the chairman
**129c**  The committee elected John to be the chairman

Our sentences are once more related as [state] to [action]. The first
two sentences we may describe as involving [identification]: John
is identified as the person who occupies a certain position, or plays
a certain role, that of chairman. The second set of sentences all
describe an action that can cause such a state.

Let us look first at the sentences **128**: it is suggested that these
are [identification] sentences. In order to discuss some of the
peculiar characteristics of such sentences we can best compare
them with sentences like **2** (*the knife is sharp*) where we were
dealing with the attribution of a quality to an object; in the
particular case of **2** we were concerned with the attribution of
'sharpness' to 'the knife'. Here we are concerned with the
identification of 'John' as filling the particular role of 'chairman'.
The distinction between [attribute] and [identification] can be
seen more clearly in a slightly different example:

> **130**   My wife is tall and beautiful
> **131**   My wife is that tall and beautiful woman over there

**130** describes my wife; **131** identifies her. Note that **131**, but not
**130**, reasonably answers the questions:

> **132**   Who is your wife?
>         Which one is your wife?

Questions like **132** are asking for an identification, not a
description.

[Identification] sentences have certain syntactic peculiarities.
We concern ourselves with two of them. Firstly, both NPs are
characteristically definite: they are usually either proper names,
like *John*, or are NPs with the definite article, like *the chairman*.
Definite NPs usually refer uniquely to some individual in the
context of utterance. With descriptive sentences, the subject NP
is often definite, but the other constituent is usually either an
adjective or, if it is an NP, usually does not contain the definite
article:

> **133**   My wife is a good cook, a teacher, etc.
>         My wife is tall and beautiful, etc.

In these examples, the adjectives and non-definite NPs do not
refer, they rather describe. Thus, for example, in **128** both *John*
and *the chairman* are NPs that could be used to refer; whereas in

**133** the NP *my wife* can be used to refer to a unique individual, but *a good cook* cannot.

The second characteristic is that the NPs in identification sentences are reversible round the verb. Thus, for example, in answer to the question:

**134** Which one is John?

we might find:

**135** John is the CHAIRman
The CHAIRman is John

The capitals indicate that CHAIR*man* is the word that appropriately in this context receives the sentence stress – it is the centre of the intonation contour. Note that whichever word order is used, the stress centres on CHAIR*man* – the NP that answers the identifying question. This particular characteristic of such sentences complicates our description, since the question can be phrased the other way:

**136** Which one is the chairman?

**137** JOHN is the chairman
The chairman is JOHN

where the intonation placement is exactly reversed. We clearly need to know what is intended by a particular sentence before we can properly assign a propositional structure to it: thus we say that with respect to the sequence **134**, **135** *chairman* is the NP that is identified with the function we describe as [role]; whereas in **137**, it is clearly *John* that has this function. The other NP we describe as realizing a [neutral] function.

What now of the sentences in **129**? Here *the committee* can be assigned the role [agent] and John the role [neutral, patient]. *Chairman* we describe as [role] as before. These characterizations are summarized as:

| | | | | |
|---|---|---|---|---|
| **138** | *neutral* | *state*<br>*identity* | *role* | (=**128**) |
| **139** | *agent* | *action*<br>*causative*<br>*directed*<br>*identification* | *neutral*<br>*patient* | *role* | (=**129**) |

Sentences like **129** are particularly good candidates for a description in terms of an embedded predication, and this is reflected in the paraphrases involving *as, to be.*

If there is a relationship between propositional frames like **138** and **139**, there is a comparable relation between pairs of sentences like:

> **140**    John is a fool
>
> **141a**   I consider John a fool
> **141b**   I consider John to be a fool
> **141c**   I consider John as a fool

Our propositional description here is of the form:

> **142**   *neutral*   *state*          *attribute*
>                       *description*
>
> **143**   *agent*     *action*         *neutral*    *attribute*
>                       *description*

The proposition structure **142** is not characterized as [causative] since there is clearly no causative relation between sentences like **135** and **141**: just because 'I consider John to be a fool', it does not mean that 'he is one'! This structure, like that in **139**, also lends itself to an analysis in terms of an embedded predication.

We may also observe that the [role] and [attribute] participants in **139** and **143** may be characterized in terms of the 'state' and 'result' distinction we observed in footnote 4 on page 298. The [causative] sentences have a 'result' implication, and the non-causative sentences a 'state' interpretation. Some other verbs that can enter these frames are shown in Figure 105.

| A Ac N/P Ro | A Ac N Att |
|:---:|:---:|
| ELECT | CONSIDER |
| NOMINATE | THINK |
| CHOOSE | ESTEEM |
| APPOINT | |

*Figure 105*    MAKE

We have obviously described only a part of the propositional structure of English – some exercises at the end of the chapter invite the reader to explore some of the many other areas that lend themselves to a description of this sort – but the part we have described includes some of the most important and fundamental relationships among propositions that are to be found in English. Relationships of this sort seem to be found in many languages. They are summarized in outline in Figure 106.

| state | | action | |
|---|---|---|---|
| | | inchoative | causative |
| descriptive | N V Att (=10) | N/P V     (=40) | A V N/P     (=9) |
| | N V Att (=10) | — | A V N Att   (=143) |
| possessive | D V N   (=77) | D V N     (=125) | A V N/P G   (=78) |
| locative | N V LP (=91) | N/P V LG (=114) | A V N/P LG (=92) |
| identifying | N V Ro  (=138) | — | A V N/P Ro (=139) |

The bracketed figures refer to the specifications of propositional structures in the text

*Examples*

| | | | | | |
|---|---|---|---|---|---|
| St | N | V | Att | | The fruit is ripe |
| Inch | N/P | V | | | The fruit is ripening |
| Caus | A | V | N/P | | The sun is ripening the fruit |
| St | N | V | Att | | John is a fool |
| Caus | A | V | N | Att | I consider John a fool |
| St | D | V | N | | John has a car |
| Inch | D | V | N | | John has acquired a car |
| Caus | A | V | N/P | LG | Mary gave a car to John |
| St | N | V | LP | | The pencil is on the floor |
| Inch | N/P | V | LG | | The pencil is falling onto the floor |
| Caus | A | V | N/P | LG | John put the pencil on the floor |
| St | N | V | Ro | | John is the chairman |
| Caus | A | V | N/P | Ro | They elected John chairman |

*Figure 106*

The sentence types defined in this figure form a matrix where sentences which can be categorized as [descriptive], [possessive], [locative] or [identifying] are cross-categorized in terms of the characterizations [state], [inchoative] and [causative]. Certain broad generalizations can be made. The [state] column involves [state] verbs, the other two columns [action] verbs with the syntactic consequences described earlier in the chapter. The [state] and [inchoative] columns involve one or two participants, neither of which is [agent]; the [causative] column always introduces a third participant, which is always [agent]; this too has syntactic consequences. We can also make some generalizations about the order of constituents in active declarative sentences. The verb is always second constituent. There is a hierarchy among the roles in terms of their ability to occur as subject, object, etc. The hierarchy is: A:D:N: etc. (where etc. represents the other roles). Thus, if there is an A it is subject; if there is no A, then D is subject; otherwise N . . . etc. Similarly in sentences with an A subject, N takes precedence over other roles as object. Stated like this, the hierarchy is too crude (and subject to a number of exceptions), but the notion of a hierarchy seems evident, and is also reflected in other languages that can be analysed in similar terms.

The symmetry of the figure is also somewhat deceptive, and only seems to apply systematically in the cases noted, and in a few others. Many propositions do not lend themselves to a comparably neat classification, for example the verbs of motion discussed in **117**. These do not seem to correlate, in any very straightforward way, with either a [state] or a non-embedded [causative] proposition. In some cases we can postulate correlations like:

**144a**   He is coming (active)
**144b**   He is here     (stative)

**145a**   He is going   (active)
**145b**   He is gone    (stative)[14]

But this does not seem to be true also of sentences like:

**146**   He is running

which have no [state] counterparts. Similarly, with causatives we can certainly construct [causative] sentences like:

14 Many English speakers make no distinction between *He has gone* (resultant state) and *He is gone* (state): see footnote on page 298. This is perhaps because in speech they would be homophonous *He's gone*. The speech form *He's come* is usually rendered in writing as *He has come*, although *He is come* is sometimes also found. How far this can be carried is unclear – which of the following are acceptable? *He is arrived*, *He is departed*, *He is disappeared*, *He is appeared*.

**147**  John made me run

but this overtly involves an embedded predication, and such a causative can be formed on any sentence with an [agent]:

**148**  John made me put a lamp on the table
**149**  Sir Harold made the committee elect his friend Charles as chairman

In terms of a single predication, verbs of motion do not appear to correlate with either [state] or [causative] propositions, without embedding. Further examples can easily be found.

Figure 106 has one further important feature. An approach of this sort leads to a classification of verbs in terms of the propositional structures they may enter. This suggests that we can use such a classification in lexical entries. Thus, for example, we can enter in the lexicon information like:

**150**  STAND:     St., N LP
                    Ac, A N/P LG
        PUT:        Ac, A N/P LG
        TAKE:       Ac, A N/P LG
                    Ac, A N/P LS
        REMOVE:     Ac, A N/P LS

(the characterizations are taken from Figure 102). In these entries we have placed first the characterizations [state], [action], and followed them by a specification of the participant roles involved (we noted previously – page 292 – that the statement of elements in propositional structures was abstract, and, in principle, unordered). Characterizations like those in **150** bear an intimate relationship to strict sub-categorization frames discussed on pages 55–7. The difference is that the strict sub-categorization frames were there stated in purely categorical terms, i.e. in terms of categories like Adj, NP, PP, etc., whereas these categorizations are stated in functional terms, [agent] [goal], etc. We can combine the two types of statement, perhaps like:

**151**  STAND:  V, St;__PP; N LP
                 V, Ac;__NP PP; A N/P LG

where the first characterization shows categorial information (STAND is a stative verb), the second strict subcategorization information (STAND occurs in the environment __PP), and the third indicates the functional role of the non-verbal constituents (the subject of STAND is [neutral] and the PP indicates a [locative place]).

Either of these ways of characterizing verbs enable us to relate propositional information to constituent structure, and to make use of it to control such things as the applicability of transformations.

We briefly mention two ways in which this could be done. One is associated with a school of grammar that has come to be known as 'Case grammar'. This school of grammar suggests that the 'most basic' representation of a sentence should be not in 'categorial' terms (i.e. using categories like NP, VP, V etc.), as in earlier chapters of this book, but 'functional' terms. Thus:

> In the basic structure of sentences . . . we find what might be called the 'proposition', a tenseless set of relationships involving verbs and nouns . . . separated from what might be called the 'modality' constituent. This latter will include such modalities on the sentence-as-a-whole as negation, mood, and aspect. . . . The first base rule, then, is . . .

> **152**   Sentence → Modality + Proposition

(Fillmore 1968, 24)

The proposition constituent is further expanded as a verb together with a number of nodes specified in terms of such labels as [agent], [instrument], etc.[15]

Each functionally labelled node is then developed as Preposition + NP — we have already seen the typical association between prepositions and roles and this formalizes it. Such rules would develop structures like those in Figures 107–9. The grammar would then contain rules of the following sort:

> Every English sentence has a surface subject, if only formally so. . . . In general the 'unmarked' subject choice seems to follow the following rule: If there is an [agent] it becomes subject; otherwise, if there is an [instrument], it becomes subject; otherwise the subject is [patient]. . . . The normal choice of subject for sentences containing an [agent] . . . is the [agent]. (Fillmore 1968, 33)

15 For Fillmore the specification of the participant roles, which he refers to as 'cases', is somewhat different from that we have adopted, although the basic idea is very much the same. In order not to confuse the reader we have adapted Fillmore's scheme to our terminology, and silently amended the quotations.

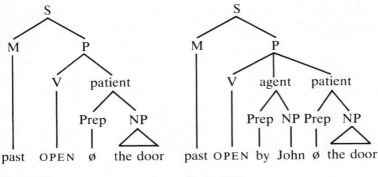

*Figure 107*     *Figure 108*

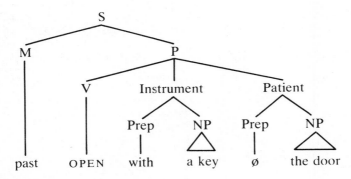

*Figure 109*

This rule is clearly in line with our previous remarks about a hierarchy of roles (page 320). This approach can deal with such things as the active:passive relationship, by deriving passive sentences directly from a propositional structure rather than by a transformational rule. The following is proposed: A verb like OPEN permits [patient] to occur as subject

as long as this 'non-normal' choice is 'registered' in the V. This 'registering' of a 'non-normal' subject takes place via the association of the feature [+passive] with the V. (Fillmore 1968, 37)

The effect of these informally stated rules is shown in Figures 110–12. Note that a further rule is required deleting prepositions from roles that occur in subject position (cf. Figure 111).

There are many problems about formulating a grammar in this

way, but we do not explore them further here (but see the discussion in Brown and Miller, in press). The only point at issue is that there are those who would wish to exploit functional information in the grammar of a language.

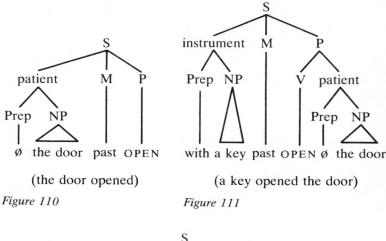

(the door opened)                (a key opened the door)

*Figure 110*                    *Figure 111*

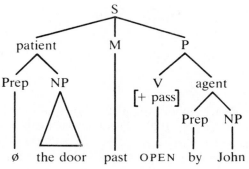

*Figure 112*          (the door was opened by John)

Another way in which functional information can be exploited is as follows. We still use a constituent structure grammar formulated as in earlier chapters, and use an appropriately modified lexical insertion rule to mark the various categorial nodes for the relevant information. Thus the grammar generates trees such as those shown in outline in Figures 113 and 114. The first lexical entry for STAND, shown in **151** lexicalizes the tree in Figure 113, and

the second entry for STAND lexicalizes Figure 114. We have
shown this in the tree, and have annotated the nodes with the
relevant functional information.

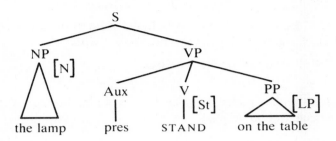

*Figure 113*

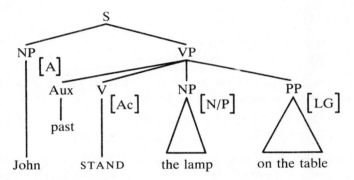

*Figure 114*

Application of the relevant realization rules produces:

**153a**  The lamp is standing on the table
**153b**  John stood the lamp on the table

The functional information can now be used to control transformations. Suppose we annotate the passive transformation along
the following lines:

**154**  SA: $NP_1 - Aux - V - NP_2$
SC: $NP_2 - Aux + PASS - V - by + NP_1$
Restriction: $NP_2$ must be [neutral, patient] *or* [neutral,
result] V must be [action]

The S A is met by the configuration in Figure 114, and it does not offend any of the restrictions, so we may derive the passive sentence:

**155**　The lamp was stood on the table by John.

Figure 113 does not meet the S A. In the same spirit we can derive and block the following active and passive pairs:

**156a**　The sun ripened the fruit
**156b**　The fruit was ripened by the sun

*The fruit* realizes [neutral, patient], RIPEN is an [action] verb, so the passive can be derived.

**157a**　John built this house
**157b**　This house was built by John

*This house* realizes [neutral result]; BUILD is an [action] verb, so the passive can be derived.

**158a**　John has a book
**158b**　*A book is had by John

A book is not [neutral patient] or [neutral result]; HAVE is [state] so the passive cannot be formed.

**159a**　John is playing tiddlywinks
**159b**　*Tiddlywinks is being played by John

*Tiddlywinks* is a [range] participant, so although PLAY is [action] the passive cannot be formed. The reader is invited to try other derivations.

We mention one final transformation not discussed previously – the imperative, which is responsible for deriving sentences like:

**160a**　Put the book on the table!
**160b**　Build a house!
**160c**　Play tiddlywinks!

Imperative sentences can only be formed from propositional structures that contain an [action] verb and an [agent] participant. These two facts have to be stated in restrictions on the formation of the imperative to account for the acceptability of sentences like those in **160** and the unacceptability of sentences like:

**161a**　*Have a book　　　(where HAVE is [state])

| 161b | *Know Chinese | (where KNOW is [state]) |
|------|---------------|-------------------------|
| 161c | *Ripen (oh, fruit) | (where RIPEN is [action], but *fruit*, does not realize an [agent] participant) |
| 161d | *Cost six pounds (oh, book) | (where *book* does not realize an [agent] participant) |

Such restrictions are difficult to formulate in straightforward categorial terms; we also need access to functional information, however this is captured in the grammar.

To close, we briefly consider two questions. How redundant are the specifications? How many propositional roles, etc. are we to recognize? As to the first question, it is clear that there is a certain amount of redundancy: for example, all [causative] structures involve an [agent]. The redundancy can be removed, but we prefer to keep it, partly for the sake of clarity, and partly because role features cannot always be predicted on the basis of process types, or *vice versa*; and until a full classification is developed in these terms it is unclear exactly what redundancy can be removed. The second question is more difficult. It seems the case that we can choose either to reduce the number of roles, thus achieving an apparently 'simpler' system, or to multiply the number of roles, thus achieving a descriptively more accurate system. For example, we can collapse together the 'locative' roles ([Lplace], [Lgoal] and [Lsource]) and the 'dative' roles [dative], [goal] and [source]. A justification for this is their very close relation, both semantically and grammatically. Typically we chose a 'dative' characterization when an animate is involved, otherwise a 'locative' characterization. Furthermore, it seems that we do not wish any nuclear proposition to contain both a 'dative' and a 'locative' participant (a dative proposition may, of course, be associated with a locative circumstantial role – *John gave Mary the money in the park* – but that is a different matter). On the other hand there are grammatical differences between the two types of proposition, and they define different classes of verb (e.g. 'locative' and 'verbs of motion', and 'dative' and 'verbs of giving and receiving'). A case where we might choose to multiply roles is [agent], which as we have observed involves a number of notions that might be stranded out – 'initiator', 'actor', 'cause', etc. As so often in linguistic descriptions, some balance must be sought between maximum generality (the 'reductionist' approach, which leads to numerous instances requiring some special treatment – as with our [agent] role) and maximum explicitness (which leads to a proliferation of roles and might eventually lead to identifying a unique structure for every use of every verb, since presumably all verbs differ, however slightly, in their grammatical and semantic behaviour). We justify our description by its offering a degree of both generality and particularity. This conclusion is uncomfortable, since it has no easily defended validity, but, there seems to be no alternative in the current state of knowledge. We can only take refuge in the fact that it is a position shared by anyone who attempts a description along these lines, and it seems to reflect the somewhat indeterminate nature of this aspect of language.

**Technical terms**

analytic; circumstantial roles; incorporation; proposition; propositional nucleus; propositional structure.

**Process terms**

descriptive, possessive, locative, identification, state, action, inchoative, directed, causative

**Participant role terms**

agent
neutral, patient, result, attribute, role
dative goal, source
locative place, locative goal, locative source, locative path
range, instrument, benefactive

**Exercise**

Consider the following 'roles' A(gent); I(nstrument); L(ocation); Dir(ection); S(ource); G(oal); D(ative); N(eutral) illustrated in the following sentences:

1   John (A) beat the dog (N) with a stick (I)
2   Mary (D) knows Chinese (N)
3   Charlie (A/S) gave the book (N) to Mary (G)
4   Mary (A/G) took the book (N) from Charlie (S)
5   The cow (A) jumped over the moon (Dir)

We can represent 'role structures' for particular verbs in the following way:

| beat: | A Vb N (I) | (the man beat the dog with a stick) |
| open: | N Vb | (the door opened) |
| | A Vb N | (the man opened the door) |
| give: | A/S Vb N to-G | (John gave the book to Mary) |
| | A/S Vb G N | (John gave Mary the book) |
| rob: | A/G Vb S of-N | (John robbed Mary of £10) |
| steal: | A/G Vb N from-S | (John stole £10 from Mary) |

The formulae are intended to indicate the particular role structure available to a given verb when the verb is *active* (i.e. it does not take account of *passive* structures). So, for example, BEAT, in active sentences, requires both an A(gent) and a N(eutral) noun (*The man beat the dog*) but cannot occur with only an A (*The man beat*) or only an N (*\*The dog beat*): it may optionally occur with an I(nstrument). With some verbs, like GIVE, there are two alternative active sentences, as shown in the examples; with other verbs, like ROB, there is only one possible order of constituents – there is no sentence *John robbed £10 of Mary* or the like.

Note that in the examples given, a passive can be formed with the NP immediately following the verb as subject: *Mary was robbed of £10 by John.*

In the groups of verbs given below:

(i) Write a statement, or statements, of possible role structures for each verb, as in the examples above. Note the prepositions that occur.

(ii) Start by considering only active sentences – can passive sentences always be formed from NPs that can become 'object' of the verb (and immediately follow it without a preposition)?

1   ROB, STEAL, PLUNDER, LOOT, RANSACK
2   SEND, TAKE, BRING, FETCH, CARRY
3   SUPPLY, ISSUE, FURNISH, DELIVER
4   GIVE, PRESENT, TAKE, OFFER, ACCEPT, RECEIVE
5   KNOW, TEACH, LEARN, INSTRUCT
6   TELL, ANNOUNCE, INFORM, MENTION, REPORT, NOTIFY
7   SMEAR, PAINT, FESTOON, SPREAD, ENGRAVE, MARK, SPATTER, SPRAY

# 19 Subjects, objects, complements and adjuncts

The traditional apparatus of grammatical description includes the set of terms: subject, object, oblique object, indirect object, complement and adjunct. Their definitions are typically an amalgam of features deriving from their grammatical characteristics, from syntactico-semantic characterizations as discussed in the preceding chapter, and from characteristics of their behaviour in texts. Criteria of the first two sorts, grammatical and syntactico-semantic, are chiefly involved in this chapter. We cannot entirely avoid textual criteria, but largely leave these until the next chapter. We shall be concerned to establish whether any or all of these notions has a special role in a grammatical description. The discussion concerns itself with English, since the grammatical characteristics of these notions vary from language to language: the general principles involved, however, do seem to be widely applicable.

## Subject

A distinction is frequently drawn between the 'grammatical' subject (characterized by grammatical considerations, such as being the controller of number agreement), the 'logical' subject (characterized by syntactico-semantic considerations – in sentences with an [agent] NP this is usually held to be the logical subject) and the 'thematic' or 'psychological' subject (characterized by textual considerations – 'this is what the sentence is about'). These can be illustrated in the sentences **1a**, **b**, **c** where G,L and T indicate respectively the grammatical, logical and thematic subjects:

**1a** John (G,L,T) took the largest kitten
**1b** The largest kitten (G,T) was taken by John (L)
**1c** The largest kitten (T), we (G,L) gave away

As can be seen the three characterizations do not necessarily coincide. We defer consideration of the thematic subject until the next chapter, and concentrate here on the notions of grammatical and logical subject.

We first consider the grammatical subject. All full declarative sentences must have a subject. This is an NP. With few exceptions the grammatical subject immediately precedes the main verb and is in number concord with it. Grammatical subjects are never marked with a preposition. NPs that fulfill these characteristics we call grammatical subjects. As we have seen before, for some actual sentence the structural configuration 'NP that is immediately dominated by S' typically identifies the grammatical subject.

The subject is frequently a 'full' lexical NP, like *John* or *the largest kitten* in **1a**, **1b**, or a pronoun, like *we* in **1c**, but it may also be a nominalized sentence or sentence-like constituent as in:

**2a**   *That Edinburgh's New Town is magnificent* is undeniable

**2b**   *For you to run off with Mary* would be madness

Sometimes when no such constituent is available to act as subject a 'dummy' subject is supplied: this is the case with 'weather' expressions:[1]

**3**   *It* is raining

and in cases like **4b** where a nominalized sentence is 'extraposed' (see pages 372–3):

**4a**   *That Edinburgh's New Town is magnificent* is undeniable

**4b**   *It* is undeniable that Edinburgh's New Town is magnificent

The main verb concords in the singular with the dummy subject *it*. *It* does not, however, have the full range of syntactic possibilities of a full subject – questioning is impossible; no sense is made by asking:

1 In terms of the terminology introduced in the preceding chapter, we might refer to the proposition which **3** realizes as a 'no place' proposition. In traditional grammars they are often realized by what are referred to as 'impersonal verbs'. It may be observed that not all languages permit no place propositions: in Akan the sense of **3** would be realized as *nsuo tɔ* 'water falls', 'it is raining'.

**5a**　\*What is raining?
**5b**　\*What is undeniable that Edinburgh's New Town is magnificent?

Another item that operates like a dummy subject is *there* in sentences like:

**6a**　There is a glass on the mantelpiece
**6b**　There are glasses in the drinks cupboard

Sentences like these are called 'existential' because they are typically used to assert the existence of something. We call this use of *there* the 'existential' *there*, distinct from another use of *there* in sentences like:

**7**　There is the glass

which we call the 'deictic' *there* because sentences like **7** can be used to point to something. Existential *there* has several curious features. It does not control number agreement on the verb, as can be seen in **6a** and **6b**. Unlike the deictic *there*, it cannot be stressed:

**8a**　*There* is the glass (deictic)
**8b**　\**There* are glasses in the drinks cupboard (existential)

Connected with this is the fact that it is almost invariably pronounced in a 'reduced' form: / ðəz / 'there is', / ðəra / 'there are': the deictic *there* is usually non-reduced: / ðɛərɪz / 'there is' / ðɛəra / 'there are'. Thus / ðəz ə glas / 'There is a glass', with the reduced form, is understood as existential and not deictic. Finally we note that existential *there* is always in subject position:

**9a**　There are glasses in the drinks cupboard
**9b**　\*Glasses in the drinks cupboard are there

(*It* may, of course, occur as subject of an embedded sentence: *It appears that there are a number of problems*.) By contrast, deictic *there* need not necessarily be subject:

**10a**　*There* is the glass
**10b**　The glass is *there*

Existential *there*, unlike deictic *there* cannot be questioned:

**11a**　Where is the glass? (deictic)

**11b**   *Where are the glasses in the drinks cupboard?
(*existential)

Finally, existential *there* is typically restricted to sentences with an indefinite NP:

**12a**   The glass is on the table
**12b**   ? A glass is on the table
**12c**   ?There's the glass on the table
**12d**   There is a glass on the table

(**12c** is to be understood as the reduced, existential *there*: it is acceptable as the stressed deictic *there*.[2])

Some arguments that tend to the view that subject has a special status in the grammar of English can be derived from a transformational approach to description. In this approach we distinguish an underlying from a surface level of description (see pages 123–5). Suppose that the sentence:

---

2  The total distribution of existential *there* is 'fuzzy'. It occurs with the locative copula BE, and also with verbs like:

> There appears to be some difficulty about the tickets
> There seem to be some people who still believe the earth is flat
> There should be an answer to that question
> There happens to be a party this evening
> There still exist some problems in the analysis of THERE

In all these examples the NP immediately following the verb is indefinite. If we replace this by a definite NP, then the sentences are often of dubious acceptability:

> ? There appears to be the difficulty about the tickets

Nor is it exactly clear how far this construction can be extended. The following seem only marginally acceptable with the existential *there*:

> ? There hung a picture on the wall
> ? There lay a man in the gutter

Another item that operates rather like existential *there* in some constructions is *here*:

> Here comes the procession
> Here's a pretty kettle of fish

Like existential *there*, this item is usually unstressed and reduced phonologically. It needs to be distinguished from a 'locative' here:

> Here lies John Smith
> The procession comes past here at ten o'clock

**13**   Everyone believes that Charlie is handsome

is derived from an underlying structure which we represent as:

**14**   Everyone believes (Charlie is handsome)

Suppose too that the sentence:

**15**   Everyone believes Charlie to be handsome

is an alternative realization of this underlying structure. We now observe that whereas in **13** *Charlie* is clearly the subject of the verb *is* in the embedded sentence, in **15** *Charlie* appears to operate syntactically like the object of the verb *believe* in the matrix sentence. Three pieces of evidence seem to support this observation. First, if we replace *Charlie* by a pronoun, then we must have *he*, the subject form, in **13**, but must have *him*, the object form in **15**:

**16a**   Everyone believes that he (*him) is handsome
**16b**   Everyone believes him (*he) to be handsome

Secondly, consider the following sentences with reflexive pronouns:

**17a**   $Charlie_1$ believes that $he_1$ (*himself) is handsome
**17b**   $Charlie_1$ believes $himself_1$ to be handsome
**17c**   $Charlie_1$ believes $him_2$ to be handsome

We have followed here the convention of marking subscripts on co-referential items (pages 274–7). The distribution of the reflexive and non-reflexive pronouns here strongly suggests that *himself* is the object of *believe*. Thirdly, we note that the passive sentence:

**18**   Charlie is believed by everyone to be handsome

is well formed. The passive is largely restricted to objects – and this suggests that *Charlie* can be considered to have been at some stage the object of *believe*. There is, of course, no passive corresponding to **13**:

**19**   *Charlie is believed by everyone that is handsome

If we accept that such sentences are related to the structure shown in **14**, then it seems that this structure has been 're-analysed' along the lines shown in **20**:

**20a**   Everyone believes (Charlie is handsome)
**20b**   Everyone believes Charlie (to be handsome)

Transformational grammarians postulate a rule of 'subject raising' to account for this.[3] The rule only applies to subjects, as its name implies. Consider the following sentences:

**21a**   Everyone believes (Charlie has killed Mary)
**21b**   Everyone believes Charlie (to have killed Mary)
**21c**   Charlie is believed by everyone (to have killed Mary)

**22a**   Everyone believes (Charlie has killed Mary)
**22b**   Everyone believes (Mary has been killed by Charlie) (Passive in embedded S)
**22c**   Everyone believes Mary (to have been killed by Charlie)
**22d**   Mary is believed by everyone (to have been killed by Charlie)

Note that *Mary*, the object of KILL in **22a** cannot be raised:

**23**   *Everyone believes Mary (Charlie to have killed)

but once it has become the subject of the embedded sentence by passivization, then it can be raised – yielding **22c**, and subsequently **22d**.

Returning briefly to *there*, we note that this item also operates like a subject for these purposes:

**24a**   Everyone believes (there is a solution to this problem)
**24b**   Everyone believes there (to be a solution to this problem)
**24c**   There is believed (to be a solution to this problem)

The argument suggests that the grammatical subject has an important role. Another argument offered by a transformational approach can be illustrated by the following sentence:

**25**   John$_1$ expected that the committee would choose him$_1$/ him$_2$

The subscripts indicate two possible readings, one in which *him*

3 As we have remarked before, this volume does not attempt to present a full account of the formal machinery involved in a transformational grammar. For a full discussion of this transformation the reader is referred to one of the books listed on pages 386–7.

cross-refers to *John*, and another where *him* refers deictically to some other individual in the context (see pages 276–7). Let us suppose that **25** is related to the underlying structure:

**26**   John expected (the committee would choose him)

after the fashion already established in discussing **13–15**. In the same spirit as before we consider the sentence:

**27**   John$_1$ expected the committee to choose him$_1$/him$_2$

is another way of describing the same situation. As before, *him* can have two interpretations. Let us now passivize the embedded sentence:

**28**   John expected (he would be chosen by the committee)

which is realized as:

**29**   John$_1$ expected that he$_1$/he$_2$ would be chosen by the committee

then *he* has two readings as in **25**. However, if we passivize the embedded sentence in the structure corresponding to **27** we get:

**30**   John$_1$ expected him$_2$ (*him$_1$) to be chosen by the committee

*him* can only have one reading, with deictic reference. It cannot cross-refer to the subject of *expected*. But the sentence:

**31**   John expected to be chosen by the committee

has the other reading: i.e. *John* is understood not only as the subject of *expected* but also as the subject of *be chosen*. There is, however, no overt subject present. For the purposes of discussion we represent this situation like this:

**32**   John$_1$ expected $\theta_1$ to be chosen by the committee

Once again we see that the subject, in this case an 'understood' subject, has a special role.[4] This relationship is quite general:

---

4 The phenomena briefly outlined here are treated by transformational grammarians as the result of another transformational operation known as 'Equi NP Deletion' or 'Co-referential subject deletion'. Once again the reader is referred to Further reading, pages 386–7. This transformation is believed by many to be somewhat dubious, but the phenomenon it is intended to account for lends some further support to the status of 'subject', which is our particular concern.

**33a** $I_1$ expect $\theta_1$ to go to America this summer
**33b** $Gill_1$ wants $\theta_1$ to come with me
**33c** $Gill_1$ expects $her_2$ (*$her_1$) to go with me

Our concern is not with the machinery of the putative transformational rules involved, but with the observation that the grammatical subject seems from the discussion to have a special status in English grammar.

So far all our discussion has involved declarative affirmative sentences. Let us briefly consider interrogative sentences. These can be illustrated by the **b** sentences here:

**34a** Katie is writing a French essay
**34b** Is Katie writing a French essay?

**35a** Sarah plays the trombone
**35b** Does Sarah play the trombone?

We have discussed the formation rules for interrogative sentences on page 127. In outline the rule is: invert the first auxiliary verb (*is* in **34**) and the grammatical subject; if there is no auxiliary supply an appropriate form of DO, as in **35**. Note that after the operation of this rule, the subject NP still precedes the main verb, and it still controls number agreement on the auxiliary, or DO. Subject-auxiliary inversion is also typical of certain sentences involving certain 'negative adverbs':

**36a** Never have I heard such nonsense
**36b** Seldom have I tasted a more magnificent claret

Our final observation on the grammatical subject is that there are a few constructions in which it follows rather than precedes the main verb. Thus we find:

**37** Down comes the flag, off goes the gun and away go the boats

Such sentences have a distinctly literary flavour, and we consider them to be a stylistic device, discussed further in the next chapter. Note that number concord between subject and verb is preserved even though the subject follows rather than precedes the verb.

The arguments strongly suggest that, for English at least, the grammatical relation of subject has a special role in grammatical description.

We now turn to the notion of logical subject. This, as we

observed on page 330, usually relates to the question of the participant role a subject realizes. As the preceding chapter made clear, the grammatical subject can realize any of a number of such roles. Perhaps the most typical role for the subject is agentive:

**38a**   John beat the dog
**38b**   William invaded England in 1066

Instrumental subjects can be seen in:

**39a**   The axe smashed the door
**39b**   A brush could clear those drains

The fact that such subjects are instrumental is established by the passive forms of the sentences; where the instrumental preposition *with* occurs:

**40a**   The door was smashed with an axe
**40b**   Those drains could be cleared with a brush

Dative subjects are shown in:

**41a**   Harry knows that his wife is unfaithful
**41b**   I am interested in linguistics

and this description is supported by paraphrases with *to*:

**42a**   That his wife is unfaithful is known to Harry
**42b**   Linguistics is interesting to me

where the dative preposition *to* occurs.

Goal subjects are to be observed in:

**43a**   Harry received a gold medallion from the Royal Society
**43b**   Charlie obtained a licence from the local authority

and this analysis is supported by the fact that the preposition *to* occurs in sentences like:

**44a**   The Royal Society presented a gold medallion to Harry
**44b**   The local authority issued a licence to Charlie

Source subjects are to be seen in **44**; and note the paraphrase with the preposition *from* in **43**.

Place locative subjects occur in sentences like:

**45a**   Edinburgh is cold, wet and windy
**45b**   This box contains fifty-two matches

where alternative formulations of the proposition contain a locative proposition:

**46a** It is cold, wet and windy in Edinburgh
**46b** Fifty-two matches are contained in this box

Patient subjects are found in the sentences:

**47a** The butter is melting
**47b** The ice is cooling

Finally we note neutral subjects in:

**48a** Mary is very tired
**48b** Harry is the Professor of Linguistics

All the participant roles identified in chapter 18 may occur in some sentence as the grammatical subject. The traditional notion of logical subject is usually related to sentences involving an [agent] participant. Thus in:

**49** William invaded England in 1066

*William*, the [agent] participant, is referred to as both the logical and the grammatical subject. In the corresponding passive sentence:

**50** England was invaded by William in 1066

*William* remains the logical subject, but *England* is now the grammatical subject. The notion of logical subject appears to relate to the unmarked subject choice in some particular propositional structure. By analogy *the axe* and *a brush* are the logical subjects in **39**; *Harry* and *I* in **41** and so on. We have already noted, page 322, that given the participant roles [agent], [instrument] and [neutral], the active declarative sentence chooses the [agent] participant as subject over the [instrument] and the [neutral], and the [instrument] over the [neutral]: these choices are reflected in **38** and **39**. Similarly, given [dative] and [neutral], the most unmarked order, all other things being equal, chooses [dative] as subject, and this is reflected in **41**. These facts suggest that if we introduce the notion of participant roles together with appropriate statements about unmarked subject choice we can dispense with the notion of logical subject, since this new machinery gives a more precise characterization of the notions involved.

## Object

The grammatical object, like the subject, is realized by an NP. In active declarative sentences with unmarked word order four grammatical features characterize the object: **i** it directly follows the verb; **ii** it is not in construction with a preposition; **iii** it can become the subject of the corresponding passive sentence; and **iv** it is an obligatory constituent with transitive verbs.

The most clear-cut cases of objects are those constituents traditionally referred to as the direct or affected object. These are NPs that realize what we called (page 290) [neutral, patient] participant roles in two place propositions where the verb is a verb of directed action, causative or non-causative, and the other participant, which must become subject in active sentences is described as [agent].

**51a**    Samson smote the Philistines
**51b**    The forester split the log

In such constructions no possible paraphrases involve prepositions, the relevant NPs can become the subject of the corresponding passive sentences and the direct object is an obligatory constituent. We do not find:

**52a**    *Samson smote
**52b**    *The forester split

where only an [agent] participant is realized.

Traditional grammars also recognize other types of object in two-place sentences. The names usually given to them reflect the type of propositional role that the object realizes. All of them are, to a greater or lesser extent, unable to meet the four criteria outlined above. Thus, the following sentences involve an 'object of result' (also called an 'effected' or 'factitive' object):

**53a**    Mary wove that blanket
**53b**    The workmen are digging a hole

Objects of result can typically become the subject of a passive sentence, and there are no paraphrases involving prepositions. Many verbs that occur in such sentences can also appear in one-place sentences with an agent subject but no object:

**54a**    Mary is weaving
**54b**    The workmen are digging

Sentences like:

**55a**  Mary sang a song
**55b**  I dreamed a strange dream (last night)

are sometimes described as involving 'cognate objects', since the relevant N P usually contains a noun morphologically derived from (and hence cognate with) the verb stem. We identified such participants as [range] participants but noted that, while there are no paraphrases involving prepositions, they do not always felicitously become the subjects of passive sentences.

Some grammarians have identified the object in sentences like:

**56a**  Harold is eating his lunch
**56b**  Patricia is reading *War and Peace*

as an 'object of concern': they are clearly neither affected (direct) or effected (resultant) objects. Such objects do not always appear as subjects of passive sentences with the same degree of acceptability as the other objects we have looked at, and, like objects of result, are often omissible.

The cases examined so far suggest that there is a hierarchy of 'objecthood'. The prime exemplar is the direct object. This has a particularly close tie to the main verb; it is an obligatory sentence constituent; it immediately follows the main verb; it will not occur in a paraphrase involving a preposition; and it can be the subject of the corresponding passive sentence. Other objects (of result, concern, etc.) do not meet one or more of these criteria.

We now consider sentences like:

**57a**  The Russians supplied arms to the Vietnamese
**57b**  The Russians supplied the Vietnamese with arms

In the previous chapter we described these as realizing three place propositional structures with [agent] (*the Russians*), [goal] (*the Vietnamese*) and [neutral] (*arms*) propositional roles. The [agent], as we anticipate, becomes subject of the active sentence. There is, however, a choice as to whether the [goal] or the [neutral] participant immediately follows the verb. Whichever is chosen, that participant is realized as an N P without a preposition, and the other participant is realized as a prepositional phrase. We refer to the NP that immediately follows the verb as the object. Note that it operates syntactically like an object. It cannot occur with a preposition in this position:

**58a**   *The Russians supplied with arms to the Vietnamese
**58b**   *The Russians supplied to the Vietnamese with arms

It may become the subject of the corresponding passive:

**59a**   Arms were supplied to the Vietnamese by the
          Russians
**59b**   The Vietnamese were supplied with arms by the
          Russians

And furthermore it is no longer omissible:

**60**   *The Russians supplied with arms

whereas the P P is omissible:

**61a**   The Russians supplied arms
**61b**   The Russians supplied the Vietnamese

We call the NP in the prepositional phrase an 'oblique object', recognizing that the NP in the prepositional phrase might, as it were, have become the object, had the other NP not done so. The oblique object is omissible, as we have observed, and cannot generally become the subject of a passive sentence:

**62**   *The Vietnamese were supplied arms to by the
         Russians

We furthermore suppose that both sentences realize the same propositional structure. In chapter 18 we represented this by the formulation:

**63**   agent      action       neutral          goal
                    directed          ↖     ↗
                                      patient

The arrows from [patient] indicate that this role could be associated with either the [neutral] participant (*arms*) or the [goal] participant (*the Vietnamese*): the patient participant becoming the object, and the other participant being realized as an oblique object.

In the case of verbs like SUPPLY neither of the non-agent participants is, as it were, the 'designated' object: one of the participants may become an object, but it may be either. The effect of becoming an object is important. The syntactic effect we have already discussed; but there is also a semantic effect. The semantic implications vary from verb to verb as we saw in the discussion on pages 309–10. It varies from cases like **57** where there seems to be little semantic effect to cases with considerable semantic implications:

**64a**  An archer shot at William with an arrow
**64b**  An archer shot William with an arrow
**64c**  An archer shot an arrow at William

SHOOT may occur with two oblique objects, or with a direct and an oblique object. The semantic effect may be so great here that the reader may be disinclined to treat all three sentences as deriving from the same propositional structure.

## Indirect object

We now turn to 'indirect objects': their status is very ambivalent. The term is used when a verb is followed by two NPs, neither of which is associated with a preposition. In these structures the first NP is the indirect object, and the second the direct object:

**65**  John gave Mary (IO) a book (DO)

A sentence like **65** can be paraphrased as:

**66**  John gave a book to Mary

Here the direct object directly follows the verb; what was the indirect object is now introduced in a prepositional phrase. If the direct object immediately follows the verb, then the other NP must be introduced by a prepositional phrase[5] – there is no sentence:

**67**  *John gave a book (DO) Mary (IO)

5 There are some exceptions to this generalization. Normally the IO object is animate and the DO inanimate (reflecting that normally one gives 'things' to 'people'). This need not necessarily be the case:

John gave the school a library (a library to the school)
John gave the nunnery his daughter (his daughter to the nunnery)
John gave the nurse the child (the child to the nurse)

In such cases the paraphrase with *to* seems preferred to the structure involving IO and DO: doubtless in order that the semantic relations should be clearly marked.

Further observe that if we pronominalize the DO, then only the first of the following sentences is grammatical:

Frequently the prepositional phrase in a sentence like **66** is also referred to as an indirect object. We shall not, however, do this, reserving the term indirect object for the first of two NPs in sentences like **65**. Instead we call it, as before, an oblique object.

From a semantic point of view, the indirect object frequently realizes a [goal] participant, as in **65**. But not always. We find a [benefactive] in:

> **68a**  Mary baked me a cake
> **68b**  Mary baked a cake for (*to) me

a [comitative] in:

> **69a**  Mary played John tiddlywinks
> **69b**  Mary played tiddlywinks with (*for, *to) John

and perhaps a [source] in:

> **70a**  John asked Mary a favour
> **70b**  John asked a favour from (*to, *for) Mary

Sometimes the [goal]:[benefactive] distinction is unclear (perhaps not surprising in view of the close relations between these roles – page 327):

> **71a**  Mary sang me a song
> **71b**  Mary sang a song to/for me

We call all the participants realized in prepositional phrases

> John gave it to the school
> *John gave the school it

If, however, we pronominalize the IO then both:

> John gave it a library
> John gave a library to it

are possible. If we pronominalize both NPs then, if both are animate or both inanimate sentences like·

> *John gave it it
> *John gave her him

do not seem acceptable. If however one NP is animate and the other inanimate, then we can have:

> John gave it her
> John gave her it

and whichever order is used the animate is understood as the IO and the inanimate as the DO!

oblique objects, and, if necessary, distinguish between a 'benefactive oblique object', a 'comitative oblique object', and so on.

The peculiarity about structures of this sort seems to be that one participant is, as it were, the 'designated' direct object. It retains this function even when the N P in the oblique object 'becomes' an object too – thus giving rise to a V + N P + N P structure. Before demonstrating this, let us enquire how widely the process of what we may call 'indirect object formation' applies. We illustrate with 'benefactive oblique objects', and invite the reader to determine which of the following are possible:

> **72a** Cash me a cheque (a cheque for me)
> **72b** Buy me a beer (a beer for me)
> **72c** Catch me a butterfly (a butterfly for me)
> **72d** Do me a favour (a favour for me)
> **72e** Change me a fiver (a fiver for me)
> **72f** ?Run me an errand (an errand for me)
> **72g** ?Purchase me a beer (a beer for me)
> **72h** *Feed me the cat (the cat for me)
> **72i** *Beat me the carpet (the carpet for me)
> **72j** *Pursue me the postman (the postman for me)

(We indicate our judgements, as before, with ? for questionable, and * for impossible.) Some of these structures were acceptable in earlier stages of English, and some, for some speakers, still are acceptable. This variability seems to occur with other indirect object constructions.

We now apply our criteria for objecthood to the direct and indirect objects in these sentences. We have already seen that the indirect object may occur as an oblique object, and that this is not possible for the direct object. We now observe that the indirect object, or its corresponding oblique object, can usually be omitted without affecting the grammaticality of the sentence, but the direct object cannot be omitted:

> **73a** John gave Mary a book
> **73b** John gave a book
> **73c** *John gave Mary (except in another sense)

> **74a** John bought me a beer
> **74b** John bought a beer
> **74c** *John bought me (except in another sense)

Consider now the problems of passive formation in these sentences. When the direct object immediately follows the verb, it can become the subject of the corresponding passive:[6]

**75a**   John gave that book to Mary
**75b**   That book was given to Mary by John

Similarly, the indirect object, the NP immediately following the verb, can usually become the subject of the corresponding passive:

**76a**   John bought Mary a new car
**76b**   Mary was bought a new car by John

**77a**   Mary baked me a cake
**77b**   I was baked a cake by Mary

**78a**   John bought me a beer
**78b**   I was bought a beer by John

but not always:

**79a**   John asked Mary a favour
**79b**   ?Mary was asked a favour by John

**80a**   John caught me a butterfly
**80b**   *I was caught a butterfly by John

**81a**   Mary played John tiddlywinks
**81b**   *John was played tiddlywinks by Mary

Once again the bounds of acceptability are not entirely clear.

A further difficulty is that in indirect object constructions (V + NP + NP) the direct object can still sometimes become the subject of the passive sentence:

**82a**   My grandfather gave me this watch
**82b**   This watch was given me by my grandfather

**83a**   John bought me that bottle of Glen Grant
**83b**   That bottle of Glen Grant was bought me by John

---

6 All sorts of problems arise in this area if we try to passivize indefinite NPs. Thus:

A book was given to Mary by John

seems intuitively less acceptable than:

That book was given to Mary by John

Here we deal only with definite NPs. Indefinite NPs as subjects are discussed on pages 370–1.

The NP in the oblique object cannot, however, become subject of the passive sentence (unless, of course, it has first 'become' indirect object):

**84a** My grandfather gave this watch to me
**84b** *I was given this watch to by my grandfather

The NP that immediately follows the verb has a privileged status, both syntactically and semantically. When only one NP is available for this role (i.e. in two place propositions) there would seem to be a hierarchy of 'objecthood' (page 341). When two NPs are available for this role (i.e. in three place propositions), the situation is more complex. Sometimes one NP seems to have what we have called a 'designated' object role, and retains many of its object-like features even when displaced from the position immediately following the verb (i.e. in indirect object + direct object constructions). In other circumstances neither of the NPs is a designated object, and then either one of them must become an object (e.g. with SUPPLY – pages 341–2) or neither of them need become an object (e.g. with SHOOT – page 343). The hierarchy of objecthood can be extended to accommodate this. Direct objects are most 'object-like', in terms of the criteria established at the beginning of this section, followed by objects of result, indirect objects, objects of concern, etc., eventually arriving at oblique objects.

We should not leave this discussion of objects without mentioning briefly 'phrasal' verbs, since their syntax clearly intersects with our observation on oblique objects. Phrasal verbs are items like BLOW UP in:

**85** The commandos blew up the bridge

In such cases UP seems to be related to BLOW rather than to be a constituent with *the bridge*. We have already seen (page 140) that the syntax of these constructions supports such an analysis. Furthermore the constituent *the bridge* operates syntactically like the direct object in such constructions. It is an obligatory constituent; it can occur immediately following the verb; and it can be the subject of the corresponding passive:

**86a** *The commandos blew up
**86b** The commandos blew the bridge up
**86c** The bridge was blown up by the commandos

The interested reader is referred to Quirk *et al*. (1972) for general discussion; to Bolinger (1971) for a perceptive analysis of many different constructions of this type; and to Jespersen (1927) for his many examples.

## Complement

Traditional grammars distinguish between a number of different complement types.[7] The names given to them, like the names given to different types of object, relate to the propositional roles that they realize. In two place sentences, the primary distinction is between 'attributive', 'identity' and 'locative' complements: we discuss each in turn.

The italicized constituents in **87** are attributive complements, so called because they describe the class membership of the subject noun, or ascribe an attribute to it:

**87a**    Roses are *red*
**87b**    Roses are *flowers*

Because such complements relate back to the subject noun, they are called 'subject complements', a relationship sometimes described as 'intensive' to the subject. Further distinctions can be profitably drawn. In **87b** the noun *flowers* is a 'nominal complement'. The complements in **87** are 'state complements' since they are found in stative sentences and describe states, in contrast to the complements in inchoative sentences like:

**88a**    The leaves are turning brown
**88b**    Sir Charles became a soldier

which are known as 'result complements'. The variety of terminology in this area relates to the complex propositional status of such constituents, discussed in the last chapter. It also reflects syntactic differences between the various types of complements,

7 Sometimes all NPs that follow the verb are known as complements. In this usage, what we have called the 'direct object' is called an 'extensive complement', to distinguish it from the 'intensive complement', which relates back to the subject. We do not follow this usage.

The term complement is also applied to the sentential objects that are associated with particular verbs. Thus in the sentence *John believed that he was clever* the constituent *that he was clever* is a sentence complement. The description of *that* as a 'complementizer' (cf. page 134) derives from this usage.

and between the complements and the direct object. The complement is an obligatory constituent and always follows the verb. The nominal complement is almost always an indefinite NP, and concords in number with the noun to which it is intensive (*He became a soldier*; *They became soldiers*). The complement cannot become the subject of a passive sentence. Some copular verbs (BE, SEEM) are restricted to stative sentences, others (BECOME, TURN) to non-stative sentences.

The identity complement can be illustrated in:

**89**   Harold is the man with the arrow in his eye

and is always a definite NP. The two constituents in such a sentence can be reversed round the copular verb:

**90**   The man with an arrow in his eye is Harold

In these circumstances, which constituent is to be identified as the complement depends on textual considerations (pages 316–17). In sentences in isolation the NP following the verb is most usually identified as the identity complement:

**91**   Harold is (to be identified as) the man with the arrow in his eye

The prepositional phrase in a sentence like:

**92**   Mary is *in bed*

is called the locative complement. The locative complement is usually prepositional phrase, as in **92**, or a place adverb like *upstairs, over there*, etc. The locative complement is typically, but not invariably, an obligatory constituent, and can be found with a variety of verbs in state sentences:

**93**   The newspaper is lying on the floor
Your coat is hanging in the cupboard
The Scott Monument stands on Princes Street

(See discussion on pages 307–10.) Corresponding to the locative complements in **92** and **93**, we can also recognize a 'directional complement' in sentences like:

**94**   The ball rolled under the bed
The car skidded across the road

If we distinguish between locative and directional complements, then we may also note that the latter typically occurs only in non-state sentences.

These three complement types correspond to three of the basic types of propositional structure identified in the preceding chapter (see Figure 106, page 319):

**95a**  attributive    John is a fool       (state)
                        John is clever
                        The litmus paper is turning red (result)

**95b**  identity       John is chairman

**95c**  locative       Mary is in London (place)
                        The ball rolled under the bed (direction)

It is interesting, and somewhat curious, that the fourth basic type we identified:

**96**  possessive      Mary has a little lamb
                        Mary has red hair

is not also described as involving a complement – but it isn't. (It may be observed that *Mary is a redhead* does involve a complement!). We return briefly to this point below.[8]

We now turn to sentences like:

**97a**  I consider John *a fool*
**97b**  I consider John *clever*
**97c**  Acid will turn litmus paper *red*
**97d**  The committee elected John *chairman*

---

8 In English the copula verb BE is used in all three types of complement construction. This is not the case in all languages. In Akan, for instance, we find:

attributive (Yɛ)    Kofi yɛ ɔhene bi (Kofi is chief a) *Kofi is a chief*
                    Kofi yɛ kɛsee (Kofi is big) *Kofi is big*

identity (Ne)       Kofi ne ɔhene no (Kofi is chief the) *Kofi is the chief*
                    ɔhene no ne Kofi                     *The chief is Kofi*

locative (Wɔ)       Kofi wɔ ofie no mu (Kofi is house the in) *Kofi is at home*

This can cause, and has caused, translation problems: in a Bible translation, is the copula in *God is love* to be translated with yɛ (has the attribute) or ne (is to be identified as) ?

We should also observe that in this language we also find:

possessive (Wɔ)     Kofi wɔ ofie yi      *Kofi owns this house*
                    ofie yi wɔ Kofi      *This house belongs to Kofi*

The italicized constituents are 'object complements' – so called because they are intensive to the object. The distinctions 'state', 'result', 'nominal', etc. that we drew for the subject complements in **87** and **88** can also be drawn here. In the sentences illustrated the complement is usually obligatory; constituent order is usually as shown; the nominal complement agrees in number with the N P to which it is intensive; and so on.

We have already noted (page 318) that many of the sentences in **97** correspond to paraphrases like:

**98**   I consider John to be a fool

This suggests that such sentences might be seen as derived from an embedded predication. We can illustrate this by the following sequence:

**99**   I consider (John is a fool)
I consider that John is a fool
I consider John to be a fool
I consider John a fool

**100**   They elected John (John is chairman)
They elected John to be chairman
They elected John chairman

In the case of a sentence like **97c** a more abstract representation might be more suitable:

**101**   Acid CAUSE (litmus paper turn red)

where CAUSE is a representation of the causative status of TURN. Such representations remind us of a similar analysis discussed on page 302. They also make very obvious the parallel between the two place constructions set out in **95**, and the corresponding three place sentences in **97**.

Before turning to three place sentences with locative complements, we should note that the italicized constituents in the sentences in **102** are also often called complements:

**102a**   Jane returned home *safe*
**102b**   Harriet danced the tango *naked*
**102c**   I always drink my coffee *cold*
**102d**   I always buy my meat *fresh*
**102e**   They painted the fence *yellow*

Some of these items are intensive to the subject, **102a**, **102b**, and others to the object, **102c**, **102d**; the state : result distinction can be drawn. In these sentences the complements seem to have a looser syntagmatic tie to the verb than do the complements previously discussed. They are, to begin with, both omissible and not relevant for strict subcategorization. Furthermore their status seems to be more 'adverbial' than that of the object complements of **97**: in some cases they can be substituted by adverbs (*safely* instead of *safe* in **102a**). Other cases relate to a variety of different paraphrase constructions – *I always drink my coffee after it has become cold*; *Harriet was naked when she danced the tango*; and so on.

Consider now the following three place locative sentences:

**103a**   John put the book on the table
**103b**   John rolled the ball under the bed

The prepositional phrase constituent is still described as a locative complement, and the place : direction distinction observed in **95c** still applies. As before, the relationship between the two and three place sentences is a causative one. We can represent this with the abstract formulation:

**104a**   John CAUSE(PUT) the book (the book BE on the table)
**104b**   John CAUSE(ROLL) the ball (the ball GO under the bed)

BE and GO represent, respectively, the place and directional nature of the embedded predications concerned. These abstract representations are rather distant from the actual surface form of the sentence; it is not suggested that the representations might be underlying structures, in the sense that we used this term (page 124).

We now close this section by returning to the possessive construction mentioned earlier:

**105**   Mary has a little lamb

**106a**   The shepherd gave Mary a little lamb
**106b**   The shepherd gave a little lamb to Mary

The constituent *a little lamb* is not usually described as a 'possessive complement' or the like, either in **105** or in **106**. Indeed in **106** this constituent is called the direct object, and in **106a** *Mary* is the indirect object, as we have seen (pages 343–7). We also saw that the status of the indirect object is less clear than that of the direct object. It is now clear that the relationship between the sentence in **105** and that in **106** is not very dissimilar from the relationship between the two-place locative sentences in **95c** and their three place counterparts in **103**. We might represent this with abstract representations like:

**107**    Mary HAVE a little lamb

**108a**    The shepherd CAUSE(GIVE) Mary (Mary HAVE a little lamb)

**108b**    The shepherd CAUSE(GIVE) a little lamb (a little lamb GO to Mary)

The different orderings in the embedded sentence correspond to the two different surface orderings in **106**, and perhaps correspond to a different nuance of meaning. An analysis of this sort may also go some way towards explaining the apparent difference in meaning surrounding the choice of object with verbs like SUPPLY and SHOOT discussed on pages 341–3, but to pursue this matter further would take us too far out of our way (it is discussed further in Brown and Miller, in press).

**Adjuncts**

Subjects, objects and complements form the nucleus of a sentence. They are nuclear in at least two senses, both of which are complementary. They are the constituents which, in constituent structure terms, are either obligatory or are introduced by an expansion of the VP, and hence relevant to strict subcategorization. They are also to be identified with nuclear participants in the sense discussed in the preceding chapter: many of the names given to different types of subject and object reflect this.

All other sentence constituents we call adjuncts. Adjuncts are usually adverbials, whether they are adverb phrases, prepositional phrases, adverbs or subordinate clauses of time, place, manner, etc. that distributionally function like adverbials. They are typically optional sentence constituents, and have a degree of mobility within the sentence denied to the nuclear constituents. Adjuncts are clearly a rather 'mixed bag', in that syntactically there are numerous subclasses which have different and overlapping distribution, and they fill a variety of semantic roles, as can be seen by consulting the discussion of adverbs in any standard grammar of English – for example Quirk *et al.* (1972).

## Conclusion

In the preceding chapter we characterized sentence constituents in terms of their syntactico-semantic function within a sentence as [agent], [patient], and so on. We suggested that a propositional structure characterized in these terms is an abstract structure which could be realized by any one of a number of actually occurring sentences. A given propositional role may occur in a number of syntactic positions within the sentence without affecting the way in which the role is characterized, though there will be other syntactic phenomena that reflect the different sentence positions the role occupies. We also noted that the syntactico-semantic characterization can be used to control various grammatical features, like the ability of some roles to occur with the progressive auxiliary, its ability to occur in imperative sentences and so on.

In this chapter we have looked at the functional roles of subject, object and complement, and at the various syntactic and semantic properties that can be associated with these functions. Of particular interest has been the various circumstances that permit an NP to take on the function of subject, object, etc. From a transformational point of view, deriving the various different sentence orders from a single underlying structure, the discussion may be seen to consider the ways in which sentences can be provided with subjects and objects.[9] Suppose, for example, we establish a hierarchy of functional roles in outline like this:

**109**   subject – object – indirect object – oblique object

and suppose the underlying order of constituents in the sets of sentences in **110** and **111** is as shown in the first of each set of sentences, then the italicized constituent as it were 'climbs up' the hierarchy:

9 The transformational account can of itself only deal satisfactorily with the actual formal operations of providing subjects and objects, etc. It does not handle the semantic consequences of these operations very satisfactorily, unless additional interpretive machinery is provided somewhere in the total description to take account of the semantic consequences of the operations. As we have seen, these vary from verb to verb and may sometimes be considerable.

**110** John gave the book to *Mary* (oblique object)
John gave *Mary* the book (indirect object)
*Mary* was given the book by John (subject)

**111** The Russians supplied arms to *the Vietnamese* (oblique object)
The Russians supplied *the Vietnamese* with arms (object)
*The Vietnamese* were supplied with arms by the Russians (subject)

If we also consider subject raising to be within the grammar, then a constituent can, as it were, climb to the front of its own sentence, hop up into a superordinate sentence, and then climb up that:

**112** $S_1$('People' allege $S_2$(John gave the book to *Mary*))

By the process illustrated in **110** we get:

**113** $S_1$('People' allege $S_2$(*Mary* was given the book by John))

Raising produces:

**114** $S_1$('People' allege *Mary*$_{S_2}$ (to have been given the book by John))

Passivization of S1, and the deletion of the indefinite 'people', then yields:

**115** *Mary* is alleged to have been given the book by John.

In this account, while the functional relation of the NP *Mary* changes from derivation to derivation, its propositional role does not – it is still understood as having a [goal] relation to GIVE. The conditions under which *Mary* climbed up its own sentence, hopped into the superordinate sentence and then climbed up that have little to do with its propositional role, but are instead related to its functional role as successively oblique object, indirect object, subject, and so on.[10]

10 We observed at the end of the preceding chapter that there is a school of 'case grammarians' who take propositional roles to be basic. We may now observe that there is a developing school of 'relational grammar' that takes functions such as subject, object, etc., to be basic in much the same way. There is, so far, comparatively little publicly available explaining the advantages of this approach, but see some of the articles in Cole and Sadock (1977).

There is very obviously a large degree of overlap between the two types of characterization – of propositional and of functional role. Are both types of characterizations necessary? Or could one type or the other not be 'enriched' so as to accommodate both sorts of description? We have attempted this to some degree: we used an 'arrow' notation in the preceding chapter (see, for example page 307), and have remarked that the different names given to different types of object and complement reflect their propositional status. On the other hand the two different characterizations do seem to control rather different sorts of syntactic phenomena, and in our present state of knowledge it seems best to retain both.

**Technical terms**

subject – grammatical, logical, thematic
object – affected, cognate, of concern, direct, effected, factitive, indirect, oblique, of result
complement – attributive, identity, locative, nominal
adjunct
existential sentence
raising

# 20 Theme, rheme and end focus; topic and comment; given and new

Notions like subject in the previous chapter were discussed by examining sentences in isolation. We now consider another use of the term subject: what can loosely be called the 'thematic subject', the 'psychological subject' or the 'subject of discourse'. To avoid confusion, we do not use the term subject in this connection (reserving it for the grammatical subject discussed in the preceding chapter), but instead introduce the terms theme, rheme and end focus, topic and comment, and given and new. We are concerned with those features of word order within sentences that are related to the communicative function of sentences within texts. The relevant notions clearly lead off into a study of the structure of text and it is not our intention to pursue this matter in detail.

'Theme', 'rheme' and 'end focus' refer to structural positions within the sentence. The two focal points in English sentences are the beginning and the end; the language has a number of processes that position a constituent either initially or finally. The constituent that occurs in initial position is the theme, and processes used to make some constituent initial are processes of thematization. The theme is italicized in the following:

1 *Someone* parked a large furniture van right outside our front door last night

2 *A large furniture van* was parked right outside our front door last night

3 *Right outside our front door* someone parked a large furniture van last night

4 *Last night* someone parked a large furniture van right outside our front door

The propositional structure of each of these sentences is identical: they differ in terms of which constituent is thematized. Constituents other than the theme are the rheme. Obviously some constituent must be sentence initial, and the word order shown in **1** is usually thought of as being the 'most neutral' or 'unmarked' word order in a set of sentences like **1–4**: it is an active declarative sentence with place and time adverbs in end position. Such sentences we call thematically unmarked. The other sentences are thematically marked in one way or another, and some involve what one intuitively thinks of as a greater degree of markedness than others – **3** for instance. We can also say that there is an unmarked order of constituents in the rheme. What the unmarked order is depends on which constituent is thematized; and we must use a somewhat intuitive notion of what we consider the unmarked or 'most neutral' order of rhematic constituents. It will probably be agreed that the rhemes in **1–4** show an unmarked constituent order, given that some constituent has been thematized. Now, just as some constituent must be thematized, so some constituent must occur in final position. We call the final position the 'end-focus'.[1] If all the rhemes in **1–4** are in an unmarked word order, then all the end-focuses are also unmarked. However, just as there are thematizing processes which produce marked themes, so too there are end-focusing processes that produce marked end-focus. Consider:

5    Someone parked a large furniture van last night *right outside our front door*

6    It was parked right outside our front door last night, *a large furniture van*

7    Parked right outside our front door last night it was, *a large furniture van*

8    A large furniture van, right outside our front door last night, *parked*!

1 The term end-focus is taken from Quirk *et al.* (1972). Their use of the term is derived from the fact that, in spoken language, the unmarked position for the intonation centre in an English sentence is the last lexical item in that sentence. Thus:

   The theme is the first consтɪтuent

If the intonation contour falls on any other constituent, as:

   The theme is the FIRST constituent
   The THEME is the first constituent

then the sentence is taken to be in some sense marked – the effect is often emphatic or contrastive. We do not discuss spoken language, except incidentally, and use the term end-focus simply for the last relevant sentence constituent.

Some of these end-focuses are clearly more marked than others as the reader can confirm by reading them aloud – they involve a successively more indignant intonation pattern!

Considerations that govern which constituent is to be chosen as theme and which as end-focus are related to communicative processes within text.

The terms given and new can only be understood in terms of text. In their most straightforward sense, these terms can be understood as information that has literally been 'given' in the preceding text and information that is 'new' to the sentence immediately under consideration. A number of linguistic features correlate with this. New information is characteristically spelled out in full – otherwise there is no way for the hearer or reader to get access to it. Given information is typically either assumed and not referred to at all, or is referred to by the use of proforms or other cross-reference expressions. For example, suppose you received a letter which contained:

**9**  I must tell you the news about John and Mary

**10**  They have just got married

**9** introduces the new information that there is some 'news' about 'John and Mary'. When we come to **10** this can be treated as given: hence *they* cross-refers to *John and Mary*, and no mention is made of 'news', but a piece of new information is added – that the 'news' is that 'John and Mary have got married'. It would be unnatural if the letter read:

**11**  I must tell you the news about John and Mary

**12**  The news I have to tell you is that John and Mary have got married

where all the given information is spelled out in the second sentence. In a long text such a process eventually becomes impossible, since new information is constantly being added.

Given information need not always be overtly referred to in text. It may be information 'given' in the sense that both participants share it as speakers of the same language, it may be cultural information shared between members of a linguistic community, or it may even be information privately shared between two individuals. To illustrate this, suppose the 'letter' in **9–10** continued:

**13**   I must tell you the news about John and Mary

**14**   They have just got married

**15**   A very flashy reception with lots of extravagant presents on display.

**16**   Dear old Charlie gave a toast-rack!

**17**   He does have a flair for the original!

The shared background of writer and reader includes the knowledge that marriages may involve receptions and the provision of presents. The way 'dear old Charlie' is introduced implies a certain type of relationship between the writer and 'Charlie', which is given to the reader. The last sentence can only be appreciated if one realizes that a 'toast-rack' is a totally conventional wedding present (not to say a literary convention). From a linguistic point of view, we note the pronominalization of 'given' information, and the elision of *They had* in **15**, and of the goal participant in **16** . . . *gave (them) a toast-rack*.

The importance of the notions of given and new to a study of word order lies in the fact that what is given is very frequently the constituent that is thematized. The unmarked structure for text might be schematically represented as:

**18**   given new. given new. (given) new. etc.

where the given is pronominalized and thematized, and the new information occurs in the rheme. We see several examples of this in the letter: *they* in **14**, *he* in **17**. What is given may be elided: in **15** we find (*they had*) *a very flashy reception* . . . so that the resultant sentence is all new information. We might regard *a toast-rack* in **16** as an example of end focus (note the prominence given to this constituent by the exclamation mark). Another way of presenting the same information is: *A toast-rack from dear old Charlie*, where the 'given' (and understood) *They received*, or the like, is elided and *A toast-rack* is thematized.

The notions of topic and comment can be illustrated in the following way. By topic we mean the 'perspective' from which a sentence is viewed, what the sentence is 'about'. Topic seems to correspond to what people mean by 'psychological subject'. The comment then is something said about this topic. With sentences in isolation, we normally understand a sentence like:

**19**   John patted the dog on the head

as being a sentence which takes *John* as its topic and tells us something about what 'John' did. By contrast the sentence:

**20**  The dog was patted on the head by John

seems to focus attention on 'the dog', and tells us something that happened to it. Frequently topic and theme coincide, as they do in **19** and **20**. Frequently, too, topic, theme and given coincide, as in **14** and **17**. So, in **14** for example, *they* is topic and theme and cross-refers to *John and Mary* in the previous sentence: the comment *have just got married* is then made on this topic.

Topic and theme need not, however, coincide. Consider:

**21**  There has been a lot of bullying in the school this term

**22**  The one who is always being picked on is Tom Brown

We might reasonably identify *Tom Brown* as the topic of **22**, yet here this constituent is in end-focus. The effect of putting *Tom Brown* in end-focus is precisely to delay identification of the topic, thus creating a particular communicative effect.

Before considering each of these three notions in more detail we should briefly mention the question of what 'meaning' attaches to them. At this point we enter a peculiarly difficult and shadowy area. Clearly sentences like **1–4** or **5–8** have an 'emphatic' or 'contrastive' effect, but it is difficult to characterize this with any precision. Similarly, the ability to recover 'given' information, as for example in the 'letter' in **13–17**, has communicative importance – but this again is difficult to characterize. Thematizing processes do not in general appear to affect what we may refer to as 'propositional meaning' – the underlying propositional roles of the various constituents: though even this statement needs some qualification since, as we have seen, subject and object forming processes are often significant.

In one area thematization has a particular effect. This involves sentences where one or more of the NPs involved contains a quantifying expression (like *every*, *few*, *many* or a numeral) or the sentence contains a negative element. So, for example, the sentence:

**23**  Everyone in this room speaks two languages

can be understood as asserting either that 'everyone' speaks the same two languages (say French and German); or that everyone speaks two languages, but they may be different for each individual (say French and German, Chinese and Hindi, and so on). The latter is the more usual interpretation: the sentence is understood as a comment on the linguistic ability of 'everyone in the room', which is the topic. By contrast, in the sentence:

**24**    Two languages are spoken by everyone in this room

the most usual interpretation is that just two languages, say French and German, are at issue and everybody speaks them. Some support for this may be gathered by considering ways in which the sentences may be extended:

**25**    Two languages are spoken by everyone in this room and I understand neither of them

**26**    Everyone in this room speaks two languages and I understand neither of them

The first of these sentences seems immediately comprehensible. In the second the reader may be momentarily confused by the suspicion that 'everyone' comprises only two people (*neither of them*). In some cases this effect is so strong that pairs of sentences appear to differ in meaning; sometimes one sentence of a pair is almost incomprehensible:

**27a**    Many men love few girls
**27b**    Few girls are loved by many men

**28a**    Nobody speaks seventeen languages
**28b**    Seventeen languages are spoken by nobody

**29a**    A few men marry two women
**29b**    Two women are married by a few men

The 'focusing' effect of thematization is very noticeable in sentences like these, but it varies from case to case. **23** and **24** may fairly easily be understood in either sense, though one sense is probably preferred for each sentence. Each sentence in **28** appears to have a distinct interpretation, though with a little effort the reader can contextualize the other interpretation. In cases like **29**, the **b** sentence is almost incomprehensible.

### Theme, rheme and end-focus

Of the notions just discussed, theme, rheme and end-focus offer least descriptive and conceptual difficulty, because they are formal terms identifying structural positions within the sentence. The initial, thematic, constituent is where the sentence starts; and the final, end-focus, constituent is the culmination of the sentence. In a sentence like:

**30**   Ice cream, that's the pudding I like best in the world

the speaker, as it were, announces what the topic of his sentence is and then goes on to make a comment on it. By contrast, in a sentence like:

**31**   The pudding that I like best in the world is ice cream

the speaker keeps his hearer in suspense as to what he likes until the very end. We can reasonably successfully specify the formal operations involved in forming sentences like **30** and **31**; it is much more difficult to say why a speaker might prefer **30** to **31**, or vice versa, since this involves the more difficult considerations of what sort of effect the speaker thinks he will achieve by using one or other sentence.

In this section we examine some of the formal machinery available in English to enable a speaker to thematize a constituent or bring it into end-focus. We begin with declarative sentences: interrogative and imperative sentences function somewhat differently, so we defer consideration of these.

First we consider thematization processes. These fall into four very general types.

The first type we call 'subject selection rules'. These are cases where any one propositional role within a given propositional structure may be selected as grammatical subject, and the sentence remains an active declarative sentence:

**32**   Blood flowed in the gutters
**33**   The gutters flowed with blood

The second we call 'promotion to subject rules': these are cases where a particular propositional role, which in an active declarative sentence would not be grammatical subject, is promoted to subject with some consequent alteration in the verb group (as is the case with the passive) or by the introduction of a pro-verb (like HAVE):

**34a**   The managing director sacked the strikers
**34b**   The strikers were dismissed by the managing director

**35a**  My auntie knitted a pair of gloves for me
**35b**  I had a pair of gloves knitted for me by my auntie

**35b** is to be understood as having the same general sense as **35a**, rather than in the causative sense 'I got my auntie to knit me a pair of gloves'.

The third general type is called 'left movement rules': these involve the thematization of a particular constituent without any consequent change of grammatical function: thus the subject function of *I* and the object function of *Christmas* do not alter in:

**36a**  I hate Christmas
**36b**  Christmas, I hate it

The fourth type we call 'clefting rules': these involve the distribution of the constituents of some proposition into a copular sentence:

**37a**  I am very fond of marzipan
**37b**  It's marzipan that I'm very fond of
**37c**  Marzipan is what I'm very fond of

Before discussing these processes, some general comments can be made. We cannot possibly list all possible types and subtypes exhaustively in this chapter, nor are these four general types mutually exclusive – they are not and they interact in various ways. The characterization is merely a useful *ad hoc* typology. Nor do we claim a strict paraphrase relation between pairs of sentences examined, as for example any of the pairs of sentences noted above: it does seem, however, that the propositional relations involved remain the same. The thematization processes themselves may add emphases of meaning, or predispose the reader to a particular reading in preference to some other possible reading.

We can group a number of processes together under the general heading of 'subject selection rules'. The most obvious cases involve verbs like FLOW, illustrated in **32, 33**, which are associated with two propositional roles, either of which may become subject. Another example is

**38a**  His face streamed with blood
**38b**  Blood streamed down his face

and similar sentences can be constructed with verbs like CRAWL, BENEFIT.

A large class of verbs and related adjectives that refer to psychological states occur in structures like:

**39a**   I am bored with writing
**39b**   Writing is boring to me
**40a**   I am excited at the prospect of Christmas
**40b**   The prospect of Christmas is exciting to me

and similarly AMUSE, CONFUSE, DISGUST, EXCITE, FRIGHTEN, AMAZE, PUZZLE, WORRY, etc.[2] Under the general heading of subject selection we can also include cases of lexical suppletion, since these too permit one rather than another constituent to become grammatical subject, and the resulting sentences are, in general terms, paraphrases. We have explored some converse relations (pages 305–6).

**41a**   I lent my daughter five pounds
**41b**   My daughter borrowed five pounds from me

and similarly with BUY : SELL; TEACH : LEARN; AMUSE : PLEASE; etc. We may also, under this general heading, note a number of verbs where an 'indefinite and non specific' agent role may not be realized at all, and some other constituent assumes the role of grammatical subject:

**42a**   They produce a lot of whisky in Scotland
**42b**   Scotland produces a lot of whisky

Similar verbs, permitting this construction include GROW, MAKE, MANUFACTURE.

Perhaps the paradigm case of a 'promotion to subject' rule is the passive:

**43a**   A bus knocked Mary down
**43b**   Mary was knocked down by a bus

---

2 The usage we are concerned with here is the non-passive one illustrated in **40**. Sentences like these offer some analytic interest: although a sentence like **40a** appears to contain a passive verb group, we note the preposition *at* rather than *by*. We can also observe that the item *excited* here operates more like an adjective than a 'true' passive since we can modify it with 'intensifiers' etc.:

I am extremely/very/quite excited at the prospect of Christmas

Passives formed with transitive verbs do not operate like this:

*John was very killed by Bill

A very characteristic use of the passive is illustrated by:

**44a**  Someone has eaten all the cheese
**44b**  All the cheese has been eaten

where in the **b** sentence the indefinite and non-specific agent expression has been elided. Indeed a sentence like:

**45**  All the cheese has been eaten by someone

is often held to be unacceptable, and is certainly stylistically marked. Such structures are also often used when the speaker is anxious not to mention a specific participant, or when it is contextually recoverable. Sentences involving modal verbs often lend themselves to loose paraphrases involving a promotion to subject:

**46a**  You might buy a second-hand motor-bike for £200
**46b**  £200 might buy you a second-hand motor-bike

The same sort of process is observable with many other verbs with a modal or aspectual meaning:

**47a**  You need to have your car serviced
**47b**  Your car needs to be serviced
**48a**  This novel begins to interest me
**48b**  I begin to be interested in this novel

'Raising' transformations (see discussion on pages 334–5) can also have the function of creating thematic constituents. Thus consider sentences like:

**49a**  (John will go) is certain
**49b**  That John will go is certain
**49c**  John is certain to go

The subject of the constituent sentence is raised to become the subject of the matrix sentence: similar sentences can be formed with LIKELY, SEEM, HAPPEN. A similar operation can raise the object of a constituent sentence to become the subject of the matrix sentence:

**50a**  (to please John) is difficult
**50b**  John is difficult to please

and similar sentences with verbs and adjectives like HARD, TOUGH, IMPOSSIBLE (but not POSSIBLE), EASY.

Other promotion to subject rules involve the introduction of pro-verbs like HAVE, GET, etc. HAVE seems involved in a number of constructions involving locative or benefactive roles, or participants that occur in genitive constructions:

**51a** There is a pond in my aunt's garden

**51b** My aunt's garden has a pond in it

**52a** There is an article by the Bishop of London in today's *Times*

**52b** Today's *Times* has an article by the Bishop of London (in it)

**52c** The Bishop of London has an article in today's *Times*

**53a** The policeman twisted the criminal's arm

**53b** The criminal had his arm twisted (by the policeman)

**54a** Someone bought a gold watch for the dustman

**54b** The dustman had a gold watch bought for him

In **54b** we see once again the non-realization of an indefinite and non-specific-agent participant. paraphrases with TAKE and GET often seem to involve goal roles:

**55a** The waves battered the ship

**55b** The ship took a battering from the waves

**56a** Parliament didn't approve the Devolution Bill last year

**56b** The Devolution Bill didn't get the approval of Parliament last year

(Note in these cases the nominalization of the verb – see footnote 6 on page 300.)

We turn now to our third set of rules – 'left-movement rules'. Many constituents can be thematized by simply moving them to the front of the sentence. We have already observed (page 129) that this can be done with sentence adverbs:

**57** Last night I proposed to Mary

**58** On Hogmanay in Scotland few people go to bed before midnight

When constituents are thematized in this way it does not affect their status as grammatical subject, object, etc.:

**59**   Mary, I proposed to

**60**   That soup, I find totally disgusting

**61**   The kittens, we drowned

Sometimes a pronoun is 'left behind' in the slot from which a constituent is moved:

**62**   Jane, she'll be late home this evening

**63**   That soup, I find it totally disgusting

Rules of this sort often permit a constituent to be thematized from quite 'deep down' in an embedded sentence:

**64**   That man, I thought you told me you were never going to see him again

Our last general type of thematization operation is 'clefting'. Under this head we mention two types of operation. The first is called simply clefting:

**65a**   John gave the book to Mary
**65b**   It was John who gave the book to Mary
**65c**   It was the book John gave to Mary
**65d**   It was Mary John gave the book to.

The syntax of cleft sentences is far from straightforward, and the reader is urged to do a little personal research into the extent to which the operation can be extended. It seems that almost any constituent can be clefted in English except the verb, and even this is possible in some dialects of English:

**66a**   ?It's singing John is
**66b**   ?It's delivering the mail the postman is

The distribution of tense, mood and aspect features in cleft sentences is also worth investigation:

**67a**   John might have given the book to Mary
**67b**   It might have been John who gave the book to Mary
**67c**   It is John who might have given the book to Mary

Another structure of this general type is pseudo-clefting, illustrated by sentences like:

**68a** John loves Mary
**68b** The one who loves Mary is John
**68c** John is the one who loves Mary
**68d** The one who John loves is Mary
**68e** Mary is the one who John loves

**69a** John bought a screwdriver
**69b** What John bought was a screwdriver

In such sentences the participants from a simple proposition – e.g. that relating to **68a** – are distributed into an equational sentence like **68b**. Equational sentences can be reversed round the copula (**68b** and **68c**), and some of the conditions for this reversal were discussed on page 317. Simple cleft sentences, like **65**, cannot be reversed. Also note the forms *the one*, and *what* in **68b** and **69b**: these form a particularly puzzling feature of pseudo-clefts, since we can also find sentences like:

**70**  The one/person/girl who John loves is Mary

**71**  What/the thing/the tool John bought is a screwdriver

We have discussed four types of operation that produce, or may produce, themes. The first two – subject selection and promotion to subject – have the consequence of making some constituent the grammatical subject. This frequently, but not inevitably, means that this constituent is also the theme. The third type – left-movement rules – necessarily produces themes, but has no effect on the functional relation (subject, object, etc.) of the thematized constituent. Clefting produces a theme which is the grammatical subject of the copular verb BE but does not affect the functional relations of the 'original' sentence, which now appears in a construction that resembles a relative clause.

Several syntactic consequences flow from these differences. Both subject-forming rules and left-movement rules can occur in the same sentence:

**72a**  Blood flowed in the gutters
**72b**  The gutters, blood flowed in them!

**73a**  I liked the novel, but I was disgusted with the musical
**73b**  The novel pleased me, but the musical disgusted me
**73c**  The novel I liked, but the musical I was disgusted with

Secondly, left-movement rules apply to a wider range of

constituents than subject forming processes. Many constituents cannot become grammatical subjects, but they can be thematized by left-movement rules. Thus adverbial expressions:

> Stealthily the cat stalked the mouse
> **74b**   One dark and stormy night the robbers met

constituents like *up* in:

> **75**   Up jumped John

or negative adverbs like *never* or *seldom*:

> **76a**   Never have I heard such magnificent playing!
> **76b**   Seldom have I tasted a more magnificent Stilton!

These particular constructions involve inversion as well as thematization. Perhaps most strikingly, however, note that subject-forming processes can only apply within the simple sentence (as, for example, the passive) or from a constituent sentence to the matrix sentence (in the case of raising rules). Movement rules and clefting rules seem to be able to apply, within ill-defined limits, across sentence boundaries. Thus in:

> **77a**   I am anxious that my dog will not keep on wanting to mate with *the mongrel next door*
> **77b**   It's *the mongrel next door* that I am anxious that my dog will not keep on wanting to mate with

the clefted constituent comes from a deeply embedded sentence: no subject-forming rule could extract a subject for a higher verb from so deeply embedded a sentence.

A further difference between subject forming and other thematization rules concerns the category of definiteness in the NP. From a statistical point of view, subject expressions are more likely to be definite than indefinite, not surprising in view of our previous observations about the structure of given and new information: given information characteristically precedes new information. Given information, since it is given, characteristically involves a definite NP. This is not, of course, to say that subjects cannot be indefinite NPs, merely that they are more frequently definite. Themes created by left-movement rules, on the other hand, are characteristically definite, again not surprising, in view of the emphatic nature of many such sentences. Consider subject NPs first. Both of the sentences:

**78a**　My wife gave me that camera
**78b**　That camera was given to me by my wife

seem perfectly acceptable; but of the sentences:

**79a**　My wife gave me a camera
**79b**　A camera was given to me by my wife

the latter seems much less acceptable, though it could be contextualized. If we now try thematizing the same constituents by a left-movement rule we find that:

**80**　That camera my wife gave me

is quite acceptable, but:

**81**　A camera my wife gave me

seems deviant. This is particularly true with indefinite expressions like *anybody, somebody*, etc.:

**82a**　Somebody has stolen my socks
**82b**　*Somebody, he's stolen my socks
**82c**　*It's somebody who has stolen my socks

**83a**　Anybody can ride a bicycle
**83b**　*Anybody, he can ride a bicycle

Just as a number of types of rules make some constituent thematic, so too there are rules which bring a particular constituent into end-focus. It is not so easy to characterize these into general types, and many of them turn out to be, as it were, the obverse of theme-forming rules – clearly, since if some constituent is chosen as theme, then some other constituent must be placed in end-focus. As before, we suggest four general types. Firstly, 'end-focus selection rules', the simple obverse of subject selection rules:

**84a**　The changes in the income-tax laws will benefit the lower-paid worker
**84b**　The lower-paid worker will benefit from the changes in the income-tax laws

We do not discuss these further.

Secondly, what we may call 'postponement rules':

**85a**　Getting hold of a plumber these days is difficult
**85b**　It's difficult to get hold of a plumber these days

Many of these rules, like that illustrated, involve changing the grammatical function of a constituent: thus *Getting hold of a plumber these days* is the subject of **85a**, but not of **85b**.

Our third class of rules we call 'right movement rules':

**86a**   Your mother has gone out shopping
**86b**   She's gone out shopping, your mother

These rules involve moving a particular constituent to the end of a sentence, but do not change its grammatical function. Finally pseudo-cleft sentences, discussed on page 369, can be as easily considered rules producing an end-focus, as they can be considered rules producing a theme (see examples **68** onwards on page 367). We do not discuss these again here.

Postponement rules transport a constituent to the right of the sentence. The most widespread such rule is 'extraposition', which takes a constituent, typically from subject position, and moves it to a position after the verb, leaving a dummy *it* subject behind:

**87a**   That you enjoy reading linguistics books is amazing
**87b**   It is amazing that you enjoy reading linguistics books

This operation is obligatory for a number of verbs – thus

**88a**   It happens that I am related to the Russian Royal Family
**88b**   *That I am related to the Russian Royal Family happens

Even when it is not obligatory, it is particularly frequent when the NP involved is a 'heavy' NP: i.e. when it is, in a literal sense, long – often the case when the constituent in question is an embedded sentence. Thus, while both **87a** and **87b** are acceptable, **87b** seems stylistically more acceptable. Why this should be is unclear, but it may have to do with 'processing' difficulties in understanding sentences. The point can be appreciated better if we make the subject constituent of *is amazing* even heavier:

**89a**   That you enjoy reading linguistics books even when you are lying on the beach at St Tropez surrounded by all those beautiful topless girls is amazing
**89b**   It is amazing that you enjoy . . .

The **b** sentence is undeniably less difficult! The shifting of heavy constituents can also be seen in sentences like the following:

**90a**   They presented a copy of the works of Bloomfield which was hand-printed on parchment and bound in red morocco to the retiring Professor

**90b**   They presented to the retiring professor a copy of the works of Bloomfield which was hand-printed on parchment and bound in red morocco

where the heavy direct object moves to the end of the sentence. Or again:

**91**   They presented a copy of the works of Bloomfield to the retiring professor which was hand-printed on parchment and bound in red morocco

where a heavy relative clause has been extraposed to the end of the sentence. (The reader is invited to consider the extent to which relative clauses can be extraposed, and what conditions permit or inhibit this.) In all cases the movement seems the consequence of a heavy constituent.

Right-movement rules typically operate on the subject constituent, and typically a pronoun copy is left behind:

**92**   It's disgusting, soup

Sometimes in addition to the constituent which is dislocated, a pro-verb copy of the verb is introduced:

**93**   He jilted her, John did

and frequently constituent and pro-verb are inverted:

**94**   He jilted her, did John

These processes are available in independent declarative sentences. We should briefly comment on thematization processes in non-declarative sentences and in dependent sentences. It can hardly have failed to strike the reader that one effect of thematizing operations is to bring some particular constituent into prominence – this usually involves making it appear as the topic of the sentence. So it is not surprising that the most usual thematic element in imperative and interrogative sentences is not the grammatical subject. Interrogative sentences are very frequently used to ask questions and in '*wh* questions' it is the *wh* word that is thematic:

**95a**  Who did I see you with last night?
**95b**  Where have you put my slippers?
**95c**  How are you?

The main thrust of a question is to discover the identity of the participant signalled by the *wh* word. With *wh* questions, if the *wh* word is not thematic, then, in speech, it usually bears heavy stress:

**96**  You put my slippers WHERE?

and is typically no longer a straightforward request for information, but rather a request for confirmation, an expression of surprise or the like:

**97a**  A: Where are my slippers?
**97b**  B: I put them in the dustbin
**97c**  A: You put them WHERE?

Note in passing that in terms of the four-way distinction drawn earlier, the formation of *wh* questions involves a left-movement rule: and the *wh* element can be thematized from a deeply embedded sentence:

**98**  Who do you suppose Mary told me she met yesterday?

'Yes–no' interrogatives are marked by the thematization of an auxiliary verb:

**99a**  Didn't we meet in Marakesh?
**99b**  Have you got a match?

In imperative sentences the thematic element is normally the main verb, perhaps not surprising if we think that imperative sentences are characteristically used as commands, and commands are typically requests for action:

**100a**  Go away!
**100b**  Shut up!

Sometimes a 'vocative' element is thematized:

**101**  Roger, give me a cigarette will you?

presumably to attract the attention of the person being addressed, or to single him out from among a number of possible addressees.

Finally we mention thematic processes in subordinate clauses. Almost invariably subordinating conjunctions are thematized within their sentence: from a functional point of view, this marks both the fact and the type of subordination. Thus:

**102a** *If* you don't stop, I'll scream
**102b** *When* Charlie comes home, we'll have a party
**102c** John gagged her, *so* she wouldn't scream
**102d** I won't stop *until* you ask me nicely

Complementizers occur initially in their complement sentence, and relative pronouns and other relative markers are initial in their sentences:

**103a** I know *that* my redeemer lives
**103b** The man *who* believes that will believe anything

In the same connection, though not with respect to subordinate sentences, binding elements in general (*thus, for example, in conclusion*, etc. see page 149) are usually thematic – again to mark the nature of the relation between sentences.

This section has looked at a number of syntactic processes available in the language that secure initial or final sentence position for some particular constituent. The function of such operations appears to be tied up with communicative processes of various kinds. It is not always easy in well-formed text to identify precisely what effect a given thematization has: it is, paradoxically, much easier in an ill-formed text to appreciate that the clumsiness springs, or can spring, from a failure to make an appropriate thematization. At the end of the chapter is an exercise based on this premise – to which the reader is invited to devote his ingenuity after reading the other sections.

## Given and new

As was suggested in the introductory section to this chapter, a principal syntactic consequence of the distribution of information into that which can be held to be given for some sentences and that which is new to the sentence, lies in the fact that given information is 'reduced' in some way or not mentioned at all. Reduction processes that can be observed in written text include most obviously the use of proforms of various kinds – not only pronouns, but also such proforms as the various forms of DO. The auxiliary verbs, including the modals, can be used with a proform type of effect in sequences like:

**104a**   A: Are you going to Alan's party tonight?
**104b**   B: Must I?
**104c**   A: I think you should

a usage referred to by Palmer, following Firth, as 'code' (Palmer 1965). In spoken discourse reduction is even more evident – given information is typically un-stressed, and may be phonologically reduced in various ways, many of which are discussed in Brown (1977).

A lot of given information is not mentioned at all. This is illustrated in the example above, where the complements of the modal verbs in **104b**, **104c** have been elided, and can be recovered contextually. Elision results in sentence fragments, which, as we noted (pages 150–2), can only be understood by reference to 'fuller' forms, which can be recovered contextually.

When given information is mentioned, the effect is frequently contrast of some sort, or emphasis. Thus, for example:

**105a**   A: I'm going to play squash this afternoon
**105b**   B: Squash! I didn't know you played

**106a**   A: Would you like a drink? There's whisky or gin
**106b**   B: I think I'd like a whisky

### Topics

It is appropriate to complete this chapter by returning briefly to the notion of topic. The discussion must be brief since a full examination of the issues involved leads to a consideration of the structure of text as a whole, and this is not the place for such a discussion.

Of all the notions discussed topic is the most difficult to come to grips with. We have suggested that we can view the topic as being 'what the sentence is about', the 'perspective from which the sentence is viewed', etc. In many simple sentences we can identify the topic by asking what is the implicit request or question which the sentence would be an appropriate answer to. Thus, for example we might identify 'Edinburgh' as the topic in a sentence like:

**107** Edinburgh is the most beautiful city in Scotland

if we assume it answers the implicit request:

**108** Tell me something about Edinburgh

On the other hand if **107** were to answer the implicit question:

**109** Which is the most beautiful city in Scotland?

then the topic would be 'the most beautiful city in Scotland'. We have used the phraseology 'implicit request or question' since **107** would not be a normal answer to either **108** or **109** if it were an actual question. In such circumstances we would rather find:

**110** It's the most beautiful city in Scotland

as the answer to **108**, and:

**111** Edinburgh is

or:

**112** It's Edinburgh

as the answer to **109** – illustrating the process of reduction consequent on the given new distinction mentioned earlier.

This approach to the identification of topic is all right so far as it goes. Our observations suggest, correctly, that the notion of topic cannot be divorced from considerations of given–new (with the associated grammatical consequences of pronominalization, elision, etc.) and from processes of thematization. It also suggests, correctly too, that there is no simple one-to-one correspondence between topic and theme (*Edinburgh* in **111** is theme, but not topic, if **111** is the answer to the implicit question **109**). Nor is there any necessary connection between topic and given, since **107** might be the initial contribution to a conversation, itself introducing a topic.

The approach seems reasonably satisfactory for simple exchanges, but it meets with some difficulties when applied to longer passages in text; some of them relate to the difficulties experienced in trying to identify a sentence unit (pages 149ff.). In the first place, a complex sentence can often be analysed as having either a complex topic, or several topics. Related to this is the problem of the units within which we wish to identify topics: for example, one might wish to say of this book that as a whole it has a topic, defined in general terms, that each part has a topic, and so on down through chapters, sections, paragraphs, etc. To regard topic as a notion restricted in its application to a single sentence is unrealistic, and the technique of asking 'implicit questions' can be applied as well to groups of sentences, paragraphs etc., as to single sentences. Let us briefly examine each of these two problems.

Consider first the problem of the identification of a topic in a complex sentence:

> **113** In everyday speech 'fitness' means suitability or, adaptedness or being in good condition; 'evolution' means gradual change, with the connotation of unfolding; and as for 'inheritance', we may hope to inherit money, rights or property; we might inherit too a mother's eyes or a grandfather's gift for fiddling. **114** These are the meanings . . . of fitness, evolution, and inheritance – the meanings for which scientists chose them when they were struggling to put their conceptions into words.[3]

The first orthographic sentence **113** might answer the implicit question:

> **115** What do scientists mean by 'fitness', 'evolution' and 'inheritance'?

But this seems to introduce three topics, each in turn topic for one of the succeeding clauses separated by semi-colons. We can resolve this difficulty by supposing that the sentence could be dissolved into independent simple sentences (which would involve some amendment to the text and would destroy its stylistic characteristics!) each answering one implicit question (What do scientists mean by fitness? What do scientists mean by evolution? etc.) We then have the difficulty of identifying an appropriate topic for the final clause in **113**: perhaps it answers the implicit question, 'What else can you inherit?' But this does not seem helpful, since the function of this sentence is further to exemplify what is meant by 'inherit'. The second sentence, **114**, also presents a problem. It seems better to regard both of these

---

3 The quotations here and in examples **116–118** and **120–121** are from P. B. Medawar, *The Future of Man* (1960).

sentences as relating to a single, complex topic: an elementary initial definition of what is meant by 'fitness', 'evolution' and 'inheritance'. The same sort of difficulty arises if we try to continue this method with the rest of the paragraph:

> **116** In the course of time those conceptions have become clearer . . . but the words which embody them have remained the same. **117** The change that has gone on is sometimes described by saying that scientists give the words a new precision and refinement. . . .
>
> **118** The idea scientists now have in mind when they speak of 'fitness' can be explained like this. . . .

It is perhaps appropriate to say that the topic of the two sentences **116** and **117** together answered the implicit question, 'How have scientists refined the definition of these terms?' The next paragraph, the beginning of which is shown in **118**, goes on to offer a contemporary definition of 'fitness' that itself extends over a number of sentences.

Even with declarative sentences in text, then, there are problems in identifying topics in any straightforward way. Further difficulties arise if we try to identify the topic of interrogative sentences. Take the case of **109** for example. It seems hardly appropriate to ask what question this answers since it is itself a question. We might say it answers some implicit question like:

> **119** What question would you like answered?

but this is tautologous. A more appropriate approach is to suggest that instead of 'having a topic', overt interrogative sentences like **109** 'introduce a topic'. This certainly seems the function of the 'rhetorical question' often found in expository texts:

> **120** 'Inheritance' was the second of the three words of which I said that biologists use in special or unfamiliar ways. **121** Just what is inherited when geneticists speak of inheritance?

**120**, a declarative sentence, reintroduces as a topic something previously mentioned, and **121** establishes that the author is about to define what he means by this topic. The author is using the 'implicit question' technique we started this section with as an explicit technique for defining a topic – it then hardly seems sensible to enquire what the topic of this topic-introducing question is!

This approach to the identification of topics leads to the question of what unit it is within which we wish to identify topics; it is suggested above that it is appropriate to consider there to be a hierarchy of such units. The hierarchy starts, if this is appropriate, with the clauses of which a complex sentence consists (see discussion of sentence **113**), goes through the orthographic sentence if this is relevant, and it may not always be so (see discussion of sentence **114**), to groups of sentences, then to the paragraph, and so on. If this approach is appropriate it will be noted that the orthographic sentence may not necessarily be a unit that needs to be attended to, though it generally will be.

To illustrate what is meant by groups of sentences serving as a unit for the identification of topics, consider for instance the structure of the second paragraph in this section. The first sentence is introductory, the second offers an elementary definition, the third suggests a technique of identification, the forth and fifth exemplify this technique, and so on. The implicit question technique works well on this paragraph, providing it is not applied to each individual sentence, but rather to groups of sentences as appropriate:

| | |
|---|---|
| What is this section about? | (S1) |
| What do you mean by 'topic'? | (S2) |
| How would I identify one? | (S3) |
| Can you give me an example? | (S4, 5) |

and so on. Note that this set of questions refers as much to what we might call the rhetorical structure of the paragraph as to the structure of individual sentences. Insofar as it relates to rhetorical structure, it helps account for a number of facets of sentence construction, notably the distribution of the binding expressions noted on pages 149–50.

This approach to the identification of topics may assist in untangling some of the mysteries of word order. We have already noted that what is topic is frequently also what is thematic, but this statement needs to be qualified. The thematic element may relate to the topic of some unit larger than the sentence (as is perhaps the case when binding expressions are thematic – they often identify the function of the sentence (*for instance, thus, in conclusion*, etc.)). Equally the thematic element may have nothing to do with the topic, but be some other element of the message that the speaker wishes to foreground.

## Concluding remarks

The phenomena considered in this chapter pose a peculiar difficulty for constituent structure grammars. Much of it, particularly the observations relating to theme and end-focus, clearly has to do with constituent structure, but some of it, particularly that relating to topic, while it may have implications for constituent structure, cannot usefully be brought into a constituent structure grammar of any sort that we have discussed. Even the material clearly relevant to constituent structure is of a curious sort. Some of it, particularly the thematization operations that have to do with subject selection, seems relevant to what we may call centrally grammatical processes – processes like subject selection with verbs like RUN, STREAM (page 364) and raising (pages 344–5). Other operations, particularly those like left-movement rules (page 367ff.), seem outside the centrally grammatical processes and have more to do with communicative effects in texts. Yet it is not as simple as that. We have noted (page 374) that question formation resembles a left-movement rule (in that it can take a constituent embedded deeply in the sentence and thematize it), and we surely want to think of question formation as a centrally grammatical process. Conversely the passive operation, often thought of as a central grammatical rule (transformational grammars often treat it as the first transformation to be taught) seems to have as much to do with communicative effects as anything else (see the very perceptive remarks on the functions of passivization in Jespersen (1924).

One might think it convenient to be able to distinguish the centrally grammatical rules, whatever they may be defined to be, from those rules that are concerned with text-forming processes, but this is clearly impossible. Nor should this surprise us.

## Technical terms

cleft sentence comment
given
'heavy' NPs

left dislocation
left-movement rules
new

pseudo-cleft sentence
right-movement rules
subject selection rules
postponement rules
promotion to subject rule

thematically marked/unmarked
thematization
theme
topic

**Exercise**

Each of the following two texts contains much the same propositional matter; the propositions follow each other in the same order. Each text too exhibits thematization devices of various sorts. Identify the types of thematization operations involved. Account for the fact that while the text A seems to be fairly coherently structured, text B is decidedly odd.

*A*

**1** It was in 1960 that the cave was discovered. **2** An old shepherd thought he heard 'water running underground' at the foot of a near-by mountain. **3** He told a friend of his who lived in the near-by village of Petralona. **4** The villager removed a few stones and literally fell into the cave. **5** A quick search showed that the floor was littered with animal bones. **6** What he had found was a prehistoric habitation site. **7** On a subsequent visit he found an entire human fossil, lying on its right side with its legs drawn up. **8** He told other villagers that night that he had found the remains of a 'big monkey' in a cave.

*B*

**1** What was discovered in 1960 was the cave. **2** A shepherd who was old thought that 'water running underground' had been heard by him at a near-by mountain's foot. **3** A friend of his who lived in the nearby village of Petralona was told by him. **4** A few loose stones were removed by the villager and it was the cave he literally fell into. **5** That animal bones littered the floor was shown by a quick search. **6** He had found a prehistoric habitation site. **7** Lying on its right side with its legs drawn up, he found an entire human fossil on a subsequent visit. **8** He told other villagers that night that the remains of a 'big monkey' had been found by him in a cave.

# Postscript

Part one of this book was devoted to a consideration of constituent structure grammars. We paid particular attention to this way of describing the structure of language because it has been the dominant approach since the 1930s, first with the 'structuralist' grammarians and more recently with the 'transformationalist' grammarians. Part three looked at some other equally important aspects of the structure of sentences – the function that particular constituents have within the sentence. This has traditionally been the concern of grammarians, and in recent years interest in this area has revived. We have been led to enquire whether the sorts of matters discussed in Part three can be accommodated within a constituent structure grammar of the sort developed in Part one: in many cases it cannot without the addition of new descriptive machinery.

The reason for this is clear. The elements used in the construction of constituent structure grammars are distributionally defined form classes and construction types. There is no simple way of introducing considerations of syntactic function into such a grammar – whether the function at issue is dependency, participant type, grammatical relation or textual. Such functions are relational: they specify the type of relation between two or more constituents. To take an example: we have identified, for English, the prepositional phrase as a particular construction type, with the constituents Preposition + Noun Phrase. How should we now identify the functions of such a construction in a particular sentence? Prepositional phrases serve many different functions: they may be adverbial modifiers (a dependency relation); they may be nuclear or circumstantial participants (a participant role relation); they may be oblique objects (a grammatical relation); or they may be themes (a textual function). They may be, and they typically are, more than one of these simultaneously: an adverbial modifier is typically

also a circumstantial participant; an oblique object may be a
nuclear participant; and so on. A functional characterization
of a particular constituent and its constituent structure
characterization interact in many complex ways. Part one
attempts to include some functional information in our grammar
by enriching the structure, as for example by the introduction of
the node labelled Pred (page 51), or by smuggling in functionally labelled nodes, like adverb of place (page 73). But we
cannot accommodate all the functional information we might
need in this way without considerable modifications to the
straightforward constituent structure grammars we started off
with. We saw (page 259) that some of the earlier approaches to
constituent structure grammars included some functional
information – by labelling the branching structures in various
ways, or by adding notes commenting on the constituent
structures. These ways of describing functional relations were not
perpetuated in the main stream of linguistic description, perhaps
because they could not be formalized in the way constituent
structure itself can, and because many linguists became interested
in the formal and mathematical properties of constituent
structure grammars, and later transformations, themselves. More
recently attempts have been made to re-introduce this functional
information, either directly into grammars that look rather like
constituent structure grammars (see, for example, the sort of
grammar described briefly on page 323ff.), or by enriching the
lexicon (see, for example, pages 321ff.).

A more radical departure from constituent structure grammars
is found in the grammatical theories known as 'Tagmemic' and
'Systemic' grammar. It is not possible to do more than mention
these alternative approaches here, and the reader is referred to the
Further reading on page 386. We may, however, mention one
feature. Most of the basic notions of distribution, form classes,
constructions, and so on that we discussed in Part one are used in
these grammars too, though sometimes in a slightly different way.
One way they differ is that each structural position within the
Sentence, the Noun Phrase, etc., is identified both in terms of its
function and of its constituent structure realization. So in a
sentence like *The sad girl wept*, the constituent *the sad girl* is
labelled both as a subject (of some particular kind) and as being
realized as an NP. The constituents of the NP are then labelled
as a head, realized by a noun, *girl*, preceded by two modifiers,

each of a different type and realized by items of a particular form class. Grammatical function and grammatical form are described simultaneously. This approach may, and in systemic grammar does, involve the recognition of several different layers of structure simultaneously; the structures not necessarily being coincident. Such a description does not lend itself to representation in the form of a tree diagram.

The problem lies in the fact that language serves a variety of functions simultaneously. The functions are all closely interknit and relate in a variety of ways to the actual forms of language. We have chosen to look at the forms of language first and then consider functions because we believe this to be the most readily comprehensible introduction to the complex structure of language.

# Further reading

## Introduction

We have not discussed many issues concerned with the nature of language in general; the reader is directed to Sapir (1921), Jespersen (1922) and (1929), Bloomfield (1935), Langacker (1968), Nash (1971) and the introductory chapters of books like Lyons (1968), Hockett (1958).

## Part one

The study of constituent structure (Chapter 1) and of form classes (Chapter 2) is so basic to any approach to syntax that all introductory books discuss it. Bolinger (1968), Gleason (1969), Hockett (1958), Lyons (1968), Palmer (1971), and Robins (1964) – consult the indexes for the relevant pages – are among those we have found the most useful. Each has a slightly different presentation of essentially the same view of constituent structure that we take in this book. Householder (1972) is a useful collection of articles, many of which bear on these questions. While the view of constituent structure expressed in this book is representative of the views most commonly held in contemporary linguistics, there are 'schools' of linguistics that take a somewhat different position: we may mention three – 'Tagmemics' (see Cook (1969), Longacre (1964)); 'Scale and Category grammar' (see Sinclair (1972)); 'Systemic grammar' (see Berry (1975), Muir (1972)).

Lyons (1968) contains a good, though sometimes difficult, account of the matters discussed in Chapters 3 and 5–7. The most interesting discussion of these questions is to be found in works on Transformational Generative grammar. As noted in the introduction, this book does not present a fully formalized account of such a grammar, though many of the ideas it presents derive from work on transformational grammar. The companion volume, Brown and Miller (1982), presents a formal account of this approach. The transformational approach derives from the work of Chomsky (1957). A useful overview is Lyons (1970). Introductions we find helpful include Akmajian and Heny (1975); Huddleston (1976) and Koutsoudas (1966).

Problems concerning the sentence (Chapter 10) are discussed in the introductory books mentioned in the first paragraph. The view presented here is much influenced by Lyons (1977).

**Part two**

The view of morphology presented here derives in the main from Lyons (1968). A comprehensive and useful discussion is found in Matthews (1974). The introductory books noted in Part one can be consulted with profit, but the terminology differs to some extent from author to author.

Form classes and grammatical categories (Chapter 16) are discussed in the introductory books. A useful discussion of form classes in a number of different languages is in Lingua (1967).

**Part three**

For the subjects discussed in Chapter 17 see particularly Hockett (1958), Lyons (1968), Palmer (1971), and Robins (1964).

On 'Processes and participants' (Chapter 18) see particularly Brown and Miller (1982), Fillmore (1968), Halliday (1970) Liefrinck (1973) contains an interesting discussion of some problems in this area. The works on Tagmemics cited earlier draw together notions of constituent structure and process and participants; a comprehensive account is Longacre (1976).

For the matters discussed in Chapters 19 and 20 an interesting non-technical discussion is Jespersen (1929). Halliday (1970) is also very approachable. There is some discussion in Lyons (1968).

**Exercises**

The following contain useful collection of exercise materials: Gleason (1955*b*), Langacker (1972), and Nida (1971).

# References

AKMAJIAN, A., and HENY, F. (1975), *An Introduction to the Principles of Transformational Syntax*, MIT Press

BERRY, M. (1975), *Introduction to Systemic Linguistics*, Batsford
BLOOMFIELD, L (1935), *Language*, Allen & Unwin
BOLINGER, D (1968), *Aspects of Language*, Harcourt & Brace
BOLINGER, D (1971), *The Phrasal Verb in English*, Harvard University Press
BROWN, E. K., and MILLER, J. E. (1982), *Syntax: Generative Grammar*, Hutchinson
BROWN, G. (1977), *Listening to Spoken English*, Longman

CHOMSKY, N. (1957), *Syntactic Structures*, Mouton
COLE, P., and SADOCK, J. M. (eds.) (1977) *Syntax and Semantics, vol. 8: Grammatical Relations*, Academic Press
COOK, W. A. (1969), *Introduction to Tagmemic Analysis*, Holt, Rinehart & Wilson
CRYSTAL, D. (1966), 'Specification and English tenses', *Journal of Linguistics,* vol. 2, 1–34

FILLMORE, C. J. (1968), 'The case for case', in E. Bach and R. T. Harms (eds.), *Universals in Linguistic Theory*, Holt, Rinehart & Winston
FRIES, C. C. (1952), *The Structure of English*, Harcourt Brace

GLEASON, H. A. (1955), *Workbook in Descriptive Linguistics*, Holt, Rinehart & Winston
GLEASON, H. A. (1969), *An Introduction to Descriptive Linguistics*, Holt, Rinehart & Winston
GREENBERG, J. H. (ed.) (1963), *Universals of Language*, MIT Press

HALLIDAY, M. A. K. (1970), 'Language structure and language function', in Lyons, J. (ed.), *New Horizons in Linguistics*, Pelican

HOCKETT, C. F. (1958), *A Course in Modern Linguistics*, Macmillan

HOUSEHOLDER, F. W. (1972), *Syntactic Theory 1*, Penguin

HUDDLESTON, R. (1976) *An Introduction to English Transformational Syntax*, Longman

JESPERSEN, O. (1922), *Language, Its Nature, Development and Origin*, Allen & Unwin

JESPERSEN, O. (1929), *Philosophy of Grammar*, Allen & Unwin

JESPERSEN, O. (1961) (reprint), *A Modern English Grammar*, Allen & Unwin

KOUTSOUDAS, A. (1966), *Writing Transformational Grammars*, McGraw-Hill

LANGACKER, R. W. (1968), *Language and its Structure*, Harcourt Brace

LANGACKER, R. W. (1972), *Fundamentals of Linguistic Analysis*, Harcourt Brace

LANGACKER, R. W. (1969), 'On pronominalization and the chain of command' in D. A. Reibel and S. Schane, *Modern Studies in English*, Prentice Hall

LEECH, G. (1971), *Meaning and the English Verb*, Longman

LIEFRINK, F. (1973), *Semantico-Syntax*, Longman

LINGUA (1967), *Word Classes*, North Holland

LONGACRE, R. E. (1964), *Grammar Discovery Procedures*, Mouton

LONGACRE, R. E. (1976), *An Anatomy of Speech Notions*, Peter de Ridder Press

LYONS, J. (1968), *An Introduction to Theoretical Linguistics*, Cambridge University Press

LYONS, J. (1970), *Chomsky*, Fontana

LYONS, J. (1977), *Semantics, vol. 2*, Cambridge University Press

MACKINNON, R. (1971), *Gaelic*, Teach Yourself Books

MATTHEWS, P. H. (1974), *Morphology*, Cambridge University Press

390　*References*

MUIR, J. (1972), *A Modern Approach to English Grammar*, Batsford

NASH, W. (1971), *Our Experience of Language*, St Martin's Press
NIDA, E. (1966), *A Synopsis of English Syntax*, Mouton
NIDA, E. (1971), *Morphology*, University of Michigan

PALMER, F. R. (1965), *A Linguistic Study of the English Verb*, Longman
PALMER, F. R. (1971), *Grammar*, Penguin
PARTRIDGE, E. (1958), *Origins, a Short Etymological Dictionary of Modern English*, Routledge & Kegan Paul

QUIRK, R., GREENBAUM, S., LEECH, G., and SVARTVIK, J. (1972), *A Grammar of Contemporary English*, Longman

ROBINS, R. H. (1964), *General Linguistics, an Introductory Survey*, Longman
ROBINS, R. H. (1967), *A Short History of Linguistics*, Longman

SAPIR, E. (1921), *Language, an Introduction to the Study of Speech*, Harcourt Brace
SINCLAIR, J. MCH. (1972), *A Course in Spoken English-Grammar*, Oxford University Press
STRANG, B. M. H. (1970), *A History of English*, Methuen

THOMAS, L. V. (1967), *Elementary Turkish*, Harvard University Press

# Index